NAZISM
RESISTANCE &
HOLOCAUST IN
WORLD WAR II
A Bibliography

by VERA LASKA

The Scarecrow Press, Inc.
Metuchen, N.J., & London 1985

Library of Congress Cataloging in Publication Data

Laska, Vera.
    Nazism, resistance & holocaust in World War II.

    Includes index.
    1. Holocaust, Jewish (1939-1945)--Bibliography.
2. World War, 1939-1945--Underground movements, Jewish--
Bibliography. 3. World War, 1939-1945--Underground
movements--Bibliography. 4. National socialism--Bibli-
ography. 5. World War, 1939-1945--Women--Bibliography.
I. Title. II. Title: Nazism, resistance and holocaust
in World War II.
Z6374.H6L37 1985   016.94053'15'03924   84-23586
[D810.J4]
ISBN 0-8108-1771-3

To the librarians of Regis College,
always resourceful fellow laborers
in the vineyard of history:

Sister Olivia Kidney, Director

Lily Farkas

William A. Gallup

Jeanne Hablanian

Adele Slatko

T A B L E   O F   C O N T E N T S

Foreword by Lawrence H. Fuchs   ix
Introduction   xi

 1. Jews and Anti-Semitism   1

 2. Nazism   9

 3. Resistance   33

 4. Resistance--Women   67

 5. Jewish Resistance   75

 6. Holocaust   83

 7. Holocaust--Women   115

 8. Women in Hiding   121

 9. Pre-1945 Knowledge of the Holocaust   123

10. War Crimes   127

11. Art and Photographs   141

12. Philosophy and Interpretation   147

13. Literature   151

Addenda   157
Author Index   165

Those who cannot remember the past
are condemned to repeat it.

Santayana

F O R E W O R D

Vera Laska already has given us a deep and moving tribute to human resistance against evil in her tragic and triumphant book, Women in the Resistance and in the Holocaust. Now, in this volume she provides, for the first time, a comprehensive bibliography for those who try to understand the essentially incomprehensible.

Laska's book on Women in the Resistance and in the Holocaust etched unforgettable portraits of human courage and dignity in the face of butchery. Undoubtedly, her passion to tell the story of women resisters also motivated the amazing industry which undergirds this tour de force of scholarship. The survivor of three concentration camps, including Auschwitz, Laska has found an unusually constructive way to pay her respects to the eleven million who died at the hands of Nazis and to the relatively small number of those who, like herself, survived to tell the rest of us about that long night of horror.

Like so many immigrants and refugees, the Czech-born Laska has devoted much of her scholarship to the celebration of the United States. Fascinated by the American Revolution, she has written about Benjamin Franklin, Abigail Adams and other heroes and heroines of those times. Professor of History at Regis College in Weston, Massachusetts, and Chairman of the Division of Social Sciences there, Laska also teaches a course on the resistance and the Holocaust.

In this book, her seventh, Laska's scholarship matches her prodigious industry. The nearly 2,000 entries, preceded by an unusually instructive Introduction, and organized into thirteen categories, will become an indispensable tool for researchers, scholars, journalists and anyone interested in learning about the Holocaust and the resistance. The categories are so efficient in organizing the material that it comes as a surprise to find that most of the entries also are annotated, making the job of those who use this book quite easy. In addition to the annotations, Laska gives us an excellent account of all the major existing collections on the subject.

Now, with this extraordinary bibliography, many libraries should begin to build collections of their own. At the very least, every library should obtain this book because it will be recognized upon its publication as an indispensable tool for anyone who wishes to study and/or write about the resistance and the Holocaust.

    Laska has provided a usable tribute to the heroes, heroines
and martyrs of those darkest years. We all are in her debt.

                                Lawrence H. Fuchs
                                Walter and Meyer Jaffe
                                Professor of American
                                Civilization and Politics
                                Brandeis University

I N T R O D U C T I O N

Historical Background for the Resistance and the Holocaust

Aside from the casualties due to military action, World War II exacted eleven million victims within the territory of Europe occupied by Nazi Germany.

Of these eleven million, six million were Jews, their only "sin" being that they or their forebears were born Jewish. The other five million were prisoners of war, Gypsies, homosexuals, priests, nuns, Jehovah's Witnesses and the "politicals," the latter being anyone overheard criticizing the Nazi regime or caught as a resister.

Simon Wiesenthal, the relentless pursuer of criminals against humanity (who deeply dislikes being called "the Nazi Hunter"), often emphasizes that the Jewish organizations made a strategic mistake when, after the war, they concentrated on the publicity of the Jewish Holocaust yet omitted the non-Jewish victims of Nazism. Thus, the Holocaust as a purely Jewish catastrophe lost the potential sympathies of millions of non-Jews. Now, forty years after the end of the war, this is beginning to change. Today, many of the earlier historians of the Holocaust would include the resistance of the Jews and of the others, in order to present a more complete view of the conflagration that was the Second World War, even aside from the massacres on the battlefields and in the bombed cities.

The resistance against the Nazi occupiers of European nations was another aspect of World War II. While soldiers and, to a degree, diplomats were waging a so-called legitimate war, the underground movements in the occupied countries, from Norway to Yugoslavia, from Belgium to Poland and to the temporarily occupied parts of the Soviet Union, resorted to clandestine activities in order to harass the enemy and to contribute to his defeat.

These activities were of an endless variety, from reversing highway signs to blowing up tanks. Resisters published thousands of newspapers, bulletins and broadsides; they kept in touch via secret transmitters with the Allies, informing them of all aspects of the local situation, especially of the economic picture, the details of political or racial persecutions and of troop movements.

They cooperated closely with the British Special Operations Executive (SOE), especially in France, but also in Belgium, Norway, Poland, Yugoslavia and elsewhere. Of the 10,000 members of the SOE, about one third were women, and many of both sexes lost their lives in the underground struggle. Many ended up in concentration camps where they died or were executed, as were the four SOE women in Dachau.

Resisters carried out countless cases of sabotage, slowing down production in factories, slashing tires on German military vehicles, dropping laxatives into the occupiers' coffee, blowing up Gestapo headquarters and bridges, distributing fake ration cards, providing fugitives with false identity papers, and ambushing and killing Nazis. The variety of acts defying the occupying forces was infinite. One must point out that the services of messengers, frequently women, were of essential importance and highly dangerous, as messengers or couriers often carried incriminating documents, bundles of false identification cards or food ration cards, coded messages or large amounts of money.

Czech resisters succeeded assassinating their Nazi "Protector" Reinhard Heydrich. Norwegian resisters managed to blow up Norsk Hydro, the heavy water factory at Vemork in southern Norway, thereby delaying German atomic research by at least two years.

French resister Marie-Madeleine Fourcade headed a military espionage network, nicknamed "Noah's Ark" by the Gestapo because all agents had animal code names; her 3,000 agents, men and women, supplied invaluable information to the Allies. A Belgian wisp of a girl, Andrée de Jongh, "Little Cyclone," created one of the best underground railroads of this war, the Comet Line, which spirited away about 700 Allied airmen shot down over enemy territory, from the Netherlands, Belgium and France via the Pyrenees, to neutral Spain, from whence they could rejoin their fighting units in Great Britain. Other such underground lines functioned in various parts of Europe. The resistance was sending men across several borders to join the Allied forces in the West and in the East; other lines aided Jews in escaping from the clutches of that unholy trinity of Hitler-Himmler-Eichmann. Several underground railroads did not specialize and simply helped all whom circumstances forced to flee for their lives, officers, Jews, the politically persecuted. The Danes did a great job of saving the Jews by rowing them over to Sweden.

There was quite a lively two-way traffic in Western Europe of secret agents and members of the resistance being picked up, landed by Lysanders or parachuted into occupied territories for further action; no wonder the Norwegians called one of their lines the "Shetland Bus."

Many resisters joined paramilitary units of the partisans, in France known as Maquis, who conducted clandestine guerrilla warfare and carried out strategic acts of sabotage. The strongest such movements existed in Yugoslavia and in the occupied parts of the Soviet Union, but partisan groups functioned at different times from Poland to Greece and everywhere under the Nazi occupation.

Much of this side of the Second World War is still unknown, not only to the general public but even to students of history. Resisters came from all walks of life, from the heights of academia and from humble farms, rich and poor, men, women, and, not infrequently, children.

They are, with a few exceptions, among the unsung heroes and heroines of this war. Yet hundreds and thousands of them paid the ultimate sacrifice for their patriotism. They were captured, tortured, martyred in the Gestapo dungeons, executed by being shot, hanged, beheaded or crucified and left to expire of starvation. Many of them fell victims to the medical experiments in Auschwitz and in the women's concentration camp at Ravensbrück.

Their names appear on the rosters of almost all concentration camps, from the very first ones, Dachau for men and Moringen for women, both established in 1933. They hold places of honor at Auschwitz, Buchenwald, Mauthausen, Sachsenhausen, Flossenburg, Ravensbrück, and many others. They contributed a large proportion to the five million non-Jewish victims of the Nazi madness.

Chapter 3 deals with sources on the resistance. As a residue of my work Women in the Resistance and in the Holocaust, there are separate chapters on women in the resistance, in the Holocaust, and in hiding.

The subject of the Jewish Holocaust is better known than that of the resisters. Anti-Semitism is older than Christianity. In spite of widespread anti-Semitism, few people are familiar with the history of the Jews and their cultural and socioeconomic interactions in European history. It seems that the intensity of a person's anti-Semitism is often in direct ratio to his or her ignorance of the subject. That is basically the rationale behind the first chapter in this bibliography.

The second chapter, on Nazism, serves as an overture to both the resistance and to the Holocaust. The Nazi ideology included theories according to which certain "races" such as Slavs and Gypsies were inferior, unworthy of living, and had to be dealt with accordingly. Even the French, not belonging to the Germanic peoples, were to be kept under strict control in the Nazi world order. Hence the suppression of their ethnic and cultural manifestations and the resulting resistance to the oppression.

The Jews were the ultimate scapegoats of this demonology.

There was no place for them, only for their properties, which were
confiscated and greatly contributed to the German economy. The
Jews themselves were slated for extermination by the "furor Teuton-
icus."

It is inconceivable how an intelligent nation could fall en masse
for this ideology; how a nation of Heine could also produce a Himmler, a people of Goethe a Goebbels, a folk of Hesse a Hoess, and
the soil that bore the clergyman-poet Mörike could spew forth an
abomination such as Mengele.

One may attempt to understand--if not comprehend--it by
studying the tenets of Nazism as the initial stage of the Holocaust.

The road from the Nazi takeover in 1933 via the Nuremberg
Laws and the Kristallnacht--the Night of the Broken Glass--led to
the Wannsee Conference and the Final Solution. Once the pattern
was established by the higher-ups, the machinery of extermination
went into higher gear with typical efficiency and precision.

The first concentration camps were established long before the
outbreak of World War II. Dachau was inaugurated just a few weeks
after Hitler became chancellor of Germany. The announcement in the
press sounded like that of a cultural exhibit opening or a coming-
out party for the upper crust. The inmates were the often ignored
German resisters.

But it was after the Nazis, rolling over the apathy of the large
democracies, gained foothold over one country after another on their
Drang nach Osten, that the killing machines for the Jews sprung into action. From ghettos to self-dug mass graves, from experiments
with mobile gas chambers to mass gassings, the nation of Kultur-
Trägers (carriers of culture) proceeded: Chelmno, Belzec, Treblinka, Sobibor, Majdanek, and the crowning glory of it all, Auschwitz-
Birkenau, with five gas chambers and crematoria. Commandant
Hoess boasted that his new gas chambers could "accommodate" 2,000
people at one time.

The bodies and the souls of millions of Jews died many deaths,
as at every stage of their calvary they had to suffer through a new
fear, a new anxiety, a new type of undescribable horror.

Myths die slowly. One of these is that Jews did not fight
back but let themselves be led to slaughter like sheep. That simply
was not so. Even though it is impossible for a naked body to fight
against machine guns, there was a Jewish resistance, as the many
entries in Chapter 5 show. There were revolts in several ghettos
beside the one in Warsaw. There were uprisings in several extermination camps, notably in Sobibor and in Auschwitz. There were
cases of individual heroism, as that of the Czech actress Katerina
Horowitzova, who shot her tormentor before entering the gas cham-
ber.

Aside from that, many Jews simply joined resistance movements in their countries, fighting as faithful sons and daughters of France or Czechoslovakia or Yugoslavia.

There was also a considerable movement to save Jews by taking them by land or by river transport out of the orbit of the Nazis. The underground railroad attempting to spirit them away to Palestine was staffed almost exclusively by Jewish men and women.

Chapter 9 deals with entries related to the now established fact that the atrocities perpetrated by Nazis in Europe, in the concentration camps, and indeed the mass extermination of the Jews in gas chambers, were known in the West at least in 1942 if not earlier; chances are good that they were also known in the Soviet Union. There were numerous early warnings of things to come, noticeable from the dates of some publications as far back as the first half of the 1930's. Yet, the inconceivable which was happening in Nazi-dominated Europe, was met head-on by the unthinkable in London and Washington: apathy and inaction.

Chapter 10 deals with the frustrating subject of war crimes, that forty years after the end of the war is still not a satisfactorily closed affair. While no court of law can balance the evil caused by the Nazis and Nazism, and while no judge can resurrect eleven million people, it is a poor reflection on those Allies who fell down on the job in pursuing the perpetrators of war crimes and crimes against humanity to the end of the earth, as they had officially pledged to do during the war.

The remaining three chapters cover respectively art and photographs from the ghettos and concentration camps, philosophical and other interpretations of the abomination that was the Nazi persecution of the resisters and of the Jews, and the literature that sprung up in their wake.

Research Sources in General

Most source materials for research on topics of the European resistance against Nazism originate in the home countries; exceptions are the writings of former resisters residing abroad. The materials are usually concentrated in the national archives or leading libraries.

In all formerly Nazi-occupied countries there exist federations or unions of former resisters, political prisoners and victims of Nazism.

Thus, for instance, in France it is the Fédération Nationale

des Déportés et Internés Résistants et Patriots; in Czechoslovakia
it is the Svaz osvobozených politických vězňů a pozůstalých po
obětech nazismu (Union of Liberated Political Prisoners and Survivors
of Victims of Nazism). In most countries there are also organizations joining former inmates of individual prisons and concentration
camps. The larger ones of these maintain archives of primary
sources and memoirs, and publish periodicals or irregularly appearing
circular letters. Addresses of these organizations may be obtained
from consulates or embassies of a given nation.

There are museums and/or archives at the sites of several concentration camps or extermination camps, as for instance at Auschwitz, Dachau, Mauthausen, Terezín and others. In East Germany
this holds true for the Buchenwald concentration camp at Weimar,
Sachsenhausen at Oranienburg, and the women's concentration camp
of Ravensbrück at Fürstenberg.

Gestapo or police files, where available, can yield important
primary material, aside from surprises. A Czech resister, doing
research at the historical section of the archives in Prague years
after the war, came upon her own Gestapo file and read with amaze-
ment that she had had a trial in November of 1943, almost two years
after her arrival at Ravensbrück!

In Yugoslavia, where the partisans not only cooperated with
the military but, under Tito, actually became the spearhead of the
postwar government, the Military Historical Institute in Belgrade
maintains the resistance records.

Regarding the history of the Soviet partisan movement, the
best starting point still is John A. Armstrong, ed. Soviet Partisans
in World War II, which indicates in the bibliography a large number
of Soviet sources. Additional material can be found at the Russian
Research Center at Harvard University in Cambridge, Massachusetts,
at the Archives of Russian and East European History and Culture
at Columbia University in New York, at the Institute for the Study
of the History and Institutions of the U.S.S.R. in Munich, and of
course in the Soviet Union.

Although little is heard in the United States about the history
of the partisans, in all countries where the partisan movement was
strong, as in Yugoslavia, the Soviet Union, Poland and toward the
end of the war in France, there are primary and secondary materials
available. Access to them varies, and anything but personal visits
may prove frustrating. Knowing the language of the country makes
communication and research easier in more ways than one. In all
cases it is strongly urged that contact by mail be established before
venturing abroad.

Great Britain contributed considerable support to the resistance movements in many countries of Europe, from Norway to Greece,

and especially in France. The best starting point for research in this respect are the holdings at the Public Records Office in London, and M.R.D. Foot's monumental history of the Special Operations Executive (SOE). In Paris the collections of the Comité d'Histoire de la Deuxième Guerre Mondiale may also prove helpful.

American cooperation with the resistance occurred at a later date and was carried on alongside the British by the Office of Strategic Services (OSS); its papers are deposited at the Washington National Archives.

The literature of the Jewish Holocaust is enormous, enriched by countless personal memoirs of survivors. While this type of source material is tapering off, histories and interpretations will probably keep multiplying. There are about 10,000 publications on Auschwitz alone, written by former political prisoners and Jews from all over the world. The various stages of the Holocaust are documented: the persecutions, the ghettos, the deportations to the East, the concentration and extermination camps. The researcher must remember that because the resisters and political prisoners mingled with the Jewish victims in most camps, memoirs cannot be strictly divided; political memoirs talk about the treatment of the Jews, and Jewish memoirs mention the politicals.

The chief primary sources about the Holocaust, including the Jewish resistance, can be found in Israel. Yad Vashem Martyrs' and Heroes' Memorial Authority in Jerusalem is a major depository of documents, mostly in German, Hebrew and Yiddish, but also in many other languages. Yad Vashem publishes the Yad Vashem Studies and the Bulletin, also in English since 1957. The first ten issues, covering the years 1957-1961, are available in a bound volume. The Bulletin is most helpful; it contains an abundance of informative articles and occasional bibliographical entries. Anyone reaching the stage of research that would lead to Israel should start out with the archives of Yad Vashem, but only after prior correspondence. From there the road might lead to other archives such as that of the Histadrut in Tel Aviv or at a certain kibbutz and so on.

In London the most important depositories of source materials are at the Wiener Library, which, in its catalog series, published a bibliography, Persecution and Resistance under the Nazis (London: Vallentine, Mitchell, 1960); the Imperial War Museum; and the Public Records Office. In Paris, major sources of information may be found at the Centre de Documentation Juive Contemporaine, and to a degree at the archives of the Comité d'Histoire de la Deuxième Guerre Mondiale. In Germany, it is the Bundesarchiv at Koblenz and its East German counterpart at Potsdam near Berlin; the Central Historical Commission and the Institut für Zeitgeschichte in Munich; also the Geheimes Staatsarchiv and the Document Center, both in Berlin. Further sources are the Jewish Historical Institute in Warsaw which publishes Bulletin, the State Jewish Museum in Prague and its pub-

lication Judaica Bohemiae, and the International Red Cross Archives
in Geneva.

In the United States it is the Library of Congress and the
National Archives and Records Service which hold rich sources on
the subject. These include the transcripts of the war crime trials,
which are truly gigantic; the trial of the twenty-three doctors alone
takes up 11,538 pages. Helpful guides to the maze of countless
concentration camps and their branches are: Catalog of Camps and
Prisons in Germany and German Occupied Territories, September 1st,
1939-May 8th, 1945. 2 vols. (Arolsen, Germany: International
Tracing Service, 1949-1950), a total of 821 oversize pages; and
Vorläufiges Verzeichnis der Konzentrations-lager und deren Aussen-
kommandos sowie anderen Haftstatten under dem Reichsführer-SS in
Deutschland und deutsch besetzten Gebieten, 1933-1945 (Arolsen,
Germany: International Tracing Service, 1969). Both are in the
Library of Congress.

The World War II Records Division of the Archives is in Alexandria, Virginia, just outside of Washington, D.C. The War Refugee
Board Records and the Franklin Delano Roosevelt Library at Hyde
Park, New York also hold pertinent materials, especially regarding
the question of wartime immigration. The International Law Library
at Columbia University in New York City may also be consulted, especially on war crimes.

The YIVO Institute for Jewish Research in New York houses
several collections of ghetto documents and other related materials,
and publishes the Annual of Jewish Social Science. The YIVO Institute together with Yad Vashem projected a multivolume bibliographical series on the Holocaust; the volume by Jacob Robinson, ed.
The Holocaust and After: Sources and Literature in English (New
Brunswick, N.J.: Transaction, 1973) is most helpful.

The American Jewish Historical Society in Waltham, Massachusetts, on the campus of Brandeis University, is a further source.
Also at Brandeis is the Tauber Institute, founded in 1980, that carries on scholarly research on subjects of the Holocaust in the broad-
er framework of the general crisis of Europe in the twentieth century. Among the special collections at Brandeis University is the
"Jewish Resistance Collection," containing a modest but growing nu-
cleus of books and documents on this important subject.

Other sources are the Jewish Historical Society of New York;
the Leo Baeck Institute in New York, which publishes a yearbook;
the Jewish Publication Society of America in Philadelphia and New
York; the Anti-Defamation League of B'nai B'rith in New York; and
the Simon Wiesenthal Center for Holocaust Studies at Yeshiva University in Los Angeles. Founded in 1979, it publishes an informative
bulletin called Response and a scholarly periodical, the Simon Wiesenthal Center Annual, started in 1984. Other organizations devoted to

the topic are the Jewish Book Council of America in New York and
the United States Holocaust Memorial Council in Washington, D.C.

Helpful entries are also in Isaac Landman, ed. The Universal
Jewish Encyclopedia, 10 vols. (New York: KTAV, 1969 [1939-1969]),
the Encyclopedia Judaica, 16 vols., and the American Jewish Yearbook of the American Jewish Committee, and more specialized periodicals as for instance Hungarian-Jewish Studies or Jewish Social
Studies, both published in New York.

Even more general reference books often yield clues, as for
instance B.R. Mitchell, ed. European Historical Statistics, 1750-1970
(New York: Columbia University Press, 1975); Louis L. Snyder's
Historical Guide to World War II (Westport, Conn.: Greenwood
Press, 1982); or Louis L. Snyder, ed. Encyclopedia of the Third
Reich (New York: McGraw-Hill, 1976).

The gigantic task of helping bring war criminals to justice is
carried out at the Dokumentationszentrum des Bundes jüdischer Verfolgten des Naziregimes in Vienna. It is a modest office presided
by its founder and director, Simon Wiesenthal. The progress of his
work is summarized once a year in a newsletter sent, for a voluntary
contribution, to the supporters of the center. Because of the very
limited staff, only the most serious scholars should address inquiries
to this center. In the United States, the recently created Office of
Special Investigations in the Department of Justice is looking into
cases of several hundred Nazi war criminals who are naturalized
American citizens.

About This Bibliography

This bibliography deals only with book entries and is by necessity selective. Periodical literature almost all over the world carries articles on the Holocaust and, in many countries, on the resistance as well. It yields a rich harvest, especially in Russian, Polish,
Israeli, British, and American journals, as well as in the daily press,
some of which is blessedly indexed. Hopefully in the future a full
bibliography based on periodical literature will materialize. This is
such a tremendous task that only a large group of individuals or a
consortium of institutions in various countries could afford the time,
money and energy for its undertaking.

By far the largest problem in creating this bibliography was
that of categorization of certain books. People's lives are not lived
in categories, memoirs are not written to fit into pigeonholes.
Many resisters ended up in concentration camps joining the deported
Jews; Jews were in the national resistance movements. The category
of "Jewish Resistance" is by no means all-inclusive. There are chap-

ters on or mentions of Jewish resistance in books on non-Jewish resistance and on the Holocaust. Lines separating the two are not
always possible. Hundreds went through all stages of resistance,
hiding, concentration camps; a certain amount of overlapping is in-
evitable.

Hence books on specific concentration camps can not be considered as dealing exclusively with Jews or with politicals. Some
prisoners and/or authors did not even distinguish between the two.
This is especially so in monographs dealing primarily with medical
experiments, which are here listed somewhat arbitrarily under
"Holocaust."

In order to avoid too many categories (that would just multiply
the problem), some items are listed by necessity in a certain category. Thus, for instance, collaborators--the very opponents of the
resisters--are listed under "Resistance"; the homosexuals or "pink
triangles"--automatically considered criminals under German law--
under "Holocaust."

Should books dealing with Martin Bormann be listed under
"Nazism" or under "War Crimes"? Such questions were decided ac-
cording to the orientation or emphasis of the book. It is easier to
understand that Jenö Lévai's Eichman in Hungary is listed under
"Holocaust," but Hannah Arendt's Eichmann in Jerusalem under "War
Crimes."

Books dealing with Christians saving Jews are listed under
"Resistance" but also under "Holocaust," depending on the contents.
All Wallenberg entries are under "Holocaust."

At times a few entries might seem farfetched at first glance, as
for instance Jacobo Timerman's Prisoner Without a Name, Cell Without
a Number; it is included under "Anti-Semitism" because one aspect
of the book deals with it. There is an entry or two on the Armenian
mass killings for comparison sake; a few deal with non-European
activities, both in the resistance and in the Holocaust, as for instance Andrew Gilchrist's Bangkok Top Secret and Marvin Tokayer
and Mary Schwartz' Fugu Plan; they were included as a reminder
that the fingers of totalitarianism reached also outside the limits of
Europe.

The following books have double entries because, more than
others, they combine information essential in more than one category:
    Apenszlak, Jacob, ed. The Black Book of Polish Jewry, listed
        under "Holocaust" and "Pre-1945 Knowledge of the Holo-
        caust";
    Berben, Paul. Dachau, 1933-45, listed under "Resistance" and
        "Holocaust";
    Bogusz, Josef, ed. Przegled lekarski (Medical Survey), 3
        vols., listed under "Resistance" and "Holocaust";

Czech, Danuta, et al. Auschwitz, listed under "Resistance"
   and "Holocaust";
Karski, Jan, Story of a Secret State, listed under "Resistance"
   and "Pre-1945 Knowledge of the Holocaust";
Kent, George O., ed. A Catalog of Files and Microfilms, 3
   vols. listed under "Nazism" and "War Crimes";
Krausnick, Helmut and Broszat, Martin. Anatomy of the SS
   State, listed under "Nazism" and "Holocaust";
Laska, Vera, ed. Women in the Resistance and in the Holo-
   caust, listed under "Resistance-Women" and "Holocaust
   Women";
Robinson, Jacob and Sachs, Henry, eds., The Holocaust: The
   Nuremberg Evidence listed under "Holocaust" and "War
   Crimes";
Smolen, Kazimierz, et al., eds. From the History of KL Ausch-
   witz, listed under "Resistance" and "Holocaust."

Women have three categories of their own, in the resistance,
in the Holocaust and in hiding; yet there is hardly a book on these
topics that would not mention them in passim. Many of those women
simply mentioned deserve a biographer.

A large portion of the entries are annotated. An effort has
been made to keep these annotation concise. Where subtitles existed,
they were noted; in many cases the subtitles serve as an annotation.
A title such as The Capture and Trial of Eichmann does not need an
annotation, while The House on Garibaldi Street does; that was where
Eichman lived in Buenos Aires and where he was captured.

Of course the chief annotation is the category under which a
book is listed. Double entries are annotated where first mentioned,
with a reference to the second mention.

Much has been written about Nazis and Nazism, perhaps a
morbid attraction to some, even if a scholarly effort to others.
There are too many books on Hitler. After spending a number of
years dealing with the resistance and the Holocaust, and as a survivor of Auschwitz and other concentration camps, I feel that research should be channelled into more deserving aspects of these
topics. Such are for instance histories of concentration camps aside
from the "Big Three": Auschwitz, Dachau, Buchenwald. There
are more than a dozen others of which little has been published in
English.

Too little is also known about the priests and nuns in the resistance and in the camps, and even less about those among them
who were converts from Judaism. Not much has been done about
the homosexuals ("pink triangles") and nothing about the Lesbians.
The topics of the "black" and "green triangles," that is, the asocials
and the professional criminals, are in need of a chronicler. As all
survivors know, the "green triangles" played an important role in
all camps.

In a different direction, psychologists should focus on the psyches of the people in hiding; they were not cowards but rather courageous heroes and heroines in many cases. Hiding was, in a sense, a form of resisting. Many resisters had to go into temporary or permanent hiding.

A Few Technicalities

Abbreviations have been avoided as much as possible. Only two have been used: GPO, Government Printing Office, and HMSO, His/Her Majesty's Stationary Office, for the American respectively British official government publishers.

Parentheses are used for the English translations of titles in foreign languages other than Spanish, French and German, which are not translated, assuming, perhaps optimistically, that most people either know them or have somebody nearby who can translate the titles. Names in parentheses after the author's name indicate pseudonyms.

Diacritical marks are preserved in all languages (except Polish for technical reasons). Hungarian experts will overlook, we hope, the lack of differentiation between long and short ö's and ü's. Russian words are transcribed according to the Library of Congress usage though it is cumbersome and phonetically not quite logical, but at least consistent. German umlauts are transcribed either as ae, oe, and ue and alphabetized accordingly, or as ä, ö and ü, in which case the two dots are ignored in the alphabetization.

But of course most of the entries are books in English, published in the United States and in Great Britain. Almost all of the foreign language books can be located in one of the major American libraries.

I am deeply indebted to many librarians on three continents for their patience, initiative and counsel, but especially to the ones at the National Archives, the Library of Congress, Boston Public Library, Harvard University, Brandeis University and Regis College. The latter were most instrumental in lifting me over numerous hurdles through interlibrary loans, manning the newly acquired computer terminal and freely dispensing professional advice. For that, and for the many years of selfless support and friendship, this book is dedicated to them.

Vera Laska
Weston, Massachusetts

1. J E W S   A N D   A N T I - S E M I T I S M

1. Ackerman, Nathan W. and Jahoda, Maria. Anti-Semitism and Emotional Disorder: A Psychoanalytical Interpretation. New York: Harper & Bros., 1950.

2. Adler, H.G. The Jews of Germany, from the Enlightenment to National Socialism. Notre Dame, Ind.: Notre Dame University Press, 1969.

3. American Jewish Committee. The Jewish Communities of Nazi Occupied Europe. New York: Fertig, 1982.
   Originally published in 1944; a collection of reports on Jews in seventeen countries.

4. _____. The Jews in Nazi Germany. New York: Fertig, 1982.
   Originally published in 1935; includes texts of Nazi laws affecting Jews.

5. Aronsfeld, Caesar C. The Ghosts of Fourteen-Ninety-Two. New York: Columbia University Press, 1979.

6. Aronson, Gregor, et al. Russian Jewry, 1917-1967. New York: Yoseloff, 1969.

7. Avni, Haim. Spain, the Jews and Franco. Philadelphia: Jewish Publication Society of America, 1981.

8. Ball-Kaduri, Kurt J. Das Leben der Juden in Deutschland im Jahre 1933. Frankfurt am Main: Europaeische Verlagsanstalt, 1963.

9. Banas, Josef. The Scapegoats, the Exodus of the Remnants of Polish Jewry. New York: Holmes & Meier, 1979.

10. Belth, Nathan C., ed. Barriers, Patterns of Discrimination Against Jews. New York: Anti-Defamation League, 1958.

11. _____. A Promise to Keep, a Narrative of the American Encounter with Anti-Semitism. New York: Schocken, 1981.

1

12. Blair, B., ed. Essays of Jewish Life and Thought. New York:
     Columbia University Press, 1959.

13. Bourdrel, Philippe. Histoire des Juifs de France. Paris:
     Michel, 1974.

14. Byrnes, Robert F. Anti-Semitism in Modern France. New
     Brunswick, N.J.: Rutgers University Press, 1950.

15. Cohen, Martin A. The Jewish Experience in Latin America.
     2 vols. New York: KTAV, 1971.

16. Cohn, Norman. The Pursuit of the Milleneum. New York:
     Harper & Row, 1961.

17. Cong, Joel. The Silent Millions: A History of the Jews in the
     Soviet Union. New York: Taplinger, 1969.

18. Curtiss, John S. An Appraisal of the Protocols of Zion. New
     York: Columbia University Press, 1942.

19. Dimont, Max I. Jews, God and History. New York: Simon &
     Schuster, 1962.

20. Dinnerstein, Leonard, ed. Antisemitism in the United States.
     New York: Holt, Rinehart & Winston, 1971.

21. Dunker, Ulrich. Der Reichsbund Jüdischen Frontsoldaten,
     1919-1938. Düsseldorf: Droste, 1977.
         Deals with the controversial role of the German Jewish
     soldiers' organization, especially during the first two years
     of the Nazi regime.

22. Eban, Abba. My People, the Story of the Jews. New York:
     Random House, 1968.

23. Elkin, Judith L. Jews of the Latin American Republics. Chapel
     Hill: University of North Carolina Press, 1980.

24. Fackenheim, Emil L. The Jewish Return into History: Reflec-
     tions in the Age of Auschwitz and a New Jerusalem. New
     York: Schocken, 1980.

25. Field, Geoffrey C. Evangelist of Race: The Germanic Vision
     of Houston Stewart Chamberlain. New York: Columbia Uni-
     versity Press, 1981.

26. Fishman, Joshua T., ed. Studies of Polish Jewry, 1919-1939.
     New York: YIVO Institute, 1974.

27. Flannery, Edward H. The Anguish of the Jews, Twenty-Three

Centuries of Anti-Semitism. New York: Macmillan, 1965.
Objective treatment of the subject by Catholic priest.

28. Frumkin, Jacob, et al., eds. Russian Jewry, 1860-1917 and
Russian Jewry, 1917-1967. New York: Barnes, 1966, 1969.
Includes discussion of the Holocaust.

29. Fuchs, Lawrence. The Political Behavior of American Jews.
New York: Free Press, 1956.

30. Geehr, Richard S., ed. "I Decide Who Is a Jew!" The Papers
of Dr. Karl Lueger. Washington, D.C.: University Press
of America, 1982.
Turn-of-the-century anti-Semitic organizer and Vienna
mayor, Lueger was called the greatest statesman of pre-
World War I Austria by Hitler.

31. Gilboa, Yehoshua A. The Black Years of Soviet Jewry. Boston:
Little, Brown, 1971.

32. Glassman, Bernard. Anti-Semitic Stereotypes Without Jews.
Detroit, Mich.: Wayne State University Press, 1975.

33. Glassman, Samuel. The Epic of Survival, Twenty-Five Cen-
turies of Anti-Semitism. New York: Bloch, 1981.
Survey since the fifth century B.C., showing that anti-
Semitism changed little until the arrival of the Holocaust.

34. Graupe, Heinz Moshe. The Rise of Modern Judaism, an Intellectual History of German Jewry, 1650-1942. Melbourne,
Fla.: Krieger, 1982.

35. Hay, Malcolm. Thy Brother's Blood, the Roots of Christian
Anti-Semitism. New York: Hart, 1975 (1950).

36. Heller, Celia S. On the Edge of Destruction: Jews of Poland
Between the Two World Wars. New York: Schocken, 1980.

37. Holmes, Colin. Anti-Semitism and British Society, 1876 to 1939.
New York: Holmes & Meier, 1979.

38. Hurewitz, Jacob C. The Struggle for Palestine. Westport,
Conn.: Greenwood Press, 1968 (1950).

39. The International Jew: The World's Foremost Problem. 4 vols.
Dearborn, Mich.: Dearborn Publishing House, 1920-1922.
Originally published in the Dearborn Independent, a periodical of the Ford Motor Company. Abridged 1948 edition
also exists.

40. Isaac, Jules. The Teaching of Contempt: Christian Roots of
Anti-Semitism. New York: Holt, Rinehart & Winston, 1964.

41.   Johnpoll, Bernard K. The Politics of Futility: The General
      Jewish Workers Bund of Poland, 1917-1947. Ithaca, N.Y.:
      Cornell University Press, 1967.

42.   Katz, Jacob. Exclusiveness and Tolerance: Studies in Jewish-
      Gentile Relations in Medieval and Modern Times. Westport,
      Conn.: Greenwood Press, 1980.

43.   _____. From Prejudice to Destruction: Anti-Semitism, 1700-
      1933. Cambridge, Mass.: Harvard University Press, 1980.
      A scholarly reinterpretation of modern anti-Semitism,
      speeded up after 1870 and culminating in Nazism, by pro-
      fessor of Hebrew University in Jerusalem.

44.   _____. Out of the Ghetto: The Social Background of Jew-
      ish Emancipation, 1700-1870. New York: Schocken, 1978.

45.   Kisch, Guido, et al. Jews of Czechoslovakia, Historical Studies
      and Surveys. 2 vols. Philadelphia: Jewish Publication So-
      ciety of America, and New York: Society for the History of
      Czechoslovak Jews, 1968, 1971.
      A third and final volume on the war years is to appear in
      1984.

46.   Kochan, Lionel. The Jew and His History. New York: Schoc-
      ken, 1977.

47.   _____, ed. The Jews in Soviet Russia Since 1917. New
      York: Oxford University Press, 1970.

48.   Kublin, Hyman, ed. Studies of Chinese Jews. New York:
      Paragon, 1971.

49.   Le soldat juif dans les armées du monde. Tel Aviv: Maarachot,
      1967.

50.   Lebzelter, Gisela. Political Anti-Semitism in England, 1918-1939.
      New York: Holmes & Meier, 1979.

51.   Leschnitzer, Adolf. The Magic Background of Modern Anti-
      Semitism: An Analysis of the German-Jewish Relationship.
      New York: International University Press, 1956.

52.   Leslau, Wolf. Falasha Anthology. New Haven: Yale University
      Press, 1951.

53.   Low, Alfred D. Jews in the Eyes of the Germans from the En-
      lightenment to Imperial Germany. Philadelphia: Institute
      for the Study of Human Issues, 1979.

54.   Lowenthal, Leo and Guterman, Norbert. Prophets of Deceit.
      New York: Harper & Row, 1949.

55. Lowenthal, Marvin. The Jews of Germany: A Story of Sixteen
    Centuries. New York: Russell & Russell, 1970 (1936).

56. Marr, Wilhelm. Der Sieq des Judentums über das Germantum.
    Bern: Rudolph Costenoble, 1879.

57. Massing, Paul W. Rehearsal for Destruction: A Study of Po-
    litical Anti-Semitism in Imperial Germany. New York:
    Harper & Bros., 1949.

58. May, Harry S. Francisco Franco: The Jewish Connection.
    Washington, D.C.: University Press of America, 1978.

59. Mendes-Flohr, Paul R. and Reinharz, Jehuda, eds. The Jew
    in the Modern World: A Documentary History. New York:
    Oxford University Press, 1980.

60. Meyer, Peter, et al., eds. The Jews in the Soviet Satellites.
    Syracuse, N.Y.: Syracuse University Press, 1953.

61. Michaelis, Meir. Mussolini and the Jews: German-Italian Rela-
    tions and the Jewish Question in Italy, 1922-1945. New
    York: Oxford University Press, 1978.

62. Myerson, Abraham and Goldberg, Izaac. The German Jew.
    New York: Knopf, 1933.

63. Neugroschel, Joachim, ed. The Shtetl. New York: Richard
    Marek, 1980.

64. Niewyk, Donald L. The Jews in Weimar Germany. Baton
    Rouge: Louisiana State University Press, 1980.

65. _____. Socialist, Anti-Semite, and Jew: German Social
    Democracy Confronts the Problem of Anti-Semitism, 1918-
    1933. Baton Rouge: Louisiana State University Press,
    1971.

66. Patai, Raphael. The Jewish Mind. New York: Scribner's,
    1977.

67. _____ and Wing, Jennifer Patai. The Myth of the Jewish
    Race. New York: Scribner's, 1975.

68. Perlmutter, Nathan and Ruth Ann. The Real Anti-Semitism in
    America. New York: Arbor House, 1982.

69. Pilzer, Jay M. Anti-Semitism and Jewish Nationalism. Virginia
    Beach: Donning, 1980.

70. Pollins, Harold. Economic History of the Jews in England.

London: Associated University Presses, 1983.
Good survey of Jewish contributions from c. the thir-
teenth century to the present.

71. Porter, Jack N. The Jew as Outsider, Historical and Contempo-
      rary Perspectives, Collected Essays, 1974-1980. Washington,
      D.C.: University Press of America, 1981.

72. Pulzer, Peter G.J. The Rise of Political Anti-Semitism in Ger-
      many and Austria. New York: Wiley, 1964.

73. Reinharz, Jehuda. Fatherland or Promised Land, the Dilemma
      of the German Jew, 1893-1914. Ann Arbor: University of
      Michigan Press, 1975.

74. Rezzori, Gregor von. Memoirs of an Anti-Semite. New York:
      Penguin, 1982.

75. Robinson, Nehemiah. The Spain of Franco and Its Policies
      Toward the Jews. New York: Institute of Jewish Affairs,
      1953.

76. Roblin, Michael. Les Juifs de Paris. Paris: Picard, 1952.

77. Sacher, Howard M. The Course of Modern Jewish History.
      New York: Norton, 1974.

78. Sartre, Jean-Paul. Anti-Semite and Jew. New York: Schocken,
      1965 (1948).

79. Schappes, Morris U., ed. A Documentary History of the Jews
      in the United States, 1654-1875. New York: Schocken,
      1975.

80. Schultz, Joseph P. and Klausner, Carla L. From Destruction
      to Rebirth: The Holocaust and the State of Israel. Wash-
      ington, D.C.: University Press of America, 1978.

81. Schwarz, Solomon. The Jews in the Soviet Union. Syracuse,
      N.Y.: Syracuse University Press, 1951.

82. Sofer, Eugene. From Pale to Pampa. New York: Holmes &
      Meier, 1982.

83. Steinberg, Milton. A Partisan Guide to the Jewish Problem.
      New York: Bobbs-Merrill, 1945.

84. Stemper, Charles H., et al. Jews in the Mind of America.
      New York: Basic Books, 1966.

85. Timerman, Jacobo. Prisoner Without a Name, Cell Without a
      Number. New York: Vintage, 1981.

86. Vago, Bela and Mosse, George L., eds. Jews and Non-Jews in Eastern Europe, 1918-1945. New York: Wiley, 1974.

87. Wachsman, Z.H. Jews in Czechoslovakia. New York: The Resistance, 1944.

88. Weinberg, David H. A Community on Trial: The Jews of Paris in the 1930's. Chicago: The University of Chicago Press, 1977.

89. Wirth, Louis. The Ghetto. Chicago: The University of Chicago Press, 1928.

90. Wischnitzer, Mark. To Dwell in Safety: The Story of the Jewish Migration Since 1800. Philadelphia: Jewish Publication Society of America, 1949.

91. Zisenwine, David and Rossel, Seymour, eds. Anti-Semitism in Europe, Source of the Holocaust. New York: Behrman, 1976.

2. NAZISM

92. Abel, Theodore. The Nazi Movement. New York: Atherton, 1965.

93. _____. Why Hitler Came to Power. Englewood Cliffs, N.J.: Prentice-Hall, 1938.

94. Achille-Delmas, François. Adolf Hitler: Essay de biographie psychopathologique. Paris: Librairie Marcel Rivere, 1946.

95. Allen, William S. The Nazi Seizure of Power. Chicago: The University of Chicago Press, 1965; New York: Franklin Watts, 1984.

96. Alquen, Gunther d'. Die SS: Geschichte, Aufgabe und Organisation der Schutzstaffel der NSDAP. Berlin: Junker & Duenhaupt, 1939.

97. Arendt, Hannah. The Origins of Totalitarianism. New York: Harcourt, Brace, 1951.

98. Aronson, Shlomo. Heydrich und die Anfänge des SD in der Gestapo, 1931-1935. Berlin: Free University, 1967.

99. Ayconberry, Pierre. The Nazi Question, an Essay on the Interpretations of National Socialism, 1922-1975. New York: Pantheon, 1981.

100. Bade, Wilfrid. SA erobert Berlin. Munich: Knorr & Hirth, 1941.

101. Badia, G. Histoire de l'Allemagne contemporaine (1917-1962). 2 vols. Paris: Editions sociales, 1962.

102. Barron, L. Smythe, ed. The Nazis in Africa. Salisbury, N.C.: Documentary Publications, 1978.
    Nazi penetration in former German colonies in southwest Africa.

103. Baschwitz, Kurt. Der Massenwahn. Munich: Beck, 1932.

104. Baxter, Richard. Women of the Gestapo. London: Quality,
      1943.

105. Beck, Friedrich A. Kampf und Sieg, Geschichte der NSDAP
      in Gau Westfalen Süd. Dortmund: Westfalenverlag, 1938.

106. Becker, Howard. German Youth: Bound or Free? New York:
      Oxford University Press, 1946.

107. Bell, Leland V. In Hitler's Shadow: The Anatomy of American
      Nazism. Port Washington, N.Y.: Kennikat, 1973.

108. Bennecke, Heinrich. Hitler und die SA. Munich: Olzog,
      1962.

109. Benneckenstein, Paul M., ed. Dokumente der deutschen Poli-
      tik, 1933-1944. Berlin: Junker & Duennhaupt, 1939-1944.

110. Benze, Rudolf. Erziehung im Grossdeutschen Reich.
      Frankfurt am Main: Moritz Diesterweg, 1943.

111. Besgen, Achim. Der stille Befehl: Medizinalrat Kersten und
      das Dritte Reich. Munich: Nymphenbürger Verlag, 1960.

112. Bewley, Charles. Hermann Goering and the Third Reich.
      New York: Devin-Adair, 1962.

113. Beyerchen, Alan D. Scientists under Hitler. New Haven,
      Conn.: Yale University Press, 1982.

114. Bielenberg, Christabel. Ride Out the Dark. New York:
      Norton, 1971.
          British title The Past is Myself.

115. Binion, Rudolph. Hitler Among the Germans. Amsterdam:
      Elsevier, 1976.

116. Bleuel, Hans P. Sex and Society in Nazi Germany. Philadel-
      phia: Lippincott, 1973.

117. Bley, Wulf. SA marschiert. Stuttgart: Union DVG, 1933.

118. Bloch, Charles. Die SA und die Krise des NS-Regimes, 1934.
      Frankfurt am Main: Suhrkamp, 1970.

119. Bolkonsky, Sidney. The Distorted Image: German Jewish
      Perceptions of Germans and Germany, 1918-1935. New York:
      Elsevier, 1975.

120. Borinski, Friedrich and Milch, Werner. Jugendbewegung: The
      Story of German Youth, 1896-1933. London: German Edu-
      cational Reconstruction, 1945.

121. Borkin, Joseph. The Crime and Punishment of I.G. Farben.
      New York: Macmillan, 1978.
         Collaboration of I.G. Farben, "the jackal to Hitler's
      lion," with the Nazi regime, its pioneer usage of slave la-
      bor, and its postwar trials.

122. Bormann, Martin. Le testament politique de Hitler. Paris:
      Fayard, 1945.

123. Bracher, Karl D. The German Dictatorship: The Origins,
      Structure and Effects of National Socialism. New York:
      Praeger, 1970.

124. Brandenburg, Hans C. Die Geschichte der HJ [Hitler Jugend],
      Wege und Irrwege einer Generation. Cologne: Wissenschaft
      & Politik, 1968.

125. Broszat, Martin. German National Socialism, 1919-1945. Santa
      Barbara, Cal.: ABC-Clio, 1966.

126. _____. The Hitler State. London: Longman, 1981.

127. Brown Book of the Hitler Terror and the Burning of the
      Reichstag. London: Gollancz, 1933.

128. Buchheim, Hans. Das Dritte Reich, Grundlagen und Politische
      Entwiklung. Munich: Koessel, 1958.

129. _____. Glaubenkrise im Dritten Reich. Stuttgart: Deutsche
      Verlagsanstalt, 1953.

130. _____. Totalitarian Rule, Its Nature and Characteristics.
      Middletown, Conn.: Wesleyan University Press, 1968.

131. Buchheit, Gert. Der deutsche Geheimdienst: Geschichte der
      militärischen Abwehr. Munich: List, 1966.

132. Bullock, Alan. Hitler, a Study in Tyranny. New York:
      Harper & Row, 1962.
         Standard and most frequently used biography of Hitler.

133. Butler, Rohan D. The Roots of National Socialism, 1783-1933.
      New York: Dutton, 1942.

134. Butler, Rupert. The Black Angels, the Story of the Waffen
      SS. London: Hamlyn, 1982.

135. _____. Legions of Death, the Nazi Enslavement of Eastern
      Europe. London: Hamlyn, 1983.

136a. Carr, William. Hitler, a Study in Personality and Politics.
      New York: St. Martin's, 1979.

136b. Cecil, Robert. The Myth of the Master Race: Alfred Rosen-
      berg and Nazi Ideology. New York: Dodd, Mead, 1972.

137. Cianfarra, Camille M. The Vatican and the War. New York:
     Dutton, 1944.

138. Compton, James V. The Swastika and the Eagle. Boston:
     Houghton Mifflin, 1967.

139. Conway, John S. The Nazi Persecution of the Churches, 1933-
     1945. New York: Basic Books, 1968.

140. Crankshaw, Edward. The Gestapo: Instrument of Tyranny.
     New York: Viking, 1956.

141. Dallin, Alexander. German Rule in Russia, 1941-1945, a Study
     in Occupation Policies. New York: St. Martin's, 1957.

142. Delarue, Jacques. The Gestapo, a History of Horror. New
     York: Morrow, 1964.

143. Deschner, Gunther. Reinhard Heydrich. New York: Stein
     & Day, 1982.

144. Deuel, Wallace R. People Under Hitler. New York: Harcourt,
     Brace, 1942.

145. Deutsch, Harold C. Hitler and His Generals, the Hidden Cri-
     sis, January-June, 1938. Minneapolis: University of
     Minnesota Press, 1974.

146. Deutschland erwacht, Werden, Kampf und Sieg der NSDAP.
     Hamburg: Cigaretten-Bilderdienst, 1933.

147. Devoto, Andrea. Bibliografia dell'oppressione nazista fino al
     1962 (Bibliography of Nazi Oppression till 1962). Florence:
     Leo Olschki, 1964.

148. Diamond, Sandor A. The Nazi Movement in the United States.
     Ithaca, N.Y.: Cornell University Press, 1973.

149. Dicks, Henry V. Licensed Mass Murder: A Socio-Psychologi-
     cal Study of Some SS Killers. London: Heinemann, 1972.

150. Diels, Rudolf. Lucifer ante portas: Es spricht der erste Chef
     der Gestapo. Stuttgart: Deutsche Verlagsanstalt, 1950.

151. Dietrich, Otto. The Hitler I Knew. London: Methuen, 1955.

152. Dissman, Willi and Wegner, Max, eds. Jungen und Maedel im
     Krieg. Berlin: F. Schneider, 1941.

153. Dobkowski, Michael N. and Wallimann, Isidor. Towards the
     Holocaust: The Social and Economic Collapse of the Weimar
     Republic. Westport, Conn.: Greenwood Press, 1983.

154. Documents on German Foreign Policy, 1918-1945. Series D.
     11 vols. Washington, D.C.: GPO, 1937-1945.

155. Dodd, Martha. Through Embassy Eyes. New York: Har-
     court, Brace, 1939.

156. Dodd, William E. Ambassador Dodd's Diary, 1933-1938. New
     York: Harcourt, Brace, 1941.

157. Dokumente und Materialen aus der Vorgeschichte des zweiten
     Weltkrieges aus dem Archiv des deutschen Auswärtigen
     Amtes, 1937-1938. Berlin: Ministry of Foreign Affairs of
     the U.S.S.R., n.d.

158a. Dornberg, John. Munich 1923: The First Full Story of Hit-
     ler's Early Grab for Power. New York: Harper & Row,
     1982.
         A detailed account of the beer-hall putsch.

158b. _____. Schizophrenic Germany. New York: Macmillan,
     1961.

159. Ebeling, Hans. The German Youth Movement, Its Past and
     Future. London: New Europe, 1945.

160. Eckart, Dietrich. Der Bolshewismus von Moses bis Lenin:
     Zweigespräch zwischen Adolf Hitler und mir. Munich:
     Hoheneichen, 1924.

161. Enzor, R.C.K. Self-Disclosure in "Mein Kampf." London:
     Oxford University Press, 1939.

162. Everett, Susanne. Lost Berlin. New York: St. Martin's,
     1981.
         Oversized, lavishly illustrated work.

163. Fenyo, Mario D. Hitler, Horthy, and Hungary. New Haven,
     Conn.: Yale University Press, 1972.

164. Fernandez Artucio, Hugo. Nazi Underground in South Amer-
     ica. New York: Farrar & Rinehart, 1942.

165. Fest, Joachim C. The Face of the Third Reich, Portraits of
     the Nazi Leadership. New York: Pantheon, 1970.

166. _____. Hitler. New York: Vintage, 1975.

167. Fischer, Conan. Stormtroopers, a Social, Economic and Ideo-
     logical Analysis, 1929–35. Winchester, Mass.: Allen &
     Unwin, 1983.

168. Fleming, Peter. Operation Sea Lion. New York: Simon &
     Schuster, 1957.

169. Forssmann, Werner. Experiments on Myself, Memoirs of a
     Surgeon in Germany. New York: St. Martin's, 1974.
     An amazing autobiography of a conforming Nazi doctor.

170. Friedländer, Saul. Hitler et les Etats-Unis, 1939–1941. Gen-
     eva: Droz, 1963.

171. Friedlander, W. and Meyers, Earl D. Child Welfare in Ger-
     many Before and After Nazism. Chicago: University of
     Chicago Press, 1940.

172. Frischauer, Willi. The Rise and Fall of Hermann Goering.
     Boston: Houghton Mifflin, 1951.

173. Frye, Alton. Nazi Germany and the Western Hemisphere, 1933–
     1941. New Haven, Conn.: Yale University Press, 1967.

174. Gallo, Max. The Night of the Long Knives. New York: Harp-
     er & Row, 1972.

175. Gangulee, Nagendranath, ed. The Mind and Face of Nazi Ger-
     many. London: John Murray, 1942.

176. Gasman, Daniel. Scientific Origins of National Socialism. New
     York: Elsevier, 1971.

177. Gersdorff, Ursula von. Frauen im Kriegsdienst, 1914–1945.
     Stuttgart: Deutsche Verlagsanstalt, 1969.

178. Gisevius, Hans B. Adolf Hitler. Munich: Rütten B. Löning,
     1963.

179. Goebbels, Joseph. The Goebbels Diaries. Westport, Conn.:
     Greenwood Press, 1948.

180. Goldston, Robert C. The Life and Death of Nazi Germany.
     Indianapolis: Bobbs-Merrill, 1967.

181. Gordon, Harold J. Hitler and the Beer Hall Putsch. Prince-
     ton, N.J.: Princeton University Press, 1972.

182. Graber, G.S. History of the SS: The Most Terrifying Story
     of the Century. London: Granada, 1982.

183. _____. The Life and Times of Reinhard Heydrich. New York: McKay, 1980.

184. Gray, Ronald. I Killed Martin Bormann. New York: Lancer Books, 1972.

185. Grosshans, Henry. Hitler and the Artists. New York: Holmes & Meier, 1983.

186. Grunberger, Richard. Hitler's SS. New York: Dell, 1973.

187. _____. The Twelve-Year Reich: A Social History of Nazi Germany, 1933-1945. New York: Holt, Rinehart & Winston, 1971.

188. Grunfeld, Frederic V. The Hitler File: A Social History of Germany and the Nazis. New York: Random House, 1974.

189. Grzesinski, Albert C. Inside Germany. New York: Dutton, 1939.

190. Gun, Nerin E. Eva Braun, Hitler's Mistress. London: Leslie Frewin, 1969.

191. Gurian, Waldemar. Hitler and the Christians. New York: Sheed & Ward, 1936.

192. Haffner, Sebastian. The Meaning of Hitler. New York: Macmillan, 1979.
    Analysis of Hitler's personality, his bizarre relations with women, and his misconceptions.

193. Hale, Oron J. The Captive Press in the Third Reich. Princeton, N.J.: Princeton University Press, 1973.

194. Hamilton, James D. Motive for a Mission: The Story Behind Hess's Flight to Britain. New York: St. Martin's, 1971.

195. Hamilton, Richard F. Who Voted for Hitler? Princeton, N.J.: Princeton University Press, 1982.
    Analysis of votes by cities and parties for the Reichstag elections, 1919-1933; numerous tables, appendices; indispensable for political analysts.

196. Hamlin, David. The Nazi/Skokie Conflict, a Civil Liberties Battle. Boston: Beacon, 1980.

197. Hanfstaengl, Ernst. Hitler: The Missing Years. London: Eyre & Spottiswoode, 1957.

198. _____. Unheard Witness. Philadelphia: Lippincott, 1957.

199. Hanser, Richard. Putsch. New York: Pyramid, 1971.

200. Hartshorne, Edward Y. The German Universities and National
     Socialism. Cambridge, Mass.: Harvard University Press,
     1937.

201. Hauner, Milan. Hitler: A Chronology of His Life and Times.
     New York: St. Martin's, 1982.

202. Hayes, Paul M. Quisling: The Career and Political Ideas of
     Vidkum Quisling, 1887-1945. London: Newton Abbott,
     David & Charles, 1971.

203. Heiber, Helmut. Adolf Hitler: Eine Biographie. Berlin:
     Colloquium, 1960.

204. _____. Goebbels. New York: Da Capo, 1983.
     Poet to propaganda minister's story, based on his di-
     aries, by German author.

205. _____. Himmler aux cent visages. Paris: Fayard, 1969.

206. Heiden, Konrad. Der Fuehrer: Hitler's Rise to Power. Bos-
     ton: Houghton Mifflin, 1944.

207. _____. A History of National Socialism. New York: Octa-
     gon, 1971.

208. Herwarth von Bittenfeld, Hans H. Against Two Evils: Mem-
     oirs of a Diplomat-Soldier During the Third Reich. New
     York: Rawson, Wade, 1981.

209. Herzstein, Robert E. Adolf Hitler and the German Trauma,
     1913-1945: An Interpretation of the Nazi Phenomenon.
     New York: Perigee-Putnam, 1974.
     Hitler's impact on Germany and Europe, basing his rise
     to power on the German psyche. The British title is more
     revealing: When Nazi Dreams Come True: The Third
     Reich's Internal Struggle Over the Future of Europe After
     a Germany Victory--A Look at the Nazi Mentality, 1939-
     1945. (London: Abram-Sphere Books, 1982.)

210. _____. Adolf Hitler and the Third Reich, 1933-1945. Bos-
     ton: Houghton Mifflin, 1971.

211. _____. The War That Hitler Won. New York: Putnam's,
     1978.
     Goebbels propaganda machinery and terrorization of the
     mass mind of Germany.

212. Heston, Leonard L. The Medical Casebook of Adolf Hitler.
     New York: Stein & Day, 1980.

213. Hillgruber, Andreas. Germany and the Two World Wars.
      Cambridge, Mass.: Harvard University Press, 1982 (1967).
      Deals with hotly disputed war guilt of Germany in start-
      ing two world wars, including Hitler's role.

214. Hilton, Stanley E. Hitler's Secret War in South America,
      1939-1945. New York: Ballantine, 1982.

215. Hirsch, Phil, ed. Hitler and His Henchmen. New York: Py-
      ramid, 1967.

216. Hitler, Adolf. Hitler's Secret Book. New York: Grove, 1961.

217. _____. Hitler's Words. Washington, D.C.: American
      Council on Public Affairs, 1944.

218. _____. Mein Kampf. Boston: Houghton Mifflin, 1943.

219. _____. Secret Conversations, 1941-1944. New York:
      Farrar, Straus, 1953.

220. _____. The Speeches of Adolf Hitler. 2 vols. London:
      Oxford University Press, 1942.

221. Hofer, Walter, ed. Der Nationalsozialismus: Dokumente, 1933-
      1945. Frankfurt am Main: Fischer, 1957.

222. Hoffmann, Heinrich. Hitler über Deutschland. Munich: Eher,
      1932.

223. _____. Hitler Was My Friend. London: Burke, 1955.

224. Höhne, Heinz. The Order of the Death's Head: The Story of
      Hitler's SS. London: Pan Books, 1981; New York:
      Coward, McCann & Geoghegan, 1970.
         Contains valuable appendices, maps, statistics, bibliog-
      raphy of German sources. German original published in
      1966.

225. Homze, Edward L. Foreign Labor in Nazi Germany. Prince-
      ton, N.J.: Princeton University Press, 1967.

226. Horn, Wolfgang. Führerideologie und Parteiorganisation in
      der NSDAP, 1919-1933. Düsseldorf: Droste, 1972.

227. Hory, Ladislaus and Broszat, Martin. Der Croatische Ustascha-
      Staat, 1941-1945. Stuttgart: Deutsche Verlags-Anstalt, 1964.

228. Hossbach, Friedrich. Zwischen Wehrmacht und Hitler. Göt-
      tingen, West Germany: Bandenhöck und Ruprecht, 1965
      (1949).

229. Hutton, Joseph B. Hess, the Man and His Mission. New
      York: Macmillan, 1970.

230. Igra, Samuel. Germany's National Vice. London: Quality,
      1945.

231. Infield, Glenn B. Hitler's Secret Life. London: Hamlyn,
      1980.

232. Irving, David. Hitler's War. New York: Viking, 1977.

233. _____, ed. Breach of Security: The German Secret Intel-
      ligence File on Events Leading to the Second World War.
      London: Kimber, 1968.

234. Jansen, Jon and Weyl, Stefan. The Silent War. Philadelphia:
      Lippincott, 1943.

235. Jenks, William A. Vienna and the Young Hitler. New York:
      Columbia University Press, 1960.

236a. Jong, Louis de. The German Fifth Column in the Second
      World War. Chicago: The University of Chicago Press,
      1956.

236b. Kahn, David. Hitler's Spies: German Military Intelligence in
      World War II. New York: Macmillan, 1978.

237. Kamenetsky, Ihor. German Lebensraum Policy in Eastern Eu-
      rope. Ann Arbor: University of Michigan, 1982. Micro-
      film.

238. _____. Secret Nazi Plans for Eastern Europe. New Haven,
      Conn.: College and University Press, 1961.

239. Keegan, John. Waffen SS: The Asphalt Soldiers. New York:
      Ballantine, 1970.

240. Kehr, Helen and Langmaid, Janet. The Nazi Era, 1919-1945.
      New York: H.W. Wilson, 1982.
          This is a bibliography of the Nazi era in the broader
      sense; includes items on the Holocaust.

241. Kempowski, Walter. Did You Ever See Hitler? New York:
      Avon, 1975.

242. Kent, George O., ed. A Catalog of Files and Microfilms of the
      German Foreign Ministry Archives, 1920-1943. 3 vols.
      Stanford, Cal.: Hoover Institution, 1962-1966.

243. Kersten, Felix. The Memoirs of Doctor Felix Kersten. Garden
      City, N.Y.: Doubleday, 1947.

244. Kessel, Joseph. The Man with the Miraculous Hands. New York: Dell, 1962.

245. Kessler, Harry Graf. Walter Rathenau, sein Leben und sein Werk. Wiesbaden: Rheinische Verlaganstalt, 1962.

246. Kielmansegg, Johann A. Der Fritschprozess. Hamburg: Hoffman & Campe, 1949.

247. Killinger, Manfred von. Die SA in Wort und Bild. Leipzig: Kittler, 1933.

248. Kirkpatrick, Clifford. Nazi Germany: Its Women and Family Life. Indianapolis: Bobbs-Merrill, 1938.

249. Klose, Werner. Lebensformen deutscher Jugend, vom Wander-vogel zur Popgeneration. Munich: Olzog, 1970.

250. Knight-Patterson, W.M. (W. Kulski). Germany from Defeat to Conquest. London: George Allen & Unwin, 1945.

251. Koehl, Robert L. RKFDV, German Resettlement and Population Policy, 1939-1945. Cambridge, Mass.: Harvard University Press, 1957.

252. Koenigsberg, Richard A. Hitler's Ideology, a Study in Psycho-analytic Sociology. New York: Library of Social Science, 1975.

253. Koeves, Tibor. Satan in Top Hat: Biography of Franz von Papen. New York: Alliance, 1941.

254. Kohn, Hans. The Mind of Germany: The Education of a Na-tion. New York: Scribner's, 1960.

255. Komjathy, Anthony and Stockwell, Rebecca. German Minorities and the Third Reich. New York: Holmes & Meier, 1980.

256. Krausnick, Helmut and Broszat, Martin. Anatomy of the SS State. London and New York: Granada, 1982.
      Reprint of classic and definitive German treatment on the persecution of Jews and concentration camps by two German historians.

257. Krebs, Albert. Tendenzen und Gestalten der NSDAP, Erin-nerungen an die Frühzeit der Partei. Stuttgart: DVA, 1959.

258. Krüger, Horst. The Crack in the Wall, Growing Up Under Hitler. New York: Fromm International, 1982.

259. Kubizek, August. The Young Hitler I Knew. Boston: Hough-
      ton Mifflin, 1955.

260. Kuehnl, Reinhard. Der deutsche Faschismus in Quellen und
      Dokumenten. Cologne: Pahl-Rugenstein, 1975.

261. Lackó, Miklós. Arrow-Cross Men, National Socialists, 1933-44.
      Budapest: Akadémiai kiadó, 1969.

262. Land, Barbara M. and Rupp, Leila J., eds. Nazi Ideology
      Before 1933: A Documentation. Austin: University of
      Texas Press, 1978.

263. Lang, Daniel. A Backward Look: Germans Remember. New
      York: McGraw-Hill, 1979.
          German guilt acknowledged and denied, but mostly ig-
      nored.

264. Lang, Jochen von. The Secretary: Martin Bormann the Man
      Who Manipulated Hitler. New York: Random House, 1979.
          Biography of a colorless man with immense power behind
      the throne.

265. Langer, Walter C. The Mind of Adolf Hitler: The Secret
      Wartime Report. New York: Basic Books, 1972.

266. Laqueur, Walter Z. Young Germany: A History of the Ger-
      man Youth Movement. London: Routledge & Kegan Paul,
      1962.

267. Larsen, Stein U., et al., eds. Who Were the Fascists? Oslo:
      Norwegian University Presses, 1979.

268. Lemkin, Raphael. Axis Rule in Occupied Europe. Washington,
      D.C.: Carnegie Endowment for International Peace, 1944.

269. Levy, Richard S. The Downfall of Anti-Semitic Political Par-
      ties in Imperial Germany. New Haven, Conn.: Yale Uni-
      versity Press, 1975.

270. Lewy, Guenter. The Catholic Church and Nazi Germany.
      New York: McGraw-Hill, 1964.

271. Liddell Hart, Basil H. The German Generals Talk. New York:
      Morrow, 1948.

272. Lilge, Frederic. The Abuse of Learning: The Failure of the
      German University. New York: Macmillan, 1948.

273. Ludecke, Kurt G. I Knew Hitler. New York: Scribner's,
      1957.

274. Macksey, K.J. Panzer Division: The Mailed Fist. New York:
     Ballantine, 1968.

275. Malitz, Horst. The Evolution of Hitler's Germany. New York:
     McGraw-Hill, 1973.

276. Mann, Erika. School for Barbarians: Education Under the
     Nazis. New York: Modern Age, 1938.

277. Manning, Paul. Martin Bormann--Nazi in Exile. Secaucus,
     N.J.: Lyle Stuart, 1981.

278. Manwell, Roger. SS and Gestapo: Rule of Terror. New
     York: Ballantine, 1976.

279. _____ and Fraenkel, Heinrich. Doctor Goebbels, His Life
     and Death. New York: Simon & Schuster, 1960.

280. Maser, Werner. Hitler: Legend, Myth and Reality. New
     York: Harper & Row, 1973.

281. _____, ed. Hitler's Letters and Notes. New York: Harper
     & Row, 1974.

282. Mayer, Milton. They Thought They Were Free: The Germans,
     1933-45. Chicago: The University of Chicago Press, 1966.

283. McGovern, James. Martin Bormann. London: Arthur Barker,
     1968.

284. McGovern, William M. From Luther to Hitler. Boston: Hough-
     ton Mifflin, 1941.

285. McKale, Donald M. Hitler, the Survival Myth. New York:
     Stein & Day, 1981.

286. _____. The Swastika Outside Germany. Kent, Ohio: Kent
     State University Press, 1977.
     Nazi organizations abroad.

287. Merkl, Peter H. The Making of a Stormtrooper. Princeton,
     N.J.: Princeton University Press, 1980.
     Stormtroopers' contribution to Hitler's takeover of Ger-
     many and of Europe.

288. _____. Political Violence Under the Swastika: 581 Early
     Nazis. Princeton, N.J.: Princeton University Press, 1975.

289. Mitchell, Otis C. Hitler Over Germany: The Establishment of
     the Nazi Dictatorship (1918-1934). Philadelphia: Institute
     for the Study of Human Issues, 1983.

290. _____, ed. Nazism and the Common Man: Essays in Ger-
      man History (1929–1939). Washington, D.C.: University
      Press of America, 1981.

291. Mollo, Andrew. To the Death's Head True: The Story of the
      SS. London: Methuen, 1982.

292. Mosse, George L. The Crisis of German Ideology: Intellectual
      Origins of the Third Reich. New York: Schocken, 1981
      (1964).

293. _____. Germans and Jews: The Right, the Left, & the
      Search for a "Third Force" in pre-Nazi Germany. New
      York: Fertig, 1970.

294. _____. Nazism: An Historical and Comparative Analysis of
      National Socialism. New Brunswick, N.J.: Transaction,
      1978.

295. _____. Toward the Final Solution: A History of European
      Racism. New York: Harper & Row, 1980.

296. _____, ed. Nazi Culture. New York: Schocken, 1981
      (1966).

297. Munske, Hilde. Maedel im Dritten Reich. Berlin: Freiheits-
      verlag, 1935.

298. Nagy-Talavera, Nicholas M. The Green Shirts and the Others:
      A History of Fascism in Hungary and Rumania. Stanford,
      Cal.: Hoover Institution, 1970.

299. Neuhäusler, Johann. Kreuz und Hackenkreuz. 2 vols.
      Munich: Katolische Kirche Bayerns, 1946. Later revised
      edition, under title Amboss und Hammer, Erlebnisse im
      Kirchenkampf des Dritten Reichs. Munich: Manz, 1967.
      Deals also with church resistance against nazism.

300. Neumann, Franz. Behemoth: The Structure and Practice of
      National Socialism, 1933–1934. New York: Oxford Univer-
      sity Press, 1944.

301. Neumann, Peter. The Black March, The Personal Story of an
      SS Man. New York: Bantam, 1967.

302. Noakes, Jeremy and Pridham, Geoffrey, eds. Documents of
      Nazism, 1919–1945. New York: Viking, 1975.

303. Nolte, Ernst. Three Faces of Facism: Action Française,
      Italian Facism, National Socialism. New York: Holt, Rine-
      hart & Winston, 1966.

304. O'Donnell, James P. The Bunker. Boston: Houghton Mifflin, 1978.
     The last days of Nazism.

305. Olden, Rudolf. Hitler the Pawn. London: Gollancz, 1936.
     Early biography by anti-Nazi author. Also appeared in
     the United States as Hitler, New York: Covici, 1936.

306. Orlow, Dietrich. The History of the Nazi Party, 1919-1933.
     Pittsburgh: University of Pittsburgh Press, 1969.

307. _____. The History of the Nazi Party, 1933-1945. Pitts-
     burgh: University of Pittsburgh Press, 1972.

308. _____. The Nazis in the Balkans. Pittsburgh: University
     of Pittsburgh Press, 1968.

309. Papen, Franz von. Memoirs. New York: Dutton, 1953.

310. Payne, Robert. Life and Death of Adolf Hitler. New York:
     Praeger, 1973.

311. Peterson, Edward N. Hjalmar Schacht: For and Against Hit-
     ler. Boston: Christopher, 1954.

312. Picard, Max. Hitler in Ourselves. Chicago: Regnery, 1947.

313. Picker, Henry. Hitler's Table Talk. London: Weidenfeld &
     Nicolson, 1953.

314. _____ and Hoffmann, Heinrich. Hitler Close-Up. New York:
     Macmillan, 1974.

315. Pinson, Koppel S. Modern Germany. New York: Macmillan,
     1934.

316. Piotrowski, Stanislaw, ed. Hans Frank's Diary. Warsaw:
     Panstwowe wydawnictwo naukowe, 1961.

317. Platner, Geert, et al. Schule im Dritten Reich--Erziehung zum
     Tod? Eine Dokumentation. Munich: Deutscher Taschen-
     buch Verlag, 1983.
     Study carried out by author and his high school stu-
     dents. During the process they discovered a "righteous
     gentile" saving Jewish children in Buchenwald, Wilhelm
     Hammann.

318. Pool, James and Pool, Susanne. Who Financed Hitler: The
     Secret Funding of Hitler's Rise to Power, 1919-1933. New
     York: Dial, 1979.

319. Poole, Kenyon E. German Financial Policies, 1937-1939. Cambridge, Mass.: Harvard University Press, 1939.

320. Pore, Renate. A Conflict of Interest: Women in German Social Democracy, 1919-1933. Westport, Conn.: Greenwood Press, 1981.

321. Pross, Harry. Jugend, Eros, Politik, die Geschichte der deutschen Jugendverbände. Bern: Scherz, 1964.

322. Quarrie, Bruce. Hitler's Samurai: The Waffen-SS in Action. New York: Arno, 1983.

323. Raeder, Erich. My Life. Annapolis, Md.: U.S. Naval Institute, 1960.

324. Reed, Douglas. Nemesis? The Story of Otto Strasser. Boston: Houghton Mifflin, 1940.

325. Rees, J.R., ed. The Case of Rudolf Hess. London: Heinemann, 1947.

326. Reichmann, Eva G. Hostages of Civilization, the Social Sources of National Socialist Anti-Semitism. Boston: Beacon, 1951.

327. Reitlinger, Gerald R. The House Built on Sand: Conflicts of German Policy in Russia, 1939-1945. London: Weidenfeld & Nicolson, 1960.

328. _____. The SS: Alibi of a Nation, 1922-1945. New York: Viking, 1957.

329. Remak, Joachim, ed. The Nazi Years. Englewood Cliffs, N.J.: Prentice-Hall, 1969.

330. Rhodes, James M. The Hitler Movement, a Modern Millenarian Revolution. Stanford, Cal.: Hoover Institution, 1979.

331. Ribbentrop, Joachim. The Ribbentrop Memoirs. London: Weidenfeld & Nicolson, 1954.

332. Rich, Norman. Hitler's War Aims: The Establishment of the War Order. 2 vols. New York: Norton, 1973-1974.

333. Riess, Curt. Joseph Goebbels: A Biography. Garden City, N.Y.: Doubleday, 1948.

334. Roberts, Stephen H. The House That Hitler Built. New York: Harper & Bros., 1938.

335. Roehm, Ernst. Die Geschichte eines Hochverräters. Munich: Eher, 1933.

336. Roper, Edith and Leiser, Clara. Nazi Justice. New York:
     Dutton, 1949.

337. Rosenberg, Alfred. Memoirs. New York: Ziff-Davis, 1949.

338. _____. Die Protokolle der Weisen von Zion und die Jüdische
     Weltpolitik. Munich: Deutscher Volksverlag, 1923.

339. Roxan, David and Wanstall, Ken. The Rape of Art. New York:
     Coward-McCann, 1964.

340. Sagitz, Walter. Bibliographie des Nationalsozialismus. Cott-
     bus: Heine, 1933.

341. Sanders, Marion K. Dorothy Thompson: A Legend in Her
     Time. Boston: Houghton Mifflin, 1973.

342. Sautter, Reinhold. Hitlerjugend. Munich: Roehrig, 1942.

343. Sayers, Michael and Kahn, Albert. Sabotage: The Secret
     War Against America. New York: Harper & Bros., 1942.

344. Schacht, Hjalmar. Confessions of "The Old Wizard." Boston:
     Houghton Mifflin, 1956.

345. Schirach, Baldur von. Ich glaubte an Hitler. Hamburg:
     Mozaik, 1967.

346. Schmidt, Paul. Hitler's Interpreter: The Secret History of
     German Diplomacy, 1936-1945. New York: Macmillan, 1951.

347. Schnabel, Reimund. Macht ohne Moral. Frankfurt am Main:
     Röderberg, 1957.

348. Schoenbaum, David. Hitler's Social Revolution: Class and
     Status in Nazi Germany, 1933-1939. New York: Norton,
     1980.

349. Schulz, Sigrid. Germany Will Try Again. New York: Reynal
     & Hitchcock, 1944.

350. Schuschnigg, Kurt von. Austrian Requiem. New York: Put-
     nam's, 1946.

351. Schwartz, Paul. This Man Ribbentrop: His Life and Times.
     New York: Messner, 1943.

352. Schweitzer, Arthur. Big Business in the Third Reich.
     Bloomington: Indiana University Press, 1964.

353. Seabury, Paul. The Wilhelmstrasse: A Study of German Dip-

lomats Under the Nazi Regime.   Berkeley: University of
California Press, 1954.

354.   Seaton, Albert.   The German Army, 1933-1945.   London:
       Weidenfeld & Nicolson, 1982.

355.   Second Brown Book of the Hitler Terror.   London: Bodley
       Head, 1934.

356.   Seibert, Theodore.   Das amerikanische Rätsel: Die Kriegs-
       politik der USA under Roosevelt.   Berlin: Eher, 1941.

357.   Seth, Ronald.   Operation Barbarossa: The Battle for Moscow.
       London: A. Blond, 1964.

358.   Shirer, William L.   Berlin Diary.   New York: Knopf, 1943.

359.   _____.   End of Berlin Diary.   New York: Knopf, 1947.

360.   _____.   The Rise and Fall of the Third Reich: A History
       of Nazi Germany.   New York: Simon & Schuster, 1960.
       Widely accepted history by observant journalist.

361.   Siemer, Pat.   Two Thousand and Ten Days of Hitler.   New
       York: Harper & Bros., 1940.

362.   Skorzeny, Otto.   Skorzeny's Special Missions.   New York:
       McGraw-Hill, 1957.

363.   Smith, Bradley F.   Adolf Hitler, His Family, Childhood, and
       Youth.   Stanford, Cal.:   Hoover Institution, 1967.

364.   _____.   Heinrich Himmler: A Nazi in the Making.   Stan-
       ford, Cal.:   Hoover Institution, 1971.

365.   Snyder, Louis L.   From Bismarck to Hitler: The Background
       of German Nationalism.   Williamsport, Penn.:   Bayard,
       1935.

366.   _____.   Hitler and Nazism.   New York: Bantam, 1967.

367.   _____.   (Nordicus).   Hitlerism: The Iron Fist in Germany.
       New York: Mohawk Press, 1932.

368.   _____.   Hitler's Third Reich, a Documentary History.   Chi-
       cago: Nelson-Hall, 1981.

369.   _____.   Race: A History of Modern Ethnic Theories.   Chi-
       cago: Alliance, 1939.

370.   _____, ed.   Encyclopedia of the Third Reich.   New York:

McGraw-Hill, 1976.
While only a one-volume handbook, it is indispensable.

371. Speer, Albert. Infiltration: How Heinrich Himmler Schemed
    to Build an SS Industrial Empire. New York: Macmillan,
    1981.

372. _____. Inside the Third Reich. New York: Avon, 1971.

373. Spott, Frederic. Church and Politics in Germany. Middletown,
    Conn.: Wesleyan University Press, 1973.

374. Stachura, Peter D. Gregor Strasser and the Rise of Nazism.
    London: George Allen & Unwin, 1983.
    About an SS leader who cared for Germany and was shot
    on orders of his erstwhile protégé Himmler.

375. _____. Nazi Youth in the Weimar Republic. Santa Barbara,
    Cal.: ABC-Clio, 1975.

376. _____, ed. The Nazi Machtergreifung. London: George
    Allen & Unwin, 1983.
    Ten essays about Hitler's takeover.

377. _____, ed. The Shaping of the Nazi State. New York:
    Barnes & Noble, 1978.

378a. Staudinger, Hans, ed. The Inner Nazi: A Critical Analysis
    of Mein Kampf. Baton Rouge, La.: Baton Rouge University
    Press, 1981.

378b. Stein, George H. The Waffen SS, Hitler's Elite Guard of War,
    1939-1945. Ithaca, N.Y.: Cornell University Press, 1966.

379. Steinert, Marlis G. Hitler's War and the Germans: Public
    Mood and Attitude During the Second World War. Athens:
    Ohio University Press, 1977.
    Of interest to historians and psychologists as well.

380. Stephenson, Jill. Women in Nazi Society. London: Croom
    Helm, 1975.

381. Stern, J.P. Hitler: The Führer and the People. Berkeley:
    University of California Press, 1975.

382. Stierlin, Helen. Adolf Hitler, a Family Perspective. New
    York: Psychohistory Press, 1976.

383. Strasser, Bernard P. Gregor und Otto Strasser. Baden:
    Stössel, Kühlsheim, 1954.

384. Strasser, Gregor. Mein Kampf. Frankfurt am Main: Heine, 1969.

385. Strasser, Otto. Hitler and I. London: Cape, 1940.

386. Sydnor, Charles W. Soldiers of Destruction, the SS Death's Head Division, 1933-1945. Princeton, N.J.: Princeton University Press, 1977.

387. Tauber, Kurt P. Beyond Eagle and Swastika, German Nationalism Since 1945. 2 vols. Middletown, Conn.: Wesleyan University Press, 1967.

388. Taylor, Alan J.P. Origins of the Second World War. New York: Atheneum, 1962.

389. Taylor, Telford. Sword and Swastika: Generals and Nazis in the Third Reich. New York: Simon & Schuster, 1952.

390. Thomas, Catherine. Women in Nazi Germany. London: Gollancz, 1943.

391. Thompson, Dorothy. I Saw Hitler. New York: Farrar & Rinehart, 1932.

392. Thomsen, Erich. Deutsche Besatzpolitik in Dänmark, 1940-1945. Düsseldorf: Bertelsmann, 1971.

393. Thyssen, Fritz. I Paid Hitler. New York: Farrar & Rinehart, 1941.

394. Tilton, Timothy A. Nazism, Neo-Nazism and the Peasantry. Bloomington: University of Indiana Press, 1975.

395. Toland, John. Adolf Hitler. Garden City, N.Y.: Doubleday, 1976.

396. _____. The Last 100 Days. New York: Random House, 1965.

397. Tolischus, Otto D. They Wanted War. New York: Reynal & Hitchcock, 1940.

398. Tolstoy, Nikolai. Night of the Long Knives. New York: Ballantine, 1972.

399. Trevor-Roper, H.R. The Bormann Letters. London: Weidenfeld & Nicolson, 1954.

400. _____. Hitler's War Directives, 1939-1945. London: Sidgwick & Jackson, 1964.

401. _____. The Last Days of Hitler. New York: Macmillan, 1947.

402. Turner, Henry A. Jr., ed. Nazism and the Third Reich. New York: Quadrangle, 1972.

403. Tyrell, Albrecht, ed. Führer Befiel ..., Selbstzeugnisse aus der Kampfzeit der NSDAP. Düsseldorf: Droste, 1960.

404. Unger, Michael, ed. The Memoirs of Bridget Hitler. London: Duckworth, 1979.
     Memoirs of Hitler's Irish sister-in-law.

405. Viereck, Peter. Metapolitics: The Roots of the Nazi Mind. New York: Putnam's, 1961.

406a. Volz, Hans. Daten der Geschichte der NSDAP, 10th edition. Berlin: Junker & Dünnhaupt, 1939.

406b. Von Staden, Wendelgard. Darkness Over the Valley. New York: Penguin, 1982.
     Country life of well-to-do Germans who treated their slave labor well; by niece of Hitler's first foreign minister.

407. Wagner, Jonathan F. Brothers Beyond the Sea: National Socialism in Canada. Atlantic Highlands, N.J.: Humanities Press, 1981.
     Hitler manipulated National Socialists in Canada; most were simple folk, poorly assimilated to their new land. Based on both German and Canadian sources.

408. Wagner, Ludwig. Hitler: Man of Strife. New York: Norton, 1942.

409. Waite, Robert G.L. The Psychopathic God, Adolf Hitler. New York: Signet, 1977.

410. _____. Vanguard of Nazism: The Free Corps Movement in Post-War Germany, 1918-1923. Cambridge, Mass.: Harvard University Press, 1952.

411. Walker, Lawrence D. Hitler Youth and Catholic Youth, 1933-1936. Washington, D.C.: Catholic University of America Press, 1970.

412. Walther, Herbert, ed. Hitler. New York: Frederick Fell, 1983.

413. Warlimont, Walter. Inside Hitler's Headquarters, 1939-45. New York: Praeger, 1966.

414. Weber, Hermann. Die Wandlung des deutschen Kommunismus.
      2 vols. Frankfurt: EVA, 1969.

415a. Weinreich, Max. Hitler's Professors: The Part of Scholarship
      in Germany's Crimes Against the Jewish People. New York:
      Yiddish Scientific Institute, 1946.

415b. Weinstein, Fred. The Dynamics of Nazism: Leadership, Ide-
      ology and the Holocaust. New York: Academic Press, 1980.

416. Weiszäcker, Ernst von. Memoirs. Chicago: Regnery, 1957.

417. Whaley, Barton. Codeword Barbarossa. Cambridge, Mass.:
      MIT Press, 1973.

418. Wheatley, Ronald. Operation Sea Lion. Oxford: Clarendon,
      1958.

419. Wheeler-Bennett, John W. Hindenburg, the Wooden Titan.
      London: Macmillan, 1936.

420. _____. Knaves, Fools and Heroes in Europe Between the
      Wars. London: Macmillan, 1974.

421. _____. Munich: Prologue to Tragedy. New York: Viking,
      1965 (1948).

422. _____. The Nemesis of Power: The German Army in Poli-
      tics, 1918-1945. London: Macmillan, 1953.

423. Whittlesey, Derwent. German Strategy of World Conquest.
      New York: Farrar & Rinehart, 1947.

424. Wighton, Charles. Heydrich: Hitler's Most Evil Henchman.
      Radnor, Pa.: Chilton, 1962.

425. _____ and Peis, Gunter. Hitler's Spies and Saboteurs.
      New York: Charter, 1979.

426. Winkler, Dorte. Frauenarbeit im Dritten Reich. Hamburg:
      Hoffman & Campe, 1977.

427. Wistrich, Robert. Who's Who in Nazi Germany. New York:
      Macmillan, 1982.
          Lists approximately 350 prominent Germans' biographies.

428. Wunderlich, Frieda. Farm Labor in Germany, 1810-1945.
      Princeton, N.J.: Princeton University Press, 1961.

429. Zahn, Gordon C. German Catholics and Hitler's Wars, a Study
      in Social Control. New York: Sheed & Ward, 1962.

430. Zeman, Z.A.B. Nazi Propaganda. New York: Oxford Univer-
      sity Press, 1973.

431. Ziemer, Gregor. Education for Death: The Making of a Nazi.
      New York: Octagon, 1972 (1941).

432. Zinner, Paul E. Communist Strategy and Tactics in Czecho-
      slovakia, 1918-1948. New York: Praeger, 1963.

433. Zollek, A., ed. Hitler privat, Erlebnis Bericht seiner
      Geheimsekretärin. Düsseldorf: Droste, 1949.

434. Zortman, Bruce. Hitler's Theater: Ideological Drama in Nazi
      Germany. El Paso, Tex.: Firestein, 1983.

3. RESISTANCE

435. Abramov, M., ed. Bolshevistskiye gazety v tylu vraga:
Sbornik materialov iz podpolnykh gazet leningradskoi ob-
lasti v period nemetskoi okkupatsii (Bolshevik Newspapers
in the Rear of the Enemy: A Collection of Materials from
the Underground Newspapers of the Leningrad Region in
the Period of German Occupation). Leningrad: Leningrad-
skoye gazetno-zhurnalnoye izdatelstvo, 1946.

436. Adamovich, Ales, et al. Out of the Fire. Moscow: Progress,
1980.
Personal recollections of simple folk under the occupation.

437. Adamson, Hans C. and Klem, Per. Blood on the Midnight Sun.
New York: Norton, 1964.

438. Alcorn, Robert H. No Banner, No Bands. New York: David
McKay, 1965.

439. Alsop, Stewart and Braden, Thomas. Sub Rosa: The OSS
and American Espionage. New York: Harcourt, Brace &
World, 1964 (1946).
First OSS history by insiders; no scholarly apparatus.

440. American Association for a Democratic Germany. They Fought
Hitler First: A Report on the Treatment of German Anti-
Nazis in Concentration Camps from 1933 to 1939. New
York: The Association, 1945.

441. Amery, Julian. Sons of the Eagle, a Study of Guerilla War.
London: Macmillan, 1948.

442. Amicale de Neuengamme. Le camp de concentration de Neuengamme et ses kommandos extérieurs. Paris: Amicale de
Neuengamme, 1967.

443. Andenes, Johs, et al. Norway and the Second World War.
Oslo: Tanum Norli, 1983 (1966).

444. Andreas-Friedrich, Ruth. Berlin Underground, 1933-1945.
New York: Holt, 1947.

445. Andreyev, V. Narodnaya voina--zapiski partizana (The Peo-
      ple's War--Memoirs of a Partisan). Moscow: Gosudarst-
      vennoye izdatelstvo khudozhestvennoi literatury, 1952.
      Memoirs of a history teacher turned partisan.

446. Armstrong, John A., ed. Soviet Partisans in World War II.
      Madison: University of Wisconsin Press, 1964.
          Still a classic in its limited field in the West. In its 780
      pages (plus index) it deals with partisan organization, its
      value in psychological warfare, its intelligence, supplies,
      and with case studies set up by areas. Includes docu-
      ments, starting with the first ukase of July 18, 1941. Bib-
      liography contains unpublished German documents but con-
      centrates on Soviet publications.

447. Aron, Robert. Histoire de la libération de la France. Paris:
      Fayard, 1959.

448. Auty, Phyllis. Tito, a Biography. New York: McGraw-Hill,
      1970.

449. _____ and Clogg, R. British Policy Towards Wartime Re-
      sistance in Yugoslavia and Greece. London: Macmillan,
      1975.

450. Azanjac, Dušan, et al. Otpor u žicama: sečanja zatočnika
      (Resistance Behind the Wires: Remembrances of a Captive).
      2 vols. Belgrade: Vojnoizdavački zavod, 1969.

451. Bailly, Jacques C. Un lycéen à Buchenwald. Paris: Ramsay,
      1979.

452. Balchen, Bernt. Come North with Me: An Autobiography.
      New York: Dutton, 1958.

453. Balfour, Michael and Frisby, Julian. Helmuth von Moltke: A
      Leader Against Hitler. New York: St. Martin's, 1972.

454. Ballemilla Portuondo, Aurelio. El desfile de los espectros:
      tragédia vivida por su autor, superviviente cubano del in-
      famante campo de concentración de Dachau. Havana: Im-
      presa nacional de Cuba, (1960).

455. Barker, Elisabeth. British Policy in South-East Europe in the
      Second World War. London: Macmillan, 1976.

456. Barry, R.H. European Resistance Movements. Oxford: Per-
      gamon, 1960.

457. Barta, František. Pod Goethovým dubem (Under Goethe's
      Oak). Prague: Máj, 1946.

458. Bartoszewski, Wladyslaw. The Blood-Shed Unites Us. War-
     saw: Interpress, 1970.

459. _____. The Samaritans. New York: Twayne, 1970.

460. _____. Warsaw Death Ring, 1939-1944. Warsaw: Inter-
     press, 1968.

461. _____ and Lewin, J., eds. Righteous Among Nations:
     How the Poles Helped the Jews, 1939-1945. London: Swid-
     erski, 1969.

462. Baum, Bruno. Widerstand in Auschwitz. Berlin: Kongress,
     1962.

463. Bauminger, Arieh L. Roll of Honour. Tel Aviv: Hamenora,
     1971.
     Christians saving Jews in various European countries.

464. Bazna, Elyesa and Nogby, Hans. I Was Cicero. New York:
     Harper & Row, 1962.

465. Begma, Vasilii and Kyzya, Luke. Shlyakhy neskorenykh
     (Paths of the Unhumiliated). Kiev: Radyanskyi pismennyk,
     1962.
     Begma commanded partisans.

466. Beevor, J.G. SOE--Recollections and Reflections, 1940-45.
     London: Bodley Head, 1981.
     SOE was the British Special Operations Executive work-
     ing with the resistance movements in occupied Europe, Asia
     and Africa.

467. Bellanger, Claude. Press clandestine, 1940-1944. Paris: A.
     Colin, 1961.

468. Benčík, Antonín, et al. Partyzánské hnutí v Československu
     za druhé světové války (The Partisan Movement in Czecho-
     slovakia During the Second World War). Prague: Naše
     vojsko, 1961.

469. Bennett, Jeremy. British Broadcasting and the Danish Re-
     sistance Movement, 1940-1945: A Study of the Wartime
     Broadcasts of the B.B.C. Danish Service. Cambridge,
     Eng.: Cambridge University Press, 1966.

470. Benuzzi, Felice. No Picnic on Mount Kenya: The Story of
     Three POWs' Escape to Adventure. London: Kimber, 1974.

471. Berben, Paul. L'Allentat contre Hitler. Paris: Robert Laf-
     font, 1962.

472. _____. Dachau, 1933-45, an Official History. London:
      Comité International de Dachau, 1975.
        The systematic and definitive history of Dachau concen-
      tration camp, by Belgian general and historian, who was a
      prisoner there for five years. Includes photographs, maps,
      statistics, bibliography.

473. Berdych, Václav. Mauthausen--Resistance of Prisoners at the
      KZ Mauthausen. Prague: Naše vojsko, 1959.

474. Berger, Alexander (pseud.). Kreuz hinter Stacheldraht: Der
      Leidensweg deutscher Pfarrer. Beyreuth: Hestia, 1963.

475. Bernard, Henri. L'Autre Allemagne: La résistance allemande
      à Hitler, 1933-1945. Brussels: La renaissance du livre,
      1976.

476. _____. Un géant de la résistance, Walthère Dewé. Brus-
      sels: La renaissance du livre, 1971.

477. _____. Histoire de la résistance européenne: la "quartrième
      force" de la guerre 39-45. Verviers, Belgium: Gérard,
      1968.

478. _____. La résistance, 1940-1945. Brussels: La renaissance
      du livre, 1969.

479. Bertelsen, Aage. October '43. New York: Putnam's, 1954.
      Danish resistance.

480. Best, S. Payne. The Venlo Incident. London: Hutchinson,
      1950.

481. Bethge, Eberhard. Dietrich Bonhoeffer, Man of Vision, Man
      of Courage. New York: Harper & Row, 1970.
        Biography of the extraordinary life of German theologian
      and resister Bonhoeffer, by his close associate and former
      pupil. Based among others on Bonhoeffer's Letters and
      Papers from Prison. Author compares Bonhoeffer to Gorky
      and Tolstoy. Considered a definitive biography.

482. Beyer, Wilhelm R., ed. Rückkehr unerwünscht: Joseph
      Drexels "Reise nach Mauthausen" und der Widerstandkreis
      Ernst Niekisch. Stuttgart: Deutsche Verlags-Anstalt,
      1978.

483. Bidault, Georges. Resistance--the Political Autobiography of
      Georges Bidault. New York: Praeger, 1967.

484. Blair, C.N.M. Guerilla Warfare. London: Ministry of De-
      fence, 1957.

485. Bloch, Pierre. Le vent souffle sur l'histoire, témoignages et
      documents inédits. Paris: SIPEP, 1956.

486. Blumenson, Martin. The Vildé Affair, Beginning of the French
      Resistance. Boston: Houghton Mifflin, 1977.
          Discusses Boris Vildé and the resistance group at the
      Musée de l'homme in Paris.

487. Bogusz, Josef, ed. Przeglad lekarski (Medical Survey). 3
      vols. Warsaw: International Auschwitz Commission, 1970-
      1971.
          Indispensable for the study of medicine as practiced in
      the camps, together with Francois Bayle's Croix gammée
      contre caducée (see entry 1549).

488. Bokun, Branko. Spy in the Vatican, 1941-45. New York:
      Praeger, 1973.

489. Bonhoeffer, Dietrich. Letters and Papers from Prison. Edited
      by Eberhard Bethge. New York: Macmillan, 1971.

490. _____. True Patriotism, Letters, Lectures and Notes, 1939-
      45. New York: Harper & Row, 1973.
          This is vol. III of author's collected works, of which vol.
      I and II, No Rusty Swords and The Way to Freedom, ap-
      peared in Fontana Library editions. True Patriotism reveals
      the life of German churchman Bonhoeffer, his struggle with
      his conscience, the Church and the State. Eventually he
      became a double agent, served in Buchenwald, and was
      executed in Flossenburg in 1945, at the age of 39, along
      with some members of the Canaris circle.

491. Bor-Komorowski, Tadeusz. The Secret Army. New York:
      Macmillan, 1951.
          Polish military resistance leader's memoirs.

492. Bosanquet, Mary. The Life and Death of Dietrich Bonhoeffer.
      New York: Harper & Row, 1968.

493. Bradley, John. Lidice, Sacrificial Village. New York: Bal-
      lantine, 1972.
          Story of Czech village of Lidice, which in retaliation for
      Heydrich's assassination by the Czech resistance was razed
      to the ground; all men were shot, all women taken to con-
      centration camps, and the children of Aryan appearance
      put up for adoption into German families, the rest killed.

494. Braubach, Max. Der Weg zum 20. Juli 1944. Cologne: West-
      deutscher Verlag, 1953.

495. Brickhill, Paul. The Great Escape. London: Faber, 1946.

496. _____ and Norton, Conrad. Escape to Danger. London:
      Faber, 1946.

497. Brinskii, Anton P. Po etu storonu fronta: Vospominaniya
      partizana (On the Other Side of the Front: Remembrances
      of a Partisan). Moscow: Voennoye izdatelstvo Ministerstva
      Oborony S.S.S.R., 1958.

498. Brown, Anthony C. Bodyguard of Lies. New York: Harper
      & Row, 1975.

499. _____, ed. The Secret War Report of the OSS. New York:
      Berkley, 1976.

500. Buckley, Christopher. Norway, the Commandos. London:
      HMSO, 1951.

501. Buckmaster, Maurice. Specially Employed: The Story of Brit-
      ish Aid to French Patriots of the Resistance. London:
      Batchworth, 1952.

502. Bürger, Kurt, ed. Aus Hitlers Konzentrationslagern. Mos-
      cow: Verlagsgenossenschaft ausländischen Arbeiter in der
      U.S.S.R., 1934.

503. Burgess, Alan. Seven Men at Daybreak. New York: Ban-
      tam, 1983 (1960).
           Heydrich's assassination by resistance in Prague, May,
      1942.

504. Buriánek, František. Akce 17. listopad (The November 17th
      Action). Prague: Naše vojsko, 1964.
           The day the Nazis closed Czech universities, shot and
      arrested students.

505. Butler, Rupert. Hand of Steel. London: Hamlyn, 1980.
           British commandos.

506. Cahen, Fritz M. Men Against Hitler. London: Jarrolds,
      1939.

507a. Calvocoressi, Peter. Top Secret Ultra. London: Cassell,
      1980.

507b. Central Intelligence Agency. The Rote Kapelle: The CIA's
      History of Soviet Intelligence and Espionage Networks in
      Western Europe, 1936-1945. Frederick, Md.: University
      Publications of America, 1983.

508. Chambard, Claude. The Maquis. Indianapolis: Bobbs-Merrill,
      1976.
           Story of the Maquis, i.e. the French partisans.

509. Chapman, F. Spenser. The Jungle Is Neutral. London:
      Chatto & Windus, 1948.

510. Chauvet, Paul, ed. La résistance chez les fils de Gutenberg
      dans la Deuxième guerre mondiale: témoignages. Paris:
      Chauvet, 1979.

511. Ciechanowski, Jan M. The Warsaw Rising of 1944. London:
      Cambridge University Press, 1974.

512a. Cline, Marjorie W., et al., eds. Scholar's Guide to Intelligence
      Literature, Bibliography of the Russell J. Bowen Collection.
      Frederick, Md.: University Publications of America, 1983.
      Over 5,000 titles under 372 headings.

512b. Clissold, Stephen. Whirlwind, an Account of Marshall Tito's
      Rise to Power. London: Cresset, 1949.

513. Cobb, Richard. French and Germans, Germans and French.
      Hanover, N.H.: University Press of New England, 1983.
      Interesting comparison of German occupations of France
      and Belgium in two world wars, including collaboration and
      resistance.

514. Collier, Basil. The Battle of the V-Weapons. New York:
      Morrow, 1965.

515. _____. Hidden Weapons, Allied Secret or Undercover Serv-
      ices in World War II. London: Hamish Hamilton, 1982.

516. Colvin, Ian. Admiral Canaris: Chief of Intelligence. London:
      Gollancz, 1951.

517. Cookridge, Edward H. Inside SOE: The Story of Special
      Operations in Western Europe, 1940-1945. London: Barker,
      1966.

518. _____. Set Europe Ablaze. New York: Crowell, 1967.

519. _____. They Came from the Sky. London: Heinemann,
      1965.

520. Cotta, Michèle. La collaboration. Paris: Colin, 1969.

521. Cottier, Georges M. Martin, ed. De la résistance à la revo-
      lution, Anthologie de la presse clandestine française.
      Neuchâtel: Braconnière, 1945.

522. Cowburn, Benjamin H. No Cloak, No Dagger. Toronto: Nel-
      son, Foster & Scott, 1960?.
      French resistance during Nazi occupation.

523a. Cruickshank, Charles. The Fourth Arm, Psychological War-
      fare, 1938-1945. New York: Oxford University Press,
      1981.

523b. _____. The German Occupation of the Channel Islands.
      London: Oxford University Press, 1975.

524. Czech, Danuta, et al. Auschwitz, Nazi Extermination Camp.
      New York: International Publications Service, 1978.
          The best factual description of Auschwitz history, its
      prisoners, food, lodging, extermination, resistance and
      prosecution of its war criminals; includes maps and statis-
      tics. Originally published in 1978 by Interpress in Poland
      in Polish, English, French, German and Russian editions.

525. Dalton, Hugh. The Fateful Years 1931-45. London: Fred-
      erick Muller, 1957.

526. Dank, Milton. The French Against the French: Collaboration
      and Resistance. London: Cassell, 1974.
          A controversial subject of French collaboration versus
      the resisters during the occupation and in Vichy, France.

527. Dansette, Adrien. Histoire de la liberation de Paris. Paris:
      Fayard, 1946.

528. Darling, Donald. Sunday at Large: Assignment of a Secret
      Agent. London: Kimber, 1977.

529. D'Astier, Emmanuel. Sept fois sept jours. Paris: Gallimard,
      1961.

530. Davidson, Basil. Partisan Picture. Bedford, Eng.: Bedford,
      1946.

531. _____. Special Operations Europe. London: Gollancz,
      1980.

532. Davies, A.P. When the Moon Rises. London: Leo Cooper,
      1973.

533. Deacon, Richard. The History of the British Secret Service.
      London and New York: Granada, 1980.

534. _____. The Silent War: A History of Western Naval Intel-
      ligence. London: David & Charles, 1978.

535. Deakin, Frederick W. The Embattled Mountain. New York:
      Oxford University Press, 1971.

536. _____ and Storry, Richard. The Case of Richard Sorge.
      New York: Harper & Row, 1966.

537. Deborin, G. Secrets of the Second World War. Moscow:
      Progress, 1971.

538. Dedijer, Vladimir. With Tito Through the War: Partisan Di-
      ary, 1941-1944. London: Hamilton, 1951.

539. De Lawnay, J., ed. European Resistance Movements. Oxford:
      Pergamon, 1960.

540. Derry, Sam I. The Rome Escape Line. New York: Norton,
      1960.

541a. Deutsch, Harold C. The Conspiracy Against Hitler in the Twi-
      light War. Minneapolis: University of Minnesota Press,
      1968.

541b. Dewar, Diana. The Saint of Auschwitz, the Story of Maximilian
      Kolbe. New York: Harper & Row, 1983.
          Life of Polish Franciscan priest martyred in Auschwitz in
      1941 and declared saint by Pope John Paul II in 1982.

542. D'Harcourt, Pierre. The Real Enemy. New York: Scribner's,
      1967.

543. Distel, Barbara and Jakuse, Ruth, eds. Concentration Camp
      Dachau, 1933-1945. Munich: Comité International de
      Dachau, 1978.

544. Dixon, Aubrey and Heilbrunn, Otto. Communist Guerrilla
      Warfare. New York: Praeger, 1954.
          General survey, yet focuxed on Crimea.

545. Djilas, Milovan. Wartime--With Tito and the Partisans. Lon-
      don: Secker & Warburg, 1977.
          Written by Tito's aid, who was expelled from the party
      in 1954.

546. Dokumente, Aussagen, Forschungsergebnisse und Erlebnis-
      berichte über das ehemalige Konzentrationslager Sachsen-
      hausen. East Berlin: Deutscher Verlag der Wissenschaft,
      1974.

547. Doležal, Jiří. Májové povstanie 1945 (The May Uprising of
      1945). Bratislava, Czechoslovakia: Vydavatelstvo politi-
      ckej literatury, 1965.

548. _____ and Křen, Jan, eds. Czechoslovakia's Fight, Docu-
      ments on the Resistance Movement of the Czechoslovak
      People, 1938-1945. Prague: Orbis, 1964.

549. Dourlein, Pieter. Inside North Pole, a Secret Agent's Story.
      London: Kimber, 1953.

550. Dreyfus, Paul. Vercours, citadelle de liberté. Paris:
     Arthaud, 1969.

551. Du Jinchay, R. La résistance et les communistes. Paris:
     France-Empire, 1968.

552. Dulles, Allen W. Germany's Underground. Westport, Conn.:
     Greenwood Press, 1978 (1947).

553. _____. The Secret Surrender. New York: Harper & Row,
     1966.

554. Dunin-Wazowicz, Krzysztof. La résistance dans les camps de
     concentration nazis. (Summary in English). Warsaw:
     Panstwowe wydawnictwo naukowe, 1972.

555. Edgar, Donald. The Stalag Men. London: John Clare, 1982.
     By one of the approximately 110,000 POWs in Germany.

556. Edwards, Robert. A Study of a Master Spy, Allen Dulles.
     London: Hausmans, 1961.

557. Eggers, Reinhold. Colditz: The German Viewpoint. London:
     Hale, 1961.

558. Ehrlich, Blake. Resistance: France 1940-1945. New York:
     Signet, 1966.

559. Elliot-Bateman, Michael, ed. Fourth Dimension of Warfare.
     New York: Praeger, 1970.

560. Espinola, Francisco. El infierno nazi: reportajes. Monte-
     video: Instituto ... de los periodistas libres, 1939.

561. Eudes, Dominique. The Kapetanios--Partisans and Civil War
     in Greece, 1943-1949. New York: Monthly Review Press,
     1972.

562. European Resistance Movements, 1939-1945. Proceedings of
     the First International Conference on the History of the
     Resistance Movements, Held at Liege, Brussels, Bredonk,
     September 14-17, 1958. Oxford: Pergamon, 1960.
          Includes chapter on Jewish resistance. Proceedings of
     the second conference in 1961 were published in 1964.

563. Evans, A.J. The Escaping Club. London: Panther, 1957
     (1921).

564. Farago, Ladislas. Game of the Foxes. New York: David
     McKay, 1971.

565. Fiala, Bohumír. Mříže (Bars). Brno, Czechoslovakia: Blok,
     1965.

566. Fielding, Xan. Hide and Seek. Maidenstone, England:
     George Mann, 1973 (1954).

567. Fishman, Jack. And the Walls Came Tumbling Down. London:
     Pan, 1982.
          Story of the 1944 Amiens prison raid in Operation Jeri-
     cho.

568. Fitzgibbon, Constantine. 20 July. New York: Norton, 1956.

569. Flender, Harold. Rescue in Denmark. New York: Holocaust
     Library, 1963.
          Covers the Danish resistance and the saving of Jews.

570. Flicke, W.F. Die Rote Kapelle. Kreuzlingen: Neptun, 1949.
          Communist network in Europe.

571. Foot, Michael R.D. Resistance: European Resistance to Na-
     zism, 1940-1945. New York: McGraw-Hill, 1977.
          Clear and down-to-earth history of who resisted and
     how, with explanations of technicalities. Surveys Europe
     country by country. Needs American paperback edition for
     classroom purposes.

572. _____. Six Faces of Courage. London: Methuen, 1978.
          Portraits of six major resisters: Jean Moulin, Marie-
     Madeleine Fourcade, Harry Peulevé, Victor Gerson, Andrée
     de Jongh, and Vitold Pilecki. Best collateral reading entry
     on the resistance.

573. _____. SOE in France: An Account of the British Special
     Operations Executive in France, 1940-1945. London:
     HMSO, 1966.
          Monumental and definitive history of SOE in France, its
     cooperation with the French, its achievements.
          Based on official documents; with charts, tables, maps,
     statistics and photographs. New edition: Frederick, Md.:
     University Publications of America, 1983.

574. _____ and Langley, James M. MI 9, Escape and Evasion,
     1939-1945. Boston: Little, Brown, 1980.

575. Ford, Corey. Donovan of the OSS. Boston: Little, Brown,
     1970.

576. _____ and MacBain, Alistair. Cloak and Dagger. New
     York: Random House, 1945.

577. Forman, James. Code Name Walkyrie: Count von Stauffen-
          berg and the Plot to Kill Hitler. New York: Dell, 1973.

578. Fraenkel, Heinrich. The German People Versus Hitler. Lon-
          don: George Allen & Unwin, 1940.

579. _____. The Other Germany. London: L. Drummond,
          1942.

580. Frenay, Henri. The Night Will End: Memoirs of a Revolution-
          ary. New York: McGraw-Hill, 1976.
               French resistance leader's account.

581. Frischauer, Willy and Jackson, Robert. The Altmark Affair.
          New York: Macmillan, 1955.

582. Fuchik, Julius. Notes from the Gallows. New York: New
          Century, 1948.

583. Fuchs, Gottlieb. Dolmetscher gesucht: Ein Schweitzer als
          Generaldolmetscher im Sicherheitsdienst in Südfrankreich,
          Nr. 44,110 in Buchenwald, Harzungen, Dora-Nordhausen,
          Bergen-Belsen. Luzern: By the author, 1947.

584. Fuller, Jean O. The Magical Dilemma of Victor Neuberg.
          London: George Allen & Unwin, 1965.

585. _____. The Starr Affair. London: Gollancz, 1964.

586. Fyodorov, A. The Underground Committee Carries On. Mos-
          cow: Foreign Languages Publication House, 1952.
               English translation of 1947 Russian edition by Ukrainian
          partisan leader.

587. Galante, Pierre and Silianoff, Eugene. Hitler Lives and the
          Generals Die. London: Sidgewick & Jackson, 1981.
               Deals with the generals' plotting against Führer, based
          on the recollections of General Heusinger, Chief of Opera-
          tions of Hitler's army and later top NATO commander.

588. Gallagher, J.P. Scarlet Pimpernel of the Vatican. New York:
          Coward-McCann, 1968.

589. Gallagher, Thomas. Assault in Norway. New York: Harcourt,
          Brace, Jovanovich, 1975.
               Assault by Norwegian resisters, parachuted or flown in
          from Great Britain, on the Vemork Norsk Hydro heavy water
          plant, delaying Nazi atomic research by about two years.

590. Gallin, Mary Alice. German Resistance to Hitler: Ethical and
          Religious Factors. Washington, D.C.: Catholic University
          of America Press, 1962.

591. Gardner, K., ed. Guerilla and Counter-Guerilla Warfare in
      Greece, 1940-1945. Washington, D.C.: GPO, 1962.

592. Garlinski, Jozef. Fighting Auschwitz: The Resistance Move-
      ment in the Concentration Camp. New York: Holmes &
      Meier, 1975.
         The story of Witold Pilecki and his companions in the
      Auschwitz underground.

593. _____. Hitler's Last Weapons: The Underground War
      Against the V-1 and V-2. New York: Times Books, 1978.

594. _____. Intercept, Secrets of the Enigma War. London:
      J.M. Dent, 1979.

595. _____. Poland, S.O.E. and the Allies. London: George
      Allen & Unwin, 1969.

596. Garrett, Richard. POW. London: David & Charles, 1981.
         History of POWs from the Hundred Years' War to Viet-
      nam.

597. _____. The Raiders. London: David & Charles, 1980.
         British commandos and U.S. Rangers from the Peninsular
      War to the 1970's.

598. Geraghty, Tony. Who Dares Wins: The Story of the SAS,
      1950-1982. Glasgow: Fontana, 1983.
         Post-WW II exploits of the famous Special Air Service of
      the U.K.

599. Gilchrist, Andrew. Bangkok Top Secret. London: Hutchin-
      son, 1970.

600. Gisevius, Hans B. To the Bitter End. Boston: Houghton
      Mifflin, 1947.

601. Giskes, H.J. London Calling North Pole. New York: British
      Book Centre, 1953.

602. Gjelsvik, Tore. Norwegian Resistance. London: Hurst,
      1979.

603. Glieder, Mikhail. S kino-apparatom v tylu vraga (With a Movie
      Camera Behind the Enemy). Moscow: Goskinoizdat, 1947.

604. Goddard, Donald. The Last Days of Dietrich Bonhoeffer (1906-
      45). New York: Harper & Row, 1979.

605. Gordon, Bertram M. Collaborationism in France During the
      Second World War. Ithaca, N.Y.: Cornell University
      Press, 1980.

606. Gossens, Hector. De klandestiene pers in Oost-Vlaandered
      (The Clandestine Press in East Flanders). Ghent: Rijks-
      universiteit Gent, 1978.

607. Graber, G.S. Der deutsche Widerstand gegen Hitler: Vier
      historischkritische Studien. Cologne, Germany: Kiepen-
      heuer & Witsch, 1966.
          Addresses, essays and lectures about the anti-Nazi move-
      ment.

608. _____. Stauffenberg: Resistance Movement Within the
      General Staff. New York: Ballantine, 1973.

609. Graml, Hermann, et al. The German Resistance to Hitler.
      London: Batsford, 1970.

610. Groves, Leslie. Now It Can Be Told. New York: Harper &
      Row, 1962.

611. Grudzinska-Gross, Irena, ed. War Through Children's Eyes.
      Stanford, Cal.: Hoover Institution, 1981.

612. Grünewald, Paul. KZ Osthofen. Frankfurt am Main: Röder-
      berg, 1979.

613. Gueguen-Dreyfus, Georgette. Résistance Indre et Vallée du
      Cher: Témoignages. 2 vols. Paris: Editions sociales,
      1970-72.

614. Hackett, John W. I Was a Stranger. Boston: Houghton Mif-
      flin, 1978.
          British parachutist brigadier Hackett's true adventures
      with Dutch underground.

615. Haestrup, Jørgen. Europe Ablaze. Odense: Odense Univer-
      sity Press, 1978.

616. _____. European Resistance Movements, 1939-1945: A
      Complete History. Westport, Conn.: Meckler, 1981.
          Danish entry into the field; encyclopedic, but quality
      lags behind quantity because of poor translation and copy-
      editing and small type size. Includes Soviet partisan activ-
      ities. Bibliography, maps, index; overall is useful and in-
      formative.

617. _____. Secret Alliance. 3 vols. Odense: Odense Univer-
      sity Press, 1976-1977.

618. Hahlweg, W. Guerrilla, Krieg ohne Fronten. Stuttgart:
      Kohlhammer, 1966.

619. Hajšman, Jan. The Brown Beast: Concentration Camp Europe Under the Rule of Hitler. Prague: Orbis, 1948.

620. Hallie, Philip. Lest Innocent Blood Be Shed. The Story of the Village of Le Chambon and How Goodness Happened There. New York: Harper & Row, 1980.
French Protestant village of 3,000 mobilizing to hide and save Jewish and Christian refugees.

621. Hamilton-Hill, Donald. SOE Assignment. London: Kimber, 1973.

622. Hamšík, Dušan and Pražák, Jiří. Eine Bombe für Heydrich. Berlin: Buchverlag der Morgen, 1964.

623. Hamson, Denys. We Fell Among Greeks. London: Cape, 1946.

624. Hanák, Vladimír (Blank, R.). Mrtvý se vrátil (The Dead Returned). Prague: Máj, 1946.

625. Hanser, Richard. A Noble Treason, the Revolt of the Munich Students Against Hitler. New York: Putnam's, 1979.

626. Hastings, Max. Das Reich: Resistance and the March of the 2nd SS Panzer Division Through France, June 1944. London: Michael Joseph, 1981.

627. Haukelid, Knut. Skis Against the Atom. London: Kimber, 1954.

628. Hayes, Carlton J.H. Wartime Mission in Spain, 1942-1945. New York: Macmillan, 1945.

629. Heilbrunn, Otto. Partisan Warfare. New York: Praeger, 1962.
General treatment of the subject; bibliography.

630. Heilig, Bruno. Men Crucified. London: Eyre & Spottiswoode, 1941.

631. Hellman, Peter. Avenue of the Righteous: Portraits in Uncommon Courage of Christians and the Jews They Saved from Hitler. New York: Atheneum, 1980.

632. Hinsley, F.H., et al. British Intelligence in the Second World War. 3 vols. London: HMSO, 1979-1984 (fourth volume in preparation).

633. Hochmuth, Ursel. Candidates of Humanity. Hamburg: Vereinigung der Antifaschisten und Verfolgten des Naziregimes, 1971.

634. Hoettl, Wilhelm (Walter Hagen). The Secret Front. London: Weidenfeld & Nicolson, 1953.

635. Hoffmann, Peter. The HIstory of the German Resistance, 1933-1945. Cambridge, Mass.: MIT Press, 1977.

636. _____. Hitler's Personal Security. Cambridge, Mass.: MIT Press, 1979.

637. Höhne, Heinz. Code-Word: Director: The Story of the Red Orchestra. New York: Ballantine, 1982.

638. Holub, Ota. Rovnice řešená zradou (An Equation Solved by Treason). Prague: Naše vojsko, 1983.
     Role of the communists during the Munich crisis.

639. _____. Souboj s Abwehrem (Duel with the Abwehr). Prague: Naše vojsko, 1975.

640. Horbach, Michael. Out of the Night. New York: Frederick Fell, 1967.

641. Horton, Dick. Ring of Fire. London: Secher & Warburg, 1983.
     Australian guerillas against the Japanese.

642. Hostache, René. Le Conseil National de la Résistance: Les institutions de la clandestinité. Paris: Presses Universitaires de France, 1958.

643. Howarth, David. The Shetland Bus. London: Nelson, 1951.
     Norwegian resistance "commuting" to and from Great Britain.

644. _____. We Die Alone. New York: Macmillan, 1955.

645. Howarth, Patrick. Undercover: The Men and Women of the Special Operations Executive. London: Routledge & Kegan Paul, 1980.

646. _____, ed. Special Operations. London: Routledge & Kegan Paul, 1955.

647. Howe, George. Call It Treason. New York: Viking, 1949.

648. Howell, Edgar M., ed. The Soviet Partisan Movement, 1941-1944. Washington, D.C.: GPO, 1956.
     With maps, mostly on Eastern U.S.S.R.

649. Howes, Stephen and White, Ralph, eds. Resistance in Europe, 1939-1945. London: Allen Lane, 1975.

650. Hoye, Bjarne and Ager, Trygve M. The Fight of the Norwegian Church Against Nazism. New York: Macmillan, 1943.

651. Husák, Gustav. Svedectvo o slovenskom národnom povstaní (Testimony About the Slovak National Uprising). Prague: Naše vojsko, 1954.
      Refers to the 1944 uprising against the Nazi puppet Slovak regime of Monsignor Tiso.

652. Hutak, J.B. With Blood and Iron: The Lidice Story. London: R. Hale, 1957.

653. Hyde, H. Montgomery. Secret Intelligence Agent. London: Constable, 1982; New York: St. Martin's, 1983.

654. Ignatov, P. Zapiski partizana (Partisan's Memoirs). 2 vols. Moscow: Molodaya gvardiya, 1947.
      Northern Caucasus partisan leader's reminiscences.

655. Ihlau, Olaf. Die roten Kämpfer. Meisenheim, W. Ger.: Hahn, 1969.

656. Internazionale Fäderation der Widerstandkämpfer (F.I.R.). Der Widerstand gegen Hitler-Deutschland im Spiegel der Briefmarke. Warsaw: Ruch, 1972.
      Unique book for historians and philatelists alike.

657. Iranek-Osmecki, George, ed. The Unseen and Silent: Adventures from the Underground Movement, Narrated by Paratroops of the Polish Home Army. New York: Sheed & Ward, 1954.

658. Iranek-Osmecki, Kazimierz. He Who Saves One Life: A Documented Story of the Poles Who Struggled to Save the Jews During World War II. New York: Crown, 1971.

659. Ivanov, Miroslav. Target Heydrich. New York: Macmillan, 1972.

660. Joffroy, Pierre. A Spy for God: The Ordeal of Kurt Gerstein. New York: Harcourt, Brace, 1971.

661. John, Otto. Twice Through the Lines. New York: Harper & Row, 1973.

662. Johns, Philip. Within Two Cloaks. London: Kimber, 1979.

663. Jones, Reginald V. Most Secret War: British Scientific Intelligence, 1939-1945. London: Hamish Hamilton, 1978.

664. _____. The Wizard War. New York: Coward-McCann &
      Geoghegan, 1976.

665. Jones, W.M. Twelve Months with Tito's Partisans. Bedford,
      England: Bedford, 1946.

666. Jong, Louis de. Englandspiel. Amsterdam and New York:
      Noord Hollandsche U.M., 1979.
          About "turned" resistance agents in the hands of the
      Nazis, by noted Dutch historian, author of the ten-volume
      history, The Netherlands in the Second World War (The
      Hague, 1969-76, in Dutch).

667. _____. Holland Fights the Nazis. London: Drummond,
      1941.
          Early resistance in Holland, published in London in
      English and in Dutch.

668. _____. The Lion Rampant, the Story of Holland's Resist-
      ance to the Nazis. New York: Querido, 1943.

669. Julitte, Pierre. Block 26: Sabotage at Buchenwald. Garden
      City, N.Y.: Doubleday, 1971.

670. Kamenetsky, Ihor. Hitler's Occupation of the Ukraine, 1941-
      1944. Milwaukee, Wisc.: Marquette University Press,
      1956.

671. Karov, D. Partizanskoye dvizheniye v SSSR v 1941-45 (The
      Partisan Movement in the U.S.S.R. in 1941-45). Munich:
      Institut for the Study of History and Culture in the
      U.S.S.R., 1954.
          By refugee author and former partisan, writing under
      pseudonym.

672. Karski, Jan. Story of a Secret State. Boston: Houghton
      Mifflin, 1944.
          Memoir of a member of the Polish resistance, depicting
      details of how the resistance functioned day by day. He
      was the courier who, on his 1942 mission to the Polish gov-
      ernment in exile in London, also brought reports on the
      Holocaust and the pleas of the Polish Jews for urgent help
      against extermination. Skimpy on dates, but rich in in-
      sights. Note early publication date.

673. Kastner, Rudolph. Der Bericht des jüdischen Rettungskomi-
      tées aus Budapest, 1942-1945. Basel: Vaadath Ezra Keha-
      zelah de Budapest, 1946.

674. Katz, Robert. Death in Rome. New York: Macmillan, 1966.

675. Kersten, Jakob and McMillan, James. The Secret of Torgau:
     Why the Plot to Kill Hitler Failed. London: Harrap, 1982.

676. Klein, Alexander. The Counterfeit Traitor. New York:
     Holt, Rinehart & Winston, 1958.

677. Klein, Françoise. La résistance dans la province de Luxem-
     bourg, 1940-1944. Louvain: Université Catholique de
     Louvain, 1978.

678a. Klönne, Arno. Gegen den Strom: Bericht über den Jugend-
     widerstand im Dritten Reich. Hanover, Germany: O.
     Goedel, 1956.

678b. Knight, Frida. The French Resistance. London: Lawrence
     and Wishart, 1975.

679. Koch-Kent, Henri. Sie boten Trotz: Luxemburger im Frei-
     heitskampf, 1939-1945. Luxemburg: Hermann, 1974.

680. Kogon, Eugen. The Theory and Practice of Hell: The Con-
     centration Camps and the System Behind Them. New York:
     Berkley, 1975 (1950).
         Highly respected during his six years in Buchenwald as
     a German political prisoner, Dr. Kogon produced one of the
     earliest and still best analyses on life and survival in con-
     centration camps, with feelings for details that only a former
     inmate can muster. Should be reprinted for classroom use.

681. Komitee der antifaschistischen Widerstandskämpfer in der DDR.
     Sachsenhausen. East Berlin: Kongress, 1962.

682. _____. Schwur der Nationen. East Berlin: Kongress,
     1954.

683. Konopka, Vladimír. Zde stávaly Lidice (Here Lidice Once
     Stood). Prague: Naše vojsko, 1959.

684. Konzentrationslager: Ein Appell an das Gewissen der Welt.
     Karlsbad, Czechoslovakia: Graphia, 1934.
         One of the earliest "appeals to the conscience of the
     world" about concentration camps in Nazi Germany.

685. Korbonski, Stefan. Fighting Warsaw: The Story of the Polish
     Underground. New York: Funk & Wagnalls, 1969.

686. Kousoulas, D. George. Revolution and Defeat: The Story of
     the Greek Communist Party. London: Oxford University
     Press, 1965.

687. Kovpak, Sidor Artemovich. Our Partisan Course. London:

Hutchinson, 1947.
Famous Soviet partisan leader's memoirs; throws light on both military and political affairs. Later editions show differences in text, which is not unique.

688. Kramarz, Joachim. Stauffenberg, the Architect of the Famous July 20th Conspiracy to Assassinate Hitler. New York: Macmillan, 1967.

689. Krejčí, Sylva and Oskar. Číslo 64401 mluví (Number 64401 Speaks). Prague: G. Petrů, 1945.

690. Krispyn, Egbert. Anti-Nazi Writers in Exile. Athens: University of Georgia Press, 1978.

691. Kruuse, Jens. Oradour sur Glane. Paris: Fayard, 1969. The tragedy of the French village razed to the ground and its population killed.

692. Krylová, Libuše. The Small Fortress of Terezín. Terezín, Czechoslovakia: Památník Terezín, 1975.

693. Kühnrich, Heinz. Der Partisanenkrieg in Europa, 1939-1945. Berlin: Dietz, 1968.

694. Kulski, Julian E. Dying, We Live: The Personal Chronicle of a Young Freedom Fighter in Warsaw (1939-1945). New York: Holt, Rinehart & Winston, 1979.

695. Kunc, Radimír and Bartoš, Antonín. Clay-Eva volá Londýn (Clay-Eva Is Calling London). Perth Amboy, N.J.: Universum Sokol, 1980 (1946).

696. Lacaze, André. The Tunnel at Loibl Pass. Garden City, N.Y.: Doubleday, 1981.

697. Lampe, David. The Danish Resistance. New York: Ballantine, 1960.

698. Langelaan, George. Knights of the Floating Silk. London: Hutchinson, 1959.

699. Langhoff, Wolfgang. Rubber Truncheon--Being an Account of Thirteen Months Spent in a Concentration Camp. New York: Dutton, 1935.

700. Langley, James M. Fight Another Day. London: Collins, 1974.

701. Laqueur, Walter. Guerrilla, an Historical and Critical Study. Boston: Little, Brown, 1976.

702. _____, ed. The Guerrilla Reader. New York: NAL, 1977.

703. Leasor, James. Boarding Party. London: Heinemann, 1956.

704. _____. Code Name Nimrod, the True Story of the Spy Who Ensured the Success of the Normandy Invasion. (British title: The Unknown Warrior.) Boston: Houghton Mifflin, 1981.

705. Leber, Annelore, ed. Conscience in Revolt: Sixty-Four Stories of Resistance in Germany, 1933-45. London: Vallentine, Mitchell, 1957.

706. Leboucher, Fernande. Incredible Mission. Garden City, N.Y.: Doubleday, 1969.
    Heroic French priest in Italy.

707. Le Chêne, Evelyn. Mauthausen, the History of a Death Camp. London: Methuen, 1971.

708. _____. Watch for Me by Moonlight: A British Agent with the French Resistance. London: Methuen, 1973.

709. Lee, A.S.G. Crown Against Sickle, the Story of King Michael of Rumania. London: Hutchinson, 1950.

710. Lemmer, Ernst. Manches war doch anders: Erinnerungen eines deutschen Demokraten. Frankfurt am Main: H. Scheffler, 1968.
    An anti-Nazi memoir.

711. Lend, Evelyn. The Underground Struggle in Germany. New York: League for Industrial Democracy, 1938.

712. Leslie, Peter. The Liberation of the Riviera. New York: Wyndham, 1960.

713. Leuner, Heinz D. When Compassion Was a Crime: German Silent Heroes, 1933-1945. London: O. Wolff, 1966.

714. Leverkuehn, Paul. German Military Intelligence. London: Weidenfeld & Nicolson, 1954.

715. Lewin, Ronald. Ultra Goes to War. New York: McGraw-Hill, 1978.

716. Lipgens, Walter. Europa--Föderationspläne der Widerstandsbewegungen, 1940-1945. Munich: R. Oldenburg, 1968.

717. Littlejohn, David. The Patriotic Traitors: A History of Collaboration in Europe, 1940-1945. London: Heinemann, 1971.

733. Mastný, Vojtěch. The Czechs Under Nazi Rule: The Failure
      of National Resistance, 1939-1942. New York: Columbia
      University Press, 1971.

734. Matusiak, Tadeusz. Stutthof. Gdansk: Stutthof Museum,
      1969.

735. Melchior, Marcus. A Rabbi Remembers. Secaucus, N.J.:
      Lyle Stuart, 1968.
          Nazi occupation in Denmark and the saving of the Jews.

736. Michel, Henri. Bibliographie critique de la résistance. Paris:
      Institut pédagogique national, 1964.

737. _____. Histoire de la résistance (1940-1944). Paris:
      Presses universitaires de France, 1950.

738. _____. Jean Moulin l'unificateur. Paris: Hachette, 1971.

739. _____. The Second World War. London: André Deutsch,
      1975.

740. _____. The Shadow War: Resistance in Europe, 1939-1945.
      New York: Harper & Row, 1972.
          Survey of situation by French expert on the resistance.

741. _____, et al. European Resistance Movements. Oxford:
      Pergamon, 1960.

742. Michel, Jean. Dora. New York: Holt, Rinehart & Winston,
      1980.
          Dora was "the motherhouse" of a large concentration
      camp complex; it included the infamous Tunnel, an under-
      ground factory near Nordhausen, where the tools of war,
      including the V-rockets, were manufactured by thousands
      of slave laborers, your author among them.

743. Miller, Russell. The Resistance. Alexandria, Va.: Time-
      Life, 1979.

744. Molden, Fritz. Exploding Star: A Young Austrian Against
      Hitler. New York: Morrow, 1978.

745. Moravec, František. Master of Spies, the Memoirs of General
      František Moravec. New York: Doubleday, 1975.

746. Moss, W. Stanley. Ill Met by Moonlight. London: Macmillan,
      1950.

747. Moulin, Jean. Premier Combat. Paris: Minuit, 1964.

748. Moulin, Laure. Jean Moulin. Paris: Presse de la cité, 1969.

749. Moulis, Miloslav. Neviditelná fronta (The Invisible Front).
     Prague: Naše vojsko, 1970.

750. Mountfield, David. The Partisans. Felham, Eng.: Hamlyn,
     1979.

751. Moyzisch, L.C. Operation Cicero. London: Allan Wingate,
     1969.

752. Mure, David. Master of Deception, Tangled Webs in London
     and the Middle East. London: Kimber, 1980.

753. Nansen, Odd. From Day to Day. New York: Putnam's, 1949.
     Memoirs of the famous Norwegian explorer's son of the
     resistance and concentration camp.

754. Neave, Airey. The Escape Room. Garden City, N.Y.: Dou-
     bleday, 1970.

755. _____. Saturday at MI 9: The Inside Story of the Under-
     ground Escape Lines in Europe in World War II. London:
     Hodder & Stoughton, 1969.

756. Noguères, Henri, et al. Histoire de la resistance en France.
     5 vols. Paris: Laffont, 1967-1976.

757. Nohejl, Miloslav. Holýma rukama (With Bare Hands). Prague:
     Máj, 1946.

758. Noireau, Robert (Colonel Georges). Le temps des partisans.
     Paris: Flammarion, 1979.

759. Novick, Peter. The Resistance Versus Vichy: The Purge of
     Collaborators in Liberated France. London: Chatto &
     Windus, 1968.

760. Nowak, Jan. Courier from Warsaw. Detroit: Wayne State
     University Press, 1982.

761. Outze, Børge, ed. Denmark During the German Occupation.
     Copenhagen: Scandinavian Publications, 1946.

762. Passmore, Richard. Moving Tent. London: Thomas Harns-
     worth, 1982.
     An antihero's psychological story of day-by-day life as
     a POW.

763. Passy, Colonel (André de Wavrin). Souvenirs. 3 vols. Monte
     Carlo: Raoul Solar, 1947.

764. Pearson, Michael. Tears of Glory, the Betrayal of Vercours,
      1944. London: Pan, 1980.

765. Pech, Karlheinz. An der Seite der Résistance. Frankfurt am
      Main: Röderberg, 1974.

766. Pechel, Rudolf. Deutscher Widerstand. Zurich: E. Reutsch,
      1947.

767. Pergner, Eduard and Slabý, Z.K. Děti s cedulkou (Children
      with Nametags). Prague: Práce, 1982.
          Tragedy of Lidice through the eyes of children selected
      for Germanization or death.

768. Perrault, Giles. Red Orchestra. New York: Simon & Schus-
      ter, 1969.
          Communist spy network in Europe before and during
      World War II.

769. Persen, Mirko. Ustaški logori (The Ustashi Camps). Zagreb,
      Yugoslavia: Stvarnost, 1966.
          The Ustashi were Croatian fascists.

770. Persico, Joseph. Piercing the Reich: The Penetration of Nazi
      Germany by American Secret Agents During World War II.
      New York: Viking, 1979.
          OSS infiltration of Nazi Germany by approximately two
      hundred agents.

771. Pestouric, Roger. La résistance c'était cela aussi. Paris:
      Editions Sociales, 1969.

772. Petrow, Richard. The Bitter Years: The Invasion and Oc-
      cupation of Denmark and Norway, April 1940-May 1945.
      New York: Morrow, 1979.

773. Picard, Henri. Ceux de la résistance. London: Macmillan,
      1979.

774. Picket-Wicks, Eric. Four in the Shadows: A True Story of
      Espionage in Occupied France. London: Jarrolds, 1957.

775. Ponomarenko, P.K., ed. Partizanskoye dvizheniye v Velikoi
      Otechestvennoi Voine (The Partisan Movement in the Great
      Patriotic War). Moscow: Gospolizdat, 1943.
          Early anthology, edited by the Chief of Staff of the
      partisan movement. An English version appeared as Be-
      hind the Front Lines (London: Hutchinson, 1945).

776. Popov, Duško. Spy/Counterspy. London: Granada, 1974.
          The story of a Yugoslav double agent.

777. Prevan, V. Slovenské národné povstanie (The Slovak Na-
      tional Uprising). Bratislava, Czechoslovakia: Vydavatel-
      stvo politickej literatury, 1965.

778. Prittie, Terence. Germans Against Hitler. London: Hutchin-
      son, 1964.

779. Pünter, Otto. Der Anschluss fand nicht statt: Geheimagent
      Pakbo erzählt. Erlebnisse, Tatsachen und Dokumente aus
      den Jahren 1930 bis 1945. Bern: Hallwag, 1967.
           Discusses the spy network in Switzerland, including
      communists and Sándor Radó.

780. Radó, Sándor. Code Name Dora. London: Abelard, 1977.
           No connection with concentration camp Dora. Covers
      the communist spy network in Switzerland by cartographer.

781. Ramati, Alexander. The Assisi Underground: Assisi and the
      Nazi Occupation, as Told by Padre Rufino Niccacci. Lon-
      don: Sphere, 1981.

782. Rauschning, Hermann. Men of Chaos. New York: Putnam's,
      1942.

783. _____. The Revolution of Nihilism. New York: Longmans,
      Green, 1939.

784. _____. The Voice of Destruction. New York: Putnam's,
      1940.

785. Régis, Roger. La résistance par l'humeur. Paris: Editions
      de Paris, 1945.

786. Reid, Miles. Into Colditz. Salisbury, Eng.: Michael Russell,
      1983.
           POW's story, in Greece and at infamous Colditz camp.

787. Reid, P.R. The Colditz Story. 19th edition. Sevenoaks,
      Kent, Eng.: Hodder & Stoughton, 1983 (1952).
           The dreaded and "escape-proof" POW camp and the
      escapes from it.

788. _____. The Latter Days at Colditz. 14th edition. Sev-
      enoaks, Kent, Eng.: Hodder & Stoughton, 1983 (1952).

789. Renault-Roulier, Gilbert (Colonel Rémy). Comment meurt un
      réseau. Monte Carlo: Raoul Solar, 1948.

790. _____. Memoirs d'un agent secret de la France Libre.
      Monte Carlo: Raoul Solar, 1947.

791. _____. Réseau Comète. 3 vols. Paris: Perrin, 1966–
       1969.

792. _____. La résistance francaise a commencé le 3 septembre
       1939. Paris: Peon, 1979.

793. Rings, Werner. Life with the Enemy, Collaboration and Re-
       sistance in Hitler's Europe, 1939–1945. Garden City, N.Y.:
       Doubleday, 1982.
           Author's verdict is that collaboration came as a practical
       solution, while resistance contributed little to the outcome
       of the war.

794. Riste, Olav and Nokleby, Berit. Norway, 1940–45, The Re-
       sistance Movement. Oslo: Tanum Norli, 1978 (1973).

795. Ristic, Dragica N. Yugoslavia's Revolution of 1941. Univer-
       sity Park: Pennsylvania State University Press, 1966.

796. Ritter, Gerhard. The German Resistance: Carl Goerdeler's
       Struggle Against Tyranny. New York: Praeger, 1958;
       Arno reprint 1974.

797a. Roberts, Walter R. Tito, Mihailović and the Allies, 1941–1945.
       New Brunswick, N.J.: Rutgers University Press, 1973.

797b. Roelfzema, Erik Hazelhoff. Soldier of Orange. London:
       Sphere Books, 1982.

798. Rogers, Lindsay. Guerilla Surgeon. London: Collins, 1957.

799. Roon, Ger van. German Resistance to Hitler: Count von
       Moltke and the Kreisar Circle. New York: Von Nostrand
       Reinhold, 1971.

800. Roosevelt, Kermit. The Secret War Report of the OSS. New
       York: Berkley, 1976.

801. Rootham, Jasper. Missfire: The Chronicle of a British Mis-
       sion to Mihailovich, 1943–1944. London: Collins, 1957
       (1946).

802. Rothfels, Hans. The German Opposition to Hitler: An Ap-
       praisal. Chicago: Regnery, 1963; London: Oswald Wolff,
       1981.

803. _____. The Political Legacy of the Resistance Movement.
       Bad Godesberg, Ger.: Inter Nationes, 1969.

804. Roussell, Aage. The Museum of the Danish Resistance Move-
       ment, 1940–1945. Copenhagen: National Museum, 1970.

805. Rousset, David. The Other Kingdom. New York: Fertig,
      1982 (1947).
      Deals with Buchenwald and POWs.

806. Rudnicky, K.S. The Last War Horses. London: Bachman &
      Turner, 1974.
      Memoirs of a Pole who fought with Polish cavalry against
      Hitler's tanks, was in Russian captivity, and eventually on
      the Italian front.

807. Sanguedolce, Joseph. Résistance: de Saint Etienne à Dachau.
      Paris: Editions sociales, 1973.

808. Sapfirov, Nikolai N. Do poslednego dykhania (Till the Last
      Breath). Moscow: Voennoye izdatelstvo, 1958.

809. Saralvo, Corrado. Piu morti, piu spazio (The More Dead,
      the More Space). Milan: Baldini & Castoldi, 1969.

810. Schätzle, Julius, ed. Stationen zure Hölle: Konzentrations-
      lager in Baden und Würtenberg, 1933-1945. Frankfurt am
      Main: Röderberg, 1974.

811. Schaul, Dora, ed. Resistance: Erinnerungen deutscher Anti-
      faschisten. Frankfurt am Main: Röderberg, 1975.

812. Schellenberg, Walter. The Labyrinth--Memoirs of Walter
      Schellenberg. New York: Harper & Bros., 1956.

813. Schlabrendorff, Fabian von. Revolt Against Hitler. New
      York: AMS, 1978 (1948).

814. _____. The Secret War Against Hitler. New York: Put-
      nam's, 1965.

815. Schmitthenner, Walter A. and Buchheim, Hans, eds. Der
      deutsche Widerstand gegen Hitler. Cologne: Kiepenheuer
      & Witsch, 1966.

816. Schoenbrun, David. Soldiers of the Night: The Story of the
      French Resistance. New York: Dutton, 1980.

817. Scholl, Inge. Students Against Tyranny: The Resistance of
      the White Rose, Munich, 1942-1943. Middletown, Conn.:
      Wesleyan University Press, 1970.

818. Schramm, Wilhelm von. Conspiracy Among Generals. London:
      George Allen & Unwin, 1936.

819. Schreieder, Joseph. Das War das Englandspiel. Munich: W.
      Stutz, 1950.

The famous double-cross system between German and British secret agents of the underground.

820. Schuster, Kurt G.P. Der Rote Frontkämpferbund, 1924-1929. Düsseldorf: Droste, 1975.

821. Schutz, Wilhelm W. Pens Under the Swastika. Port Washington, N.Y.: Kennikat, 1972 (1946).

822. Scott, William E. Alliance Against Hitler. Durham, N.C.: Duke University Press, 1962.

823. Seth, Ronald. Noble Saboteurs. New York: Hawthorne, 1966.

824. Seton-Watson, Hugh. East European Revolution. New York: Praeger, 1956.

825. Shapko, Yekaterina N. Partizanskoye dvizheniye v Krymu v 1941-1944 gg (The Partisan Movement in the Crimea in the Years 1941-1944). Simferopol, U.S.S.R.: Krymizdat, 1959. Brief survey with factual information.

826. Šima, Ladislav. Ležáky: Vražda mužů a žen, odvlečení dětí do ciziny, srovnání osady se zemí (Ležáky: Murder of Men and Women, Kidnapping of Children Abroad, Levelling of the Village). Prague: Ministry of Interior, 1947.

827. Skidmore, Ian. Marines Don't Hold Their Horses. London: W.H. Allen, 1981.
About Colonel Alan Werren, CBE, DSC, who led men beyond enemy lines in Europe and southeast Asia.

828. Smith, Bradley F. The Shadow Warriors, OSS and the Origins of the C.I.A. New York: Basic Books, 1983.
Includes successes and failures of World War II operations under Donovan and Allen Dulles and their connections with the resistance movements in several countries.

829. Smith, R. Harris. OSS--The Secret History of America's First Central Intelligence Agency. Berkeley: University of California Press, 1972.

830. Smolen, Kazimierz, et al., eds. From the History of KL Auschwitz. New York: Fertig, 1982.
Originally published by the Panstwowe Muzeum of Auschwitz in 1967; contains essays by Smolen and five other Poles about the various aspects of Auschwitz, including medical experiments and escapes. Offers a chronology of Auschwitz developments from January 25, 1940 to January 27, 1945.

831. _____, ed. Reminiscences of Former Auschwitz Prisoners.
     Auschwitz: Panstwowe Muzeum, 1963.
     Small volume with some powerful stories.

832. Snoek, Johan M., ed. The Greybook: A Collection of Pro-
     tests Against Anti-Semitism and the Persecution of Jews,
     Issued by Non-Roman Catholic Churches and Church Lead-
     ers During Hitler's Rule. The Hague: Van Gorcum, 1969.

833. Somerhausen, Christine. Les Belges déportés à Dora et dans
     ses kommandos. Brussels: Université Libre de Bruxelles,
     1978.

834. Soustelle, Jacques. Envers et contre tout. Paris: Fayard,
     1950.

835. Soviet Partisans: From the History of the Partisan Movement
     in the Years of the Great Patriotic War. Moscow: Gos-
     polizdat, 1960.
         In Russian; consists of sixteen studies on the subject.
     Recommended by Sovietologist John A. Armstrong, although
     Ponomarenko's anthology is of easier access. Other entries,
     especially on Jewish partisans, were published by Der
     Emes Publishing House in Moscow.

836. Stafford, David. Britain and the European Resistance, 1940-
     45: A Survey of the Special Operations Executive, with
     Documents. London: Macmillan, 1980; Toronto: University
     of Toronto Press, 1980.
         Rich on information and correlation of resistance with
     diplomatic and military objectives.

837. Steinbock, Johann. Das Ende von Dachau. Vienna: Öster-
     reicher Kulturverlag, 1948.

838. Stenin, Afrikan A. "Jermak" na Moravě ("Yermak" in Mora-
     via. Prague: Naše vojsko, 1983.
         About Czechoslovak-Soviet cooperation in the liberation
     of Czechoslovakia in 1945; originally published by the
     Politizdat (i.e. political publishing house) of the Ukraine.
     Yermak was a partisan leader.

839. Stevenson, William. A Man Called Intrepid. New York: Mac-
     millan, 1976.

840. Strobinger, Rudolf. A-54: Spion mit drei Gesichten. Munich:
     List, 1966.
         About Paul Thümmel, code name "René," the master
     double agent working with the Abwehr and supplying highly
     valuable information to the Allies via Czech resistance in
     Prague.

841. Strokach, Timofei. Partyzany Ukrainy (Partisans of the Uk-
      raine). Moscow: Gospolizdat, 1943.
         Partisan chief's memoirs.

842. Sweet-Escott, Bickham. Baker Street Irregular. London:
      Methuen, 1965.

843. Teske, Hermann. Die silbernen Spiegel: Generalstabsdienst
      unter der Lupe. Heidelberg: Kurt Vowinckel, 1952.
         German report on partisan activities.

844a. Thomas, John (Jack). No Banners, the Story of Alfred and
      Henry Newton. London: Corgi, 1974 (1956).

844b. Thomas, John Oram. The Giant Killers, the Story of the
      Danish Resistance Movement, 1940-1945. New York: Tap-
      linger, 1976.

845. Tillon, C. Les F.T.P. Paris: Julliard, 1962.
         The story of the Francs-tireurs et partisans, the mili-
      tary wing of the leftist resistance, named after the guerilla
      fighters of the 1870 war against the Germans.

846. Treece, Patricia. A Man for Others. New York: Harper &
      Row, 1982.
         Biography of Maximilian Kolbe, martyred in Auschwitz;
      published on October 10, 1982, the day Kolbe was canonized.

847. Trenowden, Ian. Operations Most Secret, SOE in the Malayan
      Theatre. London: Kimber, 1978.

848. Trepper, Leopold. Great Game. New York: McGraw-Hill,
      1977.
         Memoirs of the "director" of the communist spy ring
      "Red Orchestra."

849. Trouillé, P. Journal d'un préfet pendant l'occupation. Paris:
      Gallimard, 1964.

850. Tsatsos, Jeanne. The Sword's Fierce Edge: A Journal of the
      Occupation of Greece, 1941-1944. Nashville, Tenn.: Van-
      derbilt University Press, 1969.

851. Turner, Don. Kiriakos--A British Partisan in Wartime Greece.
      London: Robert Hale, 1982.

852. U.S. Department of the Army. German Anti-Guerilla Opera-
      tions in the Balkans, 1941-1944. Washington, D.C.: GPO,
      1954.

853. Van der Post, Laurens. The Night of the New Moon. London:
      Hogarth, 1970.

854. Vechtomova, E.A. and Ivanov, V.V.   Ljudi, pobedivšie smert:
     Vospominania byvšich uznikov fašistskih lagerai (People
     Who Conquered Death: Reminiscences of Former Prisoners
     of Fascist Camps).   Leningrad: Lenizdat, 1968.

855. Veillon, Dominique.   Le Franc Tireur.   Paris: Flammarion,
     1979.

856. Verity, Hugh B.   We Landed by Moonlight.   Shepperton,
     Eng.:   Ian Allen, 1978.

857. Vershigora, Pavlo.   Ljudi s chistoi sovestyu (People with a
     Clear Conscience).   Moscow: Sovetskii pisatel, 1951.
          Memoirs of Kovpak's assistant, later an independent
     partisan leader.

858. Veselý-Štainer, Karel.   Cestou národního odbojového hnutí v
     letech 1938-1945 (The Path of the National Resistance Move-
     ment in the Years 1938-1945).   Prague: Sfinx, 1947.

859a. Von Hassel, Ulrich.   The Von Hassel Diaries, 1938-1944.
     Westport, Conn.:   Greenwood Press, 1974 (1947).

859b. Voute, Peter.   Only a Free Man: War Memories of Two Dutch
     Doctors (1940-1945).   Santa Fé, New Mexico: Lightning
     Tree, 1982.

860. Waagener, Sam.   The Pope's Jews.   La Salle, Ill.:   Library
     Press, 1974.

861. Walter, Eugene V.   Terror and Resistance: A Study in Poli-
     tical Violence.   New York: Oxford University Press, 1969.

862. Warmbrunn, Werner.   The Dutch Under German Occupation,
     1940-1945.   Stanford, Cal.:   Stanford University Press,
     1963.

863. Warner, Philip.   Phantom.   London: Kimber, 1982.
          Special regiment of secret agents, many of them known
     personalities.

864a. West, Nigel.   A Matter of Trust: MI 5, 1945-1972.   London:
     Weidenfeld and Nicolson, 1982.
          Controversial book that the government allegedly tried
     to suppress.

864b. _____.   MI 5:   British Security Service Operations, 1909-
     1945.   London: Granada, 1983.

865. West Germany.   Ministry of Defense.   Zur Geschichte der
     deutschen antifaschistischen Widerstandsbewegung, 1933-
     1945.   Berlin: Ministerium für nationale Verteidigung, 1958.

866. Whiting, Charles. Gehlen: Germany's Master Spy. New York: Ballantine, 1973.

867. _____. Hitler's Werewolves. New York: Stein & Day, 1972.

868. _____. The Spymasters. New York: Dutton, 1976.

869. Wiener, Jan G. The Assassination of Heydrich. New York: Pyramid, 1971.

870. Wilkinson, James D. Intellectual Resistance in Europe. Cambridge, Mass.: Harvard University Press, 1981.
     Extensive bibliography.

871. Williams, Eric. The Tunnel. New York: Coward-McCann, 1952.

872. _____. The Wooden Horse. Glasgow: Fontana, 1982 (1949).
     The classic escape story from Stalag Luft III in a new, expanded edition.

873. Winterbotham, F.A. The Ultra Secret. London: Weidenfeld & Nicolson, 1974.

874. Woodhouse, Christopher M. The Struggle for Greece, 1941-1949. Frogmore, Eng.: Hart-Davis, 1976.

875. Woods, Rex. A Talent to Survive, the Wartime Exploits of Lt. Col. Richard Lowthen Broad, MC, Légion d'Honneur, Croix de Guerre. London: Kimber, 1982.
     Broad and his men ("Snow White and the seven dwarves") in SOE, from Madagascar to the Berlin bunker.

876. Yahil, Leni. The Rescue of Danish Jewry, Test of Democracy. New York: Jewish Publication Society of America, 1969.

877. Yoors, Jan. Crossing--A Journal of Survival and Resistance in World War II. New York: Simon & Schuster, 1971.
     Deals with the problem of Gypsies.

878. Zahn, Gordon C. In Solitary Witness. New York: Irvington, 1964.
     About an anti-Nazi, Christian martyr.

879. Zawodny, Janusz. Death in the Forest. Notre Dame, Ind.: Notre Dame University Press, 1962.

880. _____. Nothing but Honour, the Story of the Warsaw Uprising, 1944. Stanford, Cal.: Hoover Institution, 1978.

881. Zeller, Eberhard. The Flame of Freedom, the German Strug-
        gle Against Hitler. Coral Gables: University of Miami
        Press, 1969.

882. Zentner, Kurt. La résistance allemande, 1933-1945. Paris:
        Stock, 1968.

883. Zimmermann, Wolf-Dieter and Smith, Ronald G., eds. I Knew
        Dietrich Bonhoeffer. Cleveland: Collins, 1976.

4. RESISTANCE -- WOMEN

884. Amicale de Ravensbrück. <u>Les Françaises à Ravensbrück.</u>
     Paris: Gallimard, 1965.

885. Astrup, Helen and Jacot, B.L. <u>Oslo Intrigue, a Woman's Mem-</u>
     <u>oirs of the Norwegian Resistance.</u> New York: McGraw-
     Hill, 1954.

886. Bancroft, Mary. <u>Autobiography of a Spy.</u> New York: Mor-
     row, 1983.
     Daughter of Boston Brahmins, just out of Smith College,
     worked for Allen Dulles and OSS in Switzerland; also in-
     volved with Hans Gisevius, one of the 20th of July, 1944
     plotters against Hitler's life.

887. Bellak, Georgina, ed. <u>Donne e bambini nei lageri nazisti</u>
     <u>(Women and Children in Nazi Camps).</u> Milan: Associazione
     nazionale degli ex-deportati politici nei campi nazisti, 1960.

888. Bernadac, Christian. <u>Les Mannequins nus.</u> 3 vols. Paris:
     France-Empire, 1971-73.
     Covers women in the French resistance. A major work.

889. Bertrand, Simone. <u>Mille visages, un seul combat.</u> Paris:
     Editeurs Français réunis, 1965.

890. Breur, Dunya. <u>Een Verborgen Herinnering (Hidden Remem-</u>
     <u>brances).</u> Amsterdam: Tiebosch uitgeversmaatschappij,
     1983.
     About a Dutch artist at Ravensbrück, written touchingly
     by her daughter.

891. Buber-Neumann, Margarete. <u>Milena, Kafkas Freundin.</u> Munich:
     Gotthold Müller, 1963.
     Life of Milena Jesenská, Kafka's friend in Prague, in-
     cluding her last years in Ravensbrück, by her fellow-
     prisoner and friend. One of the best descriptions of rela-
     tions among women in concentration camps. Latest edition
     in Czech translation: <u>Kafkova přítelkyně Milena.</u> Toronto:
     Sixty-Eight Publishers, 1982.

892. Buchmann, Erika, ed. Die Frauen von Ravensbrück. Berlin: Kongress, 1961.
     Illustrated; compiled for the Committee of Anti-Fascist Resistance Fighters in the German Democratic Republic.

893. Busson, Suzanne. Dans les griffes nazies: Angers, Fresnes, Ravensbrück, Mauthausen. 2 vols. Le Mans: P. Belon, 1946-52.

894. Butler, Josephine. Churchill's Secret Agent, Codename "Jay Bee." Ashburton, Devon, England: Blaketon-Hall, 1983.

895. Carré, Mathilde Lily. I Was the Cat. London: Horwitz, 1967.

896. Chatel, Nicole, ed. Des femmes dans la résistance: Récits recueillis et presentés par Nicole Chatel. Paris: Julliard, 1972.

897. Clayton, Aileen. The Enemy Is Listening, the Story of the Y Service. London: Hutchinson, 1980.

898. Cooper, Lady Diana. Trumpets from the Steep. London: Hart-Davis, 1960.

899. Cvetkova, Nadežda, et al. V fašistskih zastenkakh: Zapiski (In the Fascist Torture Chambers: Memoirs). Minsk: Government Publication of the U.S.S.R., 1958.

900. Duboscq, Geneviève. My Longest Night. New York: Seaver, 1981.

901. Elling, Hanna. Frauen im deutschen Widerstand, 1933-1945. Frankfurt am Main: Röderberg, 1981.

902. Fourcade, Marie-Madeleine. Noah's Ark: The Secret Underground. New York: Dutton, 1974.
     The memoirs of the much decorated French woman who headed a c. 3,000-agent military espionage network for the Western Allies, greatly contributing to the success of the war. While the official name of the network was "Alliance," the Gestapo nicknamed it Noah's Ark, because of the animal code names of the agents.

903. Francos, Ania. Il était des femmes dans la résistance. Paris: Stock, 1978.

904. Fuller, Jean O. Born for Sacrifice. London: Pan, 1957.

905. _____. Madeleine. London: Gollancz, 1952.

906.   _____. Noorumisa Inayat Khan. Rotterdam: East-West,
        1971.
             The biography of an Indian-American member of SOE,
        one of the four women executed at Dachau on September
        12, 1944.

907.   Gardiner, Muriel. Code Name "Mary," Memoirs of an American
       Woman in the Austrian Underground. New Haven, Conn.:
       Yale University Press, 1983.
             About a well-to-do American woman studying in Vienna
       who saves Nazi foes, while also undergoing psychoanalysis
       and having a child.

908.   Haag, Lina. How Long the Night. London: Gollancz, 1948.
             Unusual report of one of Hitler's earliest political pris-
       oners, who spent four and a half years in jails and at the
       women's concentration camp of Lichtenburg; her husband
       was at Dachau. Reissued in Germany as Eine Handvoll
       Staub (Frankfurt am Main: Röderberg, 1977).

909.   Hájková, Dagmar, et al. Ravensbrück. Prague: Naše voj-
       sko, 1960.
             One of the best documentations of the women's concen-
       tration camp Ravensbrück by several long-term political
       prisoners from Czechoslovakia.

910.   Hornsay, Denis, D.F.C., transcriber. Rendez-Vous 127, the
       Diary of Madame Brusselmans, M.B.E. Tonbridge, Eng.:
       Ernest Benn, Ltd., 1954.
             About a half-British woman, hiding British fliers in Bel-
       gium.

911.   Housková, Hana. Ženy v odboji (Women in the Resistance).
       Prague: Svaz protifašistických bojovníků, 1964.
             Brief account of Czech women resisters' role on the home
       front, in the army in the U.S.S.R., in concentration camps,
       among partisans and during the Prague uprising in May
       1945.

912.   Hunt, Antonia. Little Resistance. London: Leo Cooper,
       1982.
             Introduction by M.R.D. Foot. Account of the German
       occupation in France by an English teenager, involved in
       the resistance, even in the "Red Orchestra."

913.   Hyde, H. Montgomery. Cynthia. New York: Farrar, Straus
       & Giroux, 1965.
             The beautiful American spy who secured two naval codes
       for the Allies.

914.   Jackson, Daphne. Java Nightmare, an Autobiography. Pad-

stow, Cornwall, Eng.: Tabb House, 1979.
Women in Japanese captivity in Southeast Asia.

915. Janovská, Jarmila. Osudy žen (The Fates of Women). Zürich:
Konfrontace, 1981.

916. Kempner, Benedicta Maria. Nonnen unter dem Hackenkreuz.
Würzburg: Naumann, 1979.
Unique compendium on European nuns' role in the re-
sistance.

917a. Kiedrzynska, Wanda. Ravensbrück. Warsaw: Academy of
Science, 1961.

917b. Kocwa, Eugenia. Flucht aus Ravensbrück. East Berlin:
Union, 1973.

918. Laska, Vera. Jedna z nás (One of Us). Chicago: Nova
Doba, 1948.

919. _____. Women in the Resistance and in the Holocaust:
Voices of Eyewitnesses. Westport, Conn.: Greenwood
Press, 1983.
The first collection of memoirs focusing on women and
combining emphasis on both the resistance and on the Holocaust, with a scholarly general Introduction surveying all
aspects of both, plus individual introductions to each woman's story which serve as frameworks for the roles of the
resisters, concentration camp inmates or women in hiding.

920. Leslie, Anita. A Story Half Told, a Wartime Autobiography.
London: Hutchinson, 1983.
Churchill's cousin as ambulance driver in Africa, Italy
and France.

921. Litten, Irmgard. A Mother Fights Hitler. London: George
Allen & Unwin, 1942.

922. Machlejd, Wanda, ed. Experimental Operations on Prisoners
of Ravensbrück Concentration Camp. Warsaw: Zachodnia
agencja prasowa, 1960.

923. Masson, Madeleine. Christine: A Search for Christine Gran-
ville. London: Hamish Hamilton, 1975.
Tragic story of Polish resistance worker.

924. Maurel, Micheline. An Ordinary Camp. New York: Simon &
Schuster, 1958.
The Neubrandenburg concentration camp.

925. Mayerhofer, Emma, ed. Was geht das mich an. Vienna:
Österreichische Lagergemeinschaft Ravensbrück, 1976.

926. Mitrani, Thérèse ["Denise"]. Service d'evasion. Paris:
     Continents, 1946.

927. Moreau, Emilienne. La guerre buissonière: Une famille fran-
     çaise dans la résistance. Paris: Solan, 1970.

928. Muser, Erna and Zavrl, Vida, eds. FKL, ženskó koncenracij-
     sko taborišče Ravensbrück (FKL, the Women's Concentration
     Camp Ravensbrück). Ljubljana, Yugoslavia: Partizanska
     knjiga, 1971.

930. Neave, Airey. Little Cyclone ["Dédée"]. New York: Coronet,
     1973.
        Story of Andrée de Jongh, the Belgian founder of the
     underground railroad, the Comet Line. The line saved over
     600 Allied men, mostly pilots, by spiriting them away from
     the Netherlands, Belgium and France, through the Pyrenees
     to Spain, and hence to Great Britain.

931. Nicholas, Elisabeth. Death Be Not Proud. London: Cresset,
     1958.

932. Novac, Anna. Les beaux jours de ma jeunesse. Paris: Julli-
     ard, 1968.

933. Orska, Irena (Bytniewska). Silent Is the Vistula: The Story
     of the Warsaw Uprising. New York: Longmans, Green,
     1946.

934. Ourisson, Dounia. Les secrets du Bureau Politique d'Ausch-
     witz. Paris: Amicale d'Auschwitz, 1946.

935. Rosen, Donia. The Forest, My Friend. New York: World
     Federation of Bergen Belsen Associates, 1971.
        About the survival of a six-year-old Ukrainian girl.

936. Saint Claire, Simone. Ravensbrück, l'enfer des femmes.
     Paris: Tallandier, 1946.

937. Salus, Grete. Eine Frau erzählt. Bonn: Bundeszentrale für
     Heimatdienst, 1958.

938. Salvesen, Sylvia. Forgive but do not Forget. London:
     Hutchinson, 1958.

939a. Sergueiew, Lily. Secret Services Rendered. London: Kimber,
     1968.
        Russo-French double agent working for Abwehr and MI
     5 under the code name of "Treasure."

939b. Sim, Kevin. Women at War: Five Heroines Who Defied the Na-
     zis and Survived. New York: Morrow, 1982.

940. Ten Boom, Corrie. The Hiding Place. New York: Bantam, 1975.
     Dutch humanitarian hiding Jews and her memoirs from Ravensbrück.

941. _____. Prison Letters. New York: Bantam, 1978.
     Written by the legendary Dutch humanitarian, jailed and sent to Ravensbrück for hiding Jews.

942. Tillion, Germaine. Ravensbrück. Garden City, N.Y.: Doubleday, 1975.
     A researched personal memoir by a French anthropologist and member of the Musée de l'homme resistance group.

943. _____, et al., eds. Ravensbrück témoignages. Neuchâtel, Switzerland: Braconnière, 1946.

944. Volanská, Hela, et al. Hrdinky bez pátosu (Heroines Without Pathos). Bratislava, Czechoslovakia: Vydavatelstvo politickej literatury, 1967.

945. Von der Lühe, Irmgard. Eine Frau im Widerstand: Elisabeth von Thadden und das Dritte Reich. Freiburg: Herder, 1980.
     Known educator defying the Nazis.

946a. Ward, Donna I. F.A.N.Y. Invicta. London: Hutchinson, 1955.

946b. Warner, Lavinia and Sandilands, John. Women Beyond the Wire: A Story of Prisoners of the Japanese, 1942-45. London: Michael Joseph, 1982.

947. Wilborts, Suzanne. Pour la France. Paris: Charles-Lavauzelle, 1946.

948. Wolf, Lore. Ein Leben ist viel zu wenig. Frankfurt am Main: Röderberg, 1981.

949. Wynne, Barry. No Drums, No Trumpets, the Story of Mary Lindell. Milton Keynes, England: Clark, 1980.
     Biography of the indomitable resister of two world wars and her exploits against the Nazis.

950. Young, Gordon. Cat with Two Faces. New York: Putnam's, 1957.

951. Zassenhaus, Hiltgunt. Walls. Boston: Beacon, 1976.
     German linguist aiding Scandinavian prisoners.

952. Zorn, Gerda and Meyer, Gertrude. Frauen gegen Hitler,

Berichte aus dem Widerstand, 1933-1945. Frankfurt am Main: Röderberg, 1974.

953. Zörner, G., et al., eds. Frauen-KZ Ravensbrück. Frankfurt am Main: Röderberg, 1982 (1971).

5. JEWISH RESISTANCE

954. Ainsztein, Reuben. Jewish Resistance in Nazi Occupied Eastern Europe, with an Historical Survey of the Jew as a Fighter and Soldier in the Diaspora. New York: Harper & Row, 1975.
    Encyclopedic design presents evidence of Jewish underground in the ghettos and concentration camps.

955. _____. The Warsaw Ghetto Revolt. New York: Schocken, 1979.

956. Apenszlak, Jacob and Polakiewicz, Moshe. Armed Resistance of the Jews in Poland. New York: American Federation for Polish Jews, 1944.

957. Arad, Yitzhak. Ghetto in Flames: The Struggle and Destruction of the Jews in Vilna in the Holocaust. New York: KTAV, 1981.

958. _____. The Partisan, from the Valley of Death to Mount Zion. New York: Schocken, 1980.
    Jewish resistance in Lithuania.

959. Barkai, Meyer, ed. The Fighting Ghettos. Philadelphia: Lippincott, 1962.
    Resistance in the ghettos among partisans and in the concentration camps.

960. Bar-On, Zwi and Levin, Dov. The Story of an Underground: The Resistance of the Jews of Kovno (Lithuania) in the Second World War. Jerusalem: Yad Vashem, 1962.
    In Hebrew, with English summary.

961. Bauer, Yehuda. Flight and Rescue. New York: Random House, 1970.

962. _____. They Chose Life. New York: American Jewish Committee, 1973.
    Illustrated, short survey of armed and unarmed resistance in ghettos, camps and fields, by Israeli authority on the Holocaust.

963. Bezwinska, Jadwiga, ed. Amidst a Nightmare of Crime: Notes
      of Prisoners of the Sonderkommando Found at Auschwitz.
      Auschwitz: Panstwowe Muzeum, 1973.

964. Bial, Morrison D., ed. Holocaust: A History of Courage and
      Resistance. New York: Behrman, 1975.

965. Blumenthal, Nachman and Kernish, Joseph, eds. Resistance
      and Revolt in the Warsaw Ghetto. Jerusalem: Yad Vashem,
      1965.
         In Hebrew, with English summary.

966. Boehm, Eric H., ed. We Survived: The Stories of Fourteen
      of the Hidden and Hunted of Nazi Germany. New Haven,
      Conn.: Yale University Press, 1949.

967. Borzkowski, Tuvia. Between Tumbling Walls. Jerusalem:
      Ghetto Fighters' Publishing House, 1972.
         By a member of the Jewish Fighting Organization in the
      Warsaw ghetto.

968. Cholawski, Shalom. City and Forest Under Siege. Tel Aviv:
      Moreshet, 1970.
         Jewish resistance in Poland.

969. _____. Soldiers from the Ghetto: Jewish Armed Resistance
      in the East, 1941-1945. South Brunswick, N.J.: A.S.
      Barnes, 1980.
         Centered around the Jewish resistance at the town of
      Nezvizh in the B.S.S.R.

970. Diamant, David. Les Juifs dans la résistance française, 1940-
      1944. Paris: Le Pavillon, 1971.

971. Eckman, Lester and Lazar, Chaim. The Jewish Resistance,
      the History of the Jewish Partisans in Lithuania and White
      Russia Under Nazi Occupation, 1940-1945. New York:
      Shengold, 1977.

972. Elkins, Michael. Forged in Fury. New York: Ballantine,
      1971.
         Discusses Jewish resistance during the war and justice
      after the war, 1938-1948.

973. Eschwege, Helmut. Der Widerstand deutscher Juden gegen
      das Naziregime, 1933-1945. Dresden: Verlag der Kunst,
      1980.

974. Friedman, Philip, ed. Martyrs and Fighters, the Epic of the
      Warsaw Ghetto. New York: Praeger, 1954.

975. Goldstein, Charles. The Bunker. New York: Atheneum,
      1973.
           Memoirs of a survivor of both the Warsaw ghetto and
      the Warsaw uprising, living for four months in a bunker.

976. Goldstein, David, ed. Chaviva. Ústredný sväz cionistický,
      1947. No place of publication indicated; printed in Prague.
           Zionist girl's return from Palestine to Banská Bystrica
      during the Slovak uprising of 1944 and her martyrdom;
      less documented but parallel story to that of Hannah Senesh.

977. Gottlieb, Moshe R. American Anti-Nazi Resistance, 1933-1941,
      an Historical Analysis. New York: KTAV, 1982.
           Boycott campaign of German goods by several Jewish
      organizations, including the American Jewish War Veterans,
      and their efforts to publicize the Nazi danger.

978. Grossman, Chaike. The Members of the Underground Move-
      ment. Tel Aviv: Moreshet, 1970.
           The Bialistok ghetto revolt.

979. Gruber, Samuel. I Chose Life. New York: Shengold, 1978.
           Escapees from the Lublin ghetto join the partisan move-
      ment.

980. Gutman, Yisrael (Israel). Jews of Warsaw, 1939-1943: Ghet-
      to, Underground, Revolt. Bloomington: Indiana Univer-
      sity Press, 1982.

981. _____. The Revolt of the Besieged: Mordechai Anilewicz
      and the Fighting in the Warsaw Ghetto. Merhavya, Israel:
      Edut Mordechai Anilewicz Memorial, 1963.
           Biography, in Hebrew, of a commander, by a participant.

982. _____ and Zuroff, Efraim, eds. Rescue Attempts During
      the Holocaust. Proceedings of the Second Yad Vashem In-
      ternational Historical Conference, Jerusalem, April 8-11,
      1974. Jerusalem: Yad Vashem, 1977; New York: KTAV,
      1979.

983. Gutteridge, Richard. Open Thy Mouth for the Dumb: The
      German Evangelical Church and the Jews, 1879-1950.
      Southampton: Camelot, 1976.

984. Hirschman, Ira A. Caution to the Winds. New York: David
      McKay, 1962.

985. _____. Lifeline to the Promised Land. New York: Van-
      guard, 1946.

986. Hoettl, Wilhelm. Hitler's Paper Weapon. London: Hart-Davis,

1955.
Discusses the counterfeiting of currency in concentration camps.

987. Kahanovich, Moshe. The War of the Jewish Partisans in Eastern Europe. Tel Aviv: Ayanot, 1954.
In Hebrew.

988. Katz, Alfred. Poland's Ghettos at War. New York: Irvington, 1978.
Concise coverage of specific ghettos.

989. Kluger, Ruth and Mann, Peggy. The Last Escape: The Launching of the Largest Secret Rescue Movement of All Times. Garden City, N.Y.: Doubleday, 1973.
Hair-raising experiences of a woman organizing the rescue of Jews by boats on the Danube and in the Mediterranean Sea.

990. Knout, David. Contribution à l'histoire de la résistance juive en France, 1940-1944. Paris: Editions du Centre, 1947.

991. Kohn, Moshe and Tartakower, Aryel, eds. Jewish Resistance During the Holocaust. Proceedings of the First International Conference on the Manifestations of Jewish Resistance, April 7-11, 1968. Jerusalem: Yad Vashem, 1971.

992. Kohn, Nahum and Roiter, Howard. A Voice from the Forest: Memoirs of a Jewish Partisan. New York: Holocaust Library, 1980.

993. Kortchak, Roika. Flames in the Ashes. Tel Aviv: Moreshet, 1965.
The Vilna resistance.

994. Kowalski, Isaac. A Secret Press in Nazi Europe: The Story of a Jewish United Partisan Organization. New York: Central Guide Publishers, 1969.
Story of the resistance in Vilna and the surrounding area, based on primary sources.

995. Kurzman, Dan. The Bravest Battle: The Twenty-Eight Days of the Warsaw Ghetto Uprising. New York: Putnam's, 1976.
By nonsurvivor, based on testimonies of eyewitnesses.

996. Lambert, Gilles. Operation Hazalah. Indianapolis: Bobbs-Merrill, 1974.
Zionist resistance in Hungary in 1944.

997. Latour, Anny. The Jewish Resistance in France (1940-1944). New York: Schocken, 1981.

998. Lavi (Loewenstein), Theodore. Rumanian Jewry in World War
      II, Fight for Survival. Jerusalem: Yad Vashem, 1965.
      Hebrew, with English summary.

999. Lazar, Chaim. Muranowska 7: The Warsaw Ghetto Rising.
      Tel Aviv: Masada, 1966.

1000. Lazar-Litai, Chaim. The Masada of Warsaw. Tel Aviv:
      Jabotinsky Institute, 1963.
      In Hebrew.

1001. Mark, Bernard. The Extermination and the Resistance of the
      Polish Jews During the Period 1939-1944. Warsaw: Jewish
      Historical Institute, 1955.

1002. _____. Uprising in the Warsaw Ghetto. New York:
      Schocken, 1976.
      Includes documents.

1003. Masters, Anthony. The Summer That Bled. New York: St.
      Martin's, 1972.
      The story of Hannah Senesh, the martyred Hungarian
      parachutist from Palestine who was executed in Budapest.

1004. Meed, Vladka (Feigele Peitel). On Both Sides of the Wall.
      New York: Schocken, 1979.
      Memoirs of the Warsaw ghetto by a survivor who, with
      false identity papers, served as a Jewish resistance couri-
      er and paymaster.

1005. Mirchuk, Petro. In the German Mills of Death, 1941-1945.
      New York: Vantage, 1976.

1006. Muszkat, M., ed. Jewish Fighters in the War Against the
      Nazis. Tel Aviv: Moreshet, 1974.

1007. Nir, Akiva. Paths in the Circle of Fire. Tel Aviv: Moreshet,
      1967.
      Experiences of a Jewish member of a Slovak partisan
      group.

1008. Nirenstein, Albert, ed. A Tower from the Enemy: Contri-
      butions to the History of Jewish Resistance in Poland.
      New York: Orion, 1959.
      Focused on ghettos, especially the Warsaw ghetto up-
      rising.

1009. Novitch, Miriam. Sobibor, Martyrdom and Revolt. New York:
      Schocken, 1980.

1010. Papanek, Ernst and Linn, Edward. Out of the Fire. New
      York: Morrow, 1975.

The saving of Jewish children in southern France by
an Austrian psychologist.

1011. Perl, William R. The Four-Front War: From the Holocaust
        to the Promised Land. New York: Crown, 1979.
            Deals with the saving of groups of Jews by the river
        routes of Europe.

1012. Porter, Jack N., ed. Jewish Partisans, a Documentary of
        Jewish Resistance in the Soviet Union During World War II.
        2 vols. Washington, D.C.: University Press of America,
        1982.
            By the son of a partisan; extensive bibliography.

1013. Prager, Moshe. Sparks of Glory. New York: Shengold,
        1974.
            Supportive roles of rabbis and others during the Holo-
        caust.

1014. Rashke, Richard. Escape from Sobibor, the Heroic Story of
        the Jews Who Escaped from a Nazi Death Camp. Boston:
        Houghton Mifflin, 1982.

1015. Ravine, Jacques. La résistance organisée des Juifs en
        France: 1940-1944. Paris: Julliard, 1973.

1016. Rose, Anna. Refugee. New York: Dial Press, 1977.

1017. Rose, Leesha. The Tulips Are Red. South Brunswick, N.J.:
        A.S. Barnes, 1979.
            Heroic and effective work of Jewish girl in the Dutch
        resistance, taking care of over one hundred people in hid-
        ing.

1018. Rothschild, Guy de. Contre Bonne Fortune. Paris: Pierre
        Belfond, 1983.
            Touches only indirectly on Jewish resistance, but is a
        good example of one important Jew's contribution to a free
        France.

1019. Samuels, Gertrude. Mottele. New York: Signet, 1976.
            Youngster's experiences with the partisans.

1020. Schneider, Gertrude. Journey into Fear: Story of the Riga
        Ghetto. New York: Ark House, 1980.

1021. Sefer Hapartizanim (Book of Jewish Partisans). 2 vols. Tel
        Aviv: Merchavia, 1958.
            Overall survey of Jewish partisan activities in occupied
        Europe.

1022. Senesh, Hannah. Hannah Senesh--Her Life and Diary. New
       York: Schocken, 1973.
            About the Palestinian girl who parachuted to Yugoslavia
       and was martyred in Hungary, her original home.

1023. Sherman, A.J. Island Refuge: Britain and Refugees from
       the Third Reich, 1933-1939. Berkeley: University of
       California Press, 1974.

1024. Solomian-Loc, Fanny. Woman Facing the Gallows. Amherst,
       Mass.: By the author, 1981.
            Translated from original Hebrew edition. It is the
       story of a partisan nurse in Russia and Poland.

1025. Stadtler, Bea. The Holocaust: A History of Courage and
       Resistance. New York: Behrman, 1975. Also listed
       under Bial, Morrison D., ed.

1026. Steinberg, Lucien. Le Comité de défense des Juifs en Bel-
       gique, 1942-1944. Brussels: Université de Bruxelles,
       1973.

1027. _____. Not as a Lamb: The Jews Against Hitler. New
       York: Atheneum, 1978.

1028. Steiner, Erich G. The Story of "Patria." New York:
       Schocken, 1982.

1029. Steiner, Jean-François. Treblinka. New York: Simon &
       Schuster, 1967.
            A partly fictionalized account which includes the revolt
       at Treblinka.

1030. Suhl, Yuri. Uncle Misha's Partisans. New York: Four
       Winds, 1973.
            Juvenile book about a Jewish partisan boy near Zhito-
       mir.

1031. _____, ed. They Fought Back: The Story of the Jewish
       Resistance in Nazi Europe. New York: Schocken, 1975.
            A mosaic of thirty three cases of resisters, male and
       female, of various lengths and strength; an excellent take-
       off point for further research.

1032. Syrkin, Marie. Blessed Is the Match: The Story of Jewish
       Resistance. Philadelphia: Jewish Publication Society,
       1948.
            Covers Hannah Senesh and others in the resistance.

1033. Tenenbaum, Joseph. Underground: The Story of a People.
       New York: Philosophical Library, 1957.

1034. Vinocour, Jack, ed. The Jewish Resistance. London: World
      Jewish Congress, 1968.

1035. Yad Vashem. The Holocaust and Resistance. Jerusalem:
      Yad Vashem, 1972.
            Illustrated brief outline.

1036. _____. Jewish Resistance During the Holocaust. Proceed-
      ings... see entry 991.

1037. _____. Patterns of Jewish Leadership in Nazi Europe,
      1933-1945. Proceedings of the Third Yad Vashem Inter-
      national Historical Conference, April, 1977. Jerusalem:
      Yad Vashem, 1979.

1038. _____. Rescue Attempts During the Holocaust, Proceed-
      ings... see entry 982.

1039. _____. Yad Vashem Studies. 13 vols. New York: KTAV,
      1957-80.

1040. _____. Yad Vashem Studies on the European Jewish Cata-
      strophe and Resistance. Jerusalem: Yad Vashem, 1968.

1041. Zuckerman, Isaac, ed. The Fighting Ghettos. New York:
      Belmont-Tower, 1971.

1042. Zuckerman, Itzhak and Basok, Moshe. The Book of the Ghet-
      to Combats. Tel Aviv: Kibbutz Hameoukhas, 1956.
            In Hebrew.

6. HOLOCAUST

1043. Adler, Cyrus and Margalith, Aaron M. With Firmness in the Right: American Diplomatic Action Affecting Jews. New York: Arno, 1977 (1946).

1044. Adler, H.G. Theresienstadt, 1941-1945, Das Antlitz einer Zwangsgemeinschaft, Geschichte, Sociologie, Psychologie. 2 vols. Tübingen, W. Ger.: Mohr, 1955.

1045. _____. Der Verwaltete Mensch: Studium zur Deportation der Juden aus Deutschland. Tübingen, W. Ger.: Mohr, 1974.

1046. _____, et al., eds. Auschwitz, Zeugnisse und Berichte. Frankfurt am Main: Europäische Verlagsanstalt, 1962.

1047. Altschuler, David A., ed. Hitler's War Against the Jews: A Young Reader's Version of 'The War Against the Jews 1933-1945' by Lucy S. Dawidowicz. New York: Behrman, 1978.

1048. American Jewish History Association. America and the Holocaust. New York: American Jewish History Series, vol. 70, 1980.

1049. Amery, Jean. At the Mind's Limit. Bloomington: Indiana University Press. 1980.

1050. Anger, Per. With Raoul Wallenberg in Budapest. New York: Schocken, 1981.

1051. Apenszlak, Jacob, ed. The Black Book of Polish Jewry: An Account of the Martyrdom of Polish Jewry Under the Nazi Occupation. New York: Fertig, 1982 (1943).
Originally published by the American Federation of Polish Jews in cooperation with the Association of Jewish Refugees and Immigrants from Poland. Sponsored by fifteen distinguished Americans including Albert Einstein, Fiorello LaGuardia, A.J. Sabath, Harold Ickes and Eleanor Roosevelt. Note original 1943 publication date.

1052. Apitz, Bruno. Nahý mezi vlky (Naked Among Wolves).
       Prague: Naše vojsko, 1960.

1053. Aptecker, George. Beyond Despair. Morristown, N.J.:
       Kahn & Kahn, 1980.

1054. Arad, Yitzhak, et al., eds. Documents on the Holocaust,
       Selected Sources on the Destruction of Jews in Germany,
       Austria, Poland and the Soviet Union. Jerusalem: Yad
       Vashem, 1981.

1055. Arieti, Silvano. The Parnas. New York: Basic Books,
       1979.

1056. Aron, Isaac. Fallen Leaves. New York: Shengold, 1982.

1057. Baker, Leonard. Days of Sorrow and Pain: Leo Baeck and
       the Berlin Jews. New York: Macmillan, 1979.
           Pulitzer Prize winning biography of Berlin rabbi, deal-
       ing with his ideas and work.

1058. Barkley, Alben. Atrocities and Other Conditions in Concen-
       tration Camps in Germany. Washington, D.C.: GPO,
       1945.
           Congressional Committee report by twelve United States
       Congressmen who visited Dachau, Buchenwald and Nord-
       hausen in April and May of 1945.

1059. Bartoszewski, Wladyslaw and Lewin, Zofia, eds. Righteous
       Among Nations: How the Poles Helped the Jews, 1939-
       1945. London: Swiderski, 1969.

1060. Bauer, Yehuda. A History of the Holocaust. New York:
       Franklin Watts, 1982.
           A factual and well-organized history, suitable for use
       as a college textbook.

1061. _____. Holocaust, a Generation Later. New York:
       Holmes & Meier, 1980.

1062. _____. The Holocaust in Historical Perspective. Seattle:
       University of Washington Press, 1978.

1063. _____. The Jewish Emergence from Powerlessness. Tor-
       onto: University of Toronto Press, 1979.

1064. _____ and Rotenstreich, Nathan, eds. The Holocaust as
       Historical Experience, Essays and Discussion. New York:
       Holmes & Meier, 1981.
           Based on the conference "The Holocaust--A Generation
       After," in New York in 1975. Of lasting importance.

1065. Baum, Rainer C. The Holocaust and the German Elite: Genocide and National Suicide in Germany, 1871-1945. Totowa, N.J.: Rowman & Littlefield, 1981.

1066. Beloff, Max, ed. On the Track of Tyranny. London:
Wiener Library, 1960.

1067. Berben, Paul. Dachau, 1933-45, an Official History. London:
Comité International de Dachau, 1975.
See entry 472 for annotation.

1068. Bergh, Siegfried van den. Deportaties (Deportations). Bus-
sum, The Netherlands: C.A.J. Van Dishoeck, 1945.

1069. Bergmann, Martin S. and Jucovy, Milton E., eds. Generations of the Holocaust. New York: Basic Books, 1982.
Includes psychological essays about survivors.

1070. Berkovits, Eliezer. With God in Hell: Judaism in the Ghettos and Deathcamps. New York: Hebrew Publishing Co.,
1979.

1071. Bernadac, Christian. Les médicins de l'impossible. Paris:
France-Empire, 1968.

1072. _____. Les médicins maudits. Paris: France-Empire,
1967.

1073. _____. Les Sourciers du ciel. Paris: France-Empire,
1969.

1074. _____. Le train de la mort. Paris: France-Empire, 1970.

1075. Bernadotte, Folke. The Curtain Falls: Last Days of the
Third Reich. New York: Knopf, 1945.
Covers several categories, deals with Bernadotte's nego-
tiations with the Nazis for the release of Scandinavian
political and Jewish prisoners.

1076. Barnard, Jean J. The Camp of Slow Death. London: Gollancz, 1945.

1077. Bettelheim, Bruno. Surviving and Other Essays. New York:
Knopf, 1979.

1078. Bezwinska, Jadwiga and Czech, Danuta, eds. KL Auschwitz
Seen by the SS: Höss, Broad, Kremer. Auschwitz:
Panstwowe Muzeum, 1978.

1079. Bierman, John. Righteous Gentile, the Story of Raoul Wallenberg, Missing Hero of the Holocaust. New York: Viking,
1981.

1080.   Billig, Joseph. Les camps de concentration dans l'économie
        du Reich hitlerien. Paris: Presses universitaires de
        France, 1973.

1081.   Biss, Andreas. A Million Jews to Save--Check to the Final
        Solution. South Brunswick, N.J.: Barnes, 1975.
        Discusses the rescue of Hungarian Jews, especially in
        1944.

1082.   Black, Floyd H. The American College of Sofia: A Chapter
        in American-Bulgarian Relations. Boston: Trustees of
        Sofia American Schools, 1958.

1083.   Blackbook of Localities Where Jewish Population Was Exter-
        minated by the Nazis. Jerusalem: Yad Vashem, 1965.

1084.   Bláha, František. Medicina na scestí (Medicine Gone Astray).
        Prague: Orbis, 1946.

1085.   Blet, Pierre, ed. Actes et documents du Saint Siège relatifs
        à la Seconde Guerre Mondiale, vols. VIII-IX. Vatican
        City: Secretariat of State, 1974-1975.

1086.   Bloch, Sam E., ed. Holocaust and Rebirth: Bergen Belsen,
        1945-1965. New York and Tel Aviv: Bergen Belsen Mem-
        orial Press, 1965.
        A remembrance book in English, Hebrew and Yiddish.

1087.   Blumenthal, Nachman. Conduct and Actions of a Judenrat:
        Documents for the Bialystok Ghetto. Jerusalem: Yad
        Vashem, 1962.

1088.   _____, ed. Dokumenty i materialy--Obozy (Documents and
        Materials--Concentration Camps). Lodz: Wydawnictvo
        centralnej żydowskiej komisji historycznej, 1946.

1089.   Bogusz, Josef, ed. Przegled lekarski (Medical Survey).
        3 vols. Warsaw: International Auschwitz Commission,
        1970-1971.
        See entry 487 for annotation.

1090.   Bor, Josef. Opuštěná panenka (The Abandoned Doll).
        Prague: Státní nakladatelství politické litaratury, 1961.
        Terezín memoirs of Bor who lost his wife and two
        daughters there.

1091.   _____. The Terezín Requiem. New York: Avon, 1978.

1092.   Bornstein, Ernst I. Die lange Nacht: Ein Bericht aus sieben
        Lagern. Frankfurt am Main: Europäische Verlagsanstalt,
        1967.

1093. Borwicz, Michal M. Univerzytet zbirow (University of Brigands). Cracow: Centralna żydowska komisja historyczna, 1946.

1094. _____, et al. Dokumenty zbrodni i meczenstva (Documents of Crime and Martyrdom). Cracow: Żydowska komisja historyczna, 1945.

1095. Bowman, Derek, ed. The Diary of David Rabinowicz. Edmonds, Wash.: Creative Options, 1982.

1096. Boyajian, Dickram H. Armenia: The Case for a Forgotten Genocide. Westwood, N.J.: Educational Book Crafters, 1972.

1097. Braham, Randolph L. Eichmann and the Destruction of Hungarian Jewry. New York: Twayne, 1961.

1098. _____. The Hungarian Jewish Catastrophe: A Selected and Annotated Bibliography. New York: YIVO Institute, 1962.

1099. _____. The Hungarian Labor Service System, 1939–1945. New York: Columbia University Press, 1977.

1100. _____. The Politics of Genocide: The Holocaust in Hungary. 2 vols. New York: Columbia University Press, 1981.

1101. Brand, Joel and Weissberg, Alex. Desperate Mission: Joel Brand's Story. New York: Criterion, 1958.
       Deals with the saving of Hungarian Jews.

1102. Brennan, William. Medical Holocausts I: Exterminative Medicine in Nazi Germany and Contemporary America. Nordland Series in Contemporary American Problems. Woodside, N.Y.: Nordland, 1980.

1103. _____. Medical Holocausts II: The Language of Exterminative Medicine in Nazi Germany and Contemporary America. Nordland Series in Contemporary American Problems. Woodside, N.Y.: Nordland, 1981.

1104. Broad, Pery. KZ Auschwitz--Reminiscences of an SS-Man. Auschwitz: Panstwowe Muzeum, 1965.

1105. Browning, Christopher R. The Final Solution and the German Foreign Office. New York: Holmes & Meier, 1978.

1106. Bubeníčková, Růžena, et al. Tábory utrpení a smrti (Camps of Suffering and Death). Prague: Svoboda, 1969.

1107. Burg, J.G. Maidanek in alle Ewigkeit. Munich: Ederer,
       1979.

1108. Cahiers d'Auschwitz. Auschwitz: Panstwowe Muzeum,
       1958- .
       German edition: Hefte von Auschwitz.

1109. Chaim, Bezalel. A Bio-Bibliographical Dictionary of Holocaust
       and Anti-Holocaust Authors. New York: Revisionist
       Press, 1980.

1110. _____. A Bio-Bibliographical Dictionary of Notable Jews
       Who Perished in German Concentration Camps and Ghettos.
       New York: Revisionist Press, 1980.

1111. Charny, Israel W. How Can We Commit the Unthinkable:
       Genocide, the Human Cancer. Boulder, Col.: Westview,
       1982.
       A search for the essence of genocide by an Israeli
       psychology professor and coordinator of the Genocide Early
       Warning System project in Jerusalem.

1112. Chartok, Roselle and Spencer, Jack, eds. The Holocaust
       Years: Society of Trial. New York: Bantam, 1978.
       Good selections, suitable for classroom use.

1113. Charvat, Joseph, et al. Medical Science Abused. Prague:
       Orbis, 1946.

1114. Chary, Frederick B. The Bulgarian Jews and the Final Solu-
       tion, 1940-1944. Pittsburgh: University of Pittsburgh
       Press, 1972.
       About Bulgarian Jews, most of whom escaped the Holo-
       caust.

1115. Choumoff, Pierre S. Les chambres à gas de Mauthausen.
       Paris: Amicale des déportés et familles des desparus du
       camp de concentration de Mauthausen, 1972.

1116. Clare, George. Last Waltz in Vienna, the Destruction of a
       Family, 1842-1942. London: Pan, 1982.
       Somewhat novelized but true-to-fact coverage of the
       Holocaust.

1117. Clarke, Comer. Eichmann, the Man and His Crimes. New
       York: Ballantine, 1960.

1118. Cohen, Elie A. The Abyss, a Concession. New York: Nor-
       ton, 1973.

1119. Cohn, Norman. Warrant for Genocide: The Myth of the

Jewish World-Conspiracy and the Protocols of the Elders
of Zion. New York: Harper & Row, 1969.

1120. Collis, Robert. Straight On: Journey to Belsen and the
Road Home. London: Methuen, 1947.

1121. Crawford, Fred R. (Introduction). Dachau. Atlanta,
Georgia: Center for Research in Social Change, 1979.

1122. Czech, Danuta, et al. Auschwitz, Nazi Extermination Camp.
New York: International Publications Service, 1978.
See entry 524 for annotation.

1123. Dabrowska, Danuta and Dobroszycki, Lucjan, eds. Kronika
getta lodzkiego (Chronicles of the Lodz Ghetto). Lodz:
Wydawnictwo lodzkie, 1965.

1124. Dawidowicz, Lucy S. The War Against the Jews, 1933-1945.
New York: Bantam, 1976.
Detailed and scholarly history of the Nazi effort to ex-
terminate the Jews of Europe; considered one of the most
complete treatments of the Holocaust, covering both the
German and Jewish sides. Good scholarly apparatus, notes
and bibliography.

1125. _____, ed. A Holocaust Reader. New York: Behrman,
1976.

1126. Delzell, Charles F., ed. The Papacy and Totalitarianism Between the Two World Wars. New York: Wiley, 1974.

1127. Demant, Ebbo, ed. Auschwitz--"Direkt von der Rampe weg..."
Kaduk, Erben, Klehr: Drei Täter geben zu Protokoll.
Reinbeck bei Hamburg: Rowohlt, 1979.

1128. Des Pres, Terence. The Survivor, an Anatomy of Life in the
Death Camps. New York: Oxford University Press, 1976.
Refutes Bettelheim in a brilliant analysis; classic inter-
pretation by a nonsurvivor with literary talents.

1129. Deutschkron, Inge. ...denn ihrer war die Hölle: Kinder in
Ghettos und Lagern. Cologne: Wissenschaft & Politik,
1965.

1130. Dimsdale, Joel E., ed. Survivors, Victims and Perpetrators,
Essays on the Nazi Holocaust. Washington, D.C.: Hemisphere, 1980.

1131. "Docteur X." Le calvaire d'un médicin polonais. Geneva:
Georg, 1946.

1132. Donat, Alexander. The Holocaust Kingdom, a Memoir. New
       York: Holt, Rinehart & Winston, 1965.

1133. _____, ed. The Death Camp Treblinka. New York:
       Holocaust Library, 1979.

1134. Donovan, John. Eichmann, Man of Slaughter. New York:
       Avon, 1960.

1135. Dorian, Emil. The Quality of Witness, a Romanian Diary,
       1937-1944. Philadelphia: Jewish Publication Society of
       America, 1983.

1136. Dubois, Josiah E. Jr. The Devil's Chemists. Boston:
       Beacon, 1952.

1137. Duszak, Stanislaw, ed. Majdanek. Lublin: Krajowa agencja
       wydawnicza, 1980.

1138. Ehrenburg, Ilya and Grossman, Vasily, eds. The Black
       Book. New York: Schocken, 1983.

1139. Ehrmann, František, et al. Terezín (Theresienstadt).
       Prague: Council of Jewish Committees in the Czech Lands,
       1965.
       In English.

1140. Eisenberg, Azriel. The Lost Generation: Children in the
       Holocaust. Princeton, N.J.: Pilgrim Press, 1982.

1141. _____. Witness to the Holocaust. Princeton, N.J.:
       Pilgrim Press, 1981.
       Includes documents, testimonies and memoirs of Jews
       and Christians.

1142. Eitinger, L. Concentration Camp Survivors in Norway and
       Israel. The Hague: Martinus Nijhoff, 1972.

1143a. Ekart, Antoni. Vanished Without Trace. London: Max Par-
       rish, 1954.

1143b. Eliach, Yaffa and Gurewitsch, Brana. The Liberators: Eye-
       witness Accounts of the Liberation of Concentration Camps,
       Liberation Day. New York: Center for the Holocaust,
       1981.

1144. Epstein, Helen. Children of the Holocaust. New York: Ban-
       tam, 1980.
       Psychological problems of survivors' children.

1145. Eschwege, Helmut, ed. Kennzeichen J: Bilder, Dokumente,

Berichte zur Geschichte der Verbrechen des Hitlerfaschis-
mus an den deutschen Juden, 1933-1945. Berlin: Deutscher Verlag der Wissenschaften, 1966.

1146. Esterer, Ingeborg, et al., eds. Das Recht ein Mensch zu
sein. Baden-Baden, W. Ger.: Signal, 1970.

1147. Federation of Czechoslovakian Jews. The Persecution of the
Jews in Nazi Slovakia. London: The Federation, 1942.

1148. Federation of Jewish Committees in Yugoslavia. The Crimes
of the Fascist Occupants and Their Collaborators Against
Jews in Yugoslavia. Belgrade: ISJOJ, 1957.
In Serbian with English summary.

1149. Feig, Konnilynn G. Hitler's Death Camps, the Sanity of
Madness. New York: Holmes & Meier, 1981.
A description of nineteen major concentration camps
and their histories, with maps and charts (even directions
for visitors), and a helpful, though somewhat carelessly
prepared, bibliography.

1150. Fein, Erich. Die Steine reden. Vienna: Europaverlag, 1975.

1151. Fein, Helen. Accounting for Genocide: National Responses
and Jewish Victimization During the Holocaust. New York:
Free Press, 1979; Chicago: University of Chicago, 1984.
Scholarly sociological analysis, with statistics, maps
and bibliography, including periodical literature.

1152. Felice, Renzo de. Storia degli Ebrei Italiani sotto il fascismo
(History of the Jews Under Fascism). Turin: Einaudi,
1972.

1153. Finker, Moshe. Young Moshe's Diary, the Spiritual Torment
of a Jewish Boy in Nazi Europe. Jerusalem: Yad Vashem,
1979.

1154. Fisher, Jules S. Transnistria: The Forgotten Cemetery.
London: Yoseloff, 1969.
Fate of the Jews in Rumania.

1155. Fitzgibbon, Louis. Unpitied and Unknown. London: Bachman & Turner, 1975.

1156. Fraenkel, Josef, ed. The Jews of Austria: Essays on Their
Life, History, and Destruction. London: Vallentine,
Mitchell, 1967.

1157. Franek, Rudolf. Terezínská škola (The School in Terezín).
Prague: Svaz protifašistických bojovníků, 1965.

1158. Frankl, Victor E. Ein Psycholog erlebt das Konzentrations-
       lager. Vienna: Jugend und Volk, 1946.

1159. Friedlander, Albert H. Leo Baeck: Teacher of Theresien-
       stadt. New York: Holt, Rinehart & Winston, 1978.

1160. Friedlander, Henry. On the Holocaust: A Critique of the
       Treatment of the Holocaust in History Textbooks, Accom-
       panied by an Annotated Bibliography. New York: Anti-
       Defamation League, 1973.
       Only thirty one pages but well to the point.

1161. _____ and Milton, Sybil, eds. The Holocaust: Ideology,
       Bureaucracy, and Genocide. Millwood, N.Y.: Kraus,
       1981.

1162. Friedländer, Saul. When Memory Comes. New York: Far-
       rar, Straus & Giroux, 1979.

1163. Friedman, Ina R. Escape or Die: True Stories of Young
       People Who Survived the Holocaust. Reading, Mass.:
       Addison-Wesley, 1982.
       Presented for young readers.

1164. Friedman, Philip. Auschwitz. Buenos Aires: Sociedad
       Hebraica Argentina, 1952.

1165. _____ . Roads to Extinction: Essays on the Holocaust.
       New York: Jewish Publication Society of America, 1980.

1166. _____ . Their Brothers' Keepers. The Christian Heroes
       and Heroines Who Helped the Oppressed Escape the Nazi
       Terror. New York: Schocken, 1978.

1167. _____ . This Was Oswiecim. London: United Jewish Re-
       lief Appeal, 1946.

1168. Friedman, Saul S. Amcha, an Oral Testament of the Holo-
       caust. Washington, D.C.: University Press of America,
       1979.

1169. Garcia, Max. As Long as I Remain Alive. Tuscaloosa, Ala.:
       Portals, 1979.

1170. Garfinkels, Betty. Les Belges Face à la persécution raciale,
       1940-1944. Brussels: Université Libre, 1965.

1171. Gershon, Karen, ed. We Came as Children. New York:
       Harcourt, Brace & World, 1966.

1172. Gerz, Jochen. Exit. Frankfurt am Main: Roter Stern, 1978.

1173. Geve, Thomas. <u>Youth in Chains</u>. Jerusalem: Rubin Mass, 1958.

1174. Gibinski, H. <u>La vérité sur les camps de concentration</u>. Warsaw: Institut des sciences médicales, 1946.

1175. Gilbert, Martin. <u>Atlas of the Holocaust</u>. New York: Macmillan, 1982.
Text and collection of detailed maps about Holocaust localities. Very useful for detailed studies.

1176. _____. <u>Final Journey, the Fate of the Jews in Nazi Europe</u>. New York: Mayflower, 1979.

1177. Gilboa, Yehoshua A. <u>Confess! Confess!</u> Boston: Little, Brown, 1968.

1178. Gillman, Peter and Leni. <u>'Collar the Lot.' How Britain Interned and Expelled Its Wartime Refugees</u>. London: Quartet Books, 1980.

1179. Goldberg, Izaac. <u>The Miracles Versus Tyranny</u>. New York: Philosophical Library, 1978.

1180. Goldberg, Michel. <u>Namesake</u>. New Haven: Yale University Press, 1982.
Spiritual biography of French Jew who once was a child in hiding during the Holocaust, and his search for identity.

1181. Goldstein, Bernard. <u>Five Years in the Warsaw Ghetto</u>. Garden City, New York: Doubleday, 1961. Former edition under <u>The Stars Bear Witness</u> New York: Viking, 1949.

1182. Goldston, Robert C. <u>Sinister Touches: The Secret War Against Hitler</u>. New York: Dial, 1982.

1183. Gollwitzer, Helmut, et al., eds. <u>Dying We Live</u>. New York: Pantheon, 1956.
Last statements of victims.

1184. Gostner, Erwin. <u>1000 Tagen im KZ</u>. Innsbruck: Wagnerische Universitäts-Buchdrukerei, 1945.

1185. Gray, Martin. <u>For Those I Loved</u>. New York: Signet, 1974.
Part of this colorful memoir deals with the Warsaw ghetto and the uprising.

1186. Grinberg, Natan. <u>Dokumenti (Documents)</u>. Sofia: Central Consistory of Jews in Bulgaria, 1945.

1187. Grobman, Alex and Landes, Daniel, eds. Genocide: Critical
       Issues of the Holocaust. Chappaqua, N.Y.: Rossel
       Books, 1982.
            Copublished by the Simon Wiesenthal Center in Los
       Angeles, as a tie-in with the motion picture Genocide.

1188. Gross, Leonard. The Last Jews in Berlin. New York: Simon
       & Schuster, 1982.
            Story of a dozen Jewish men and women living as "U-
       boats" hidden in Berlin, by a known journalist.

1189. Grossman, Vassili. L'enfer de Treblinka. Paris: Arthaud,
       1966.

1190. Gryn, Edward and Murawska, Zofia. Majdanek Concentration
       Camp. Lublin: Wydawnictvo lubelskie, 1966.

1191. Grzesiuk, Stanislaw. Piec lat kacetu (Five Years of Concen-
       tration Camp). Warsaw: Ksiazka i Wiedza, 1978.

1192. Gumkowski, J. and Rutkowski, A., eds. Treblinka. Warsaw:
       Council for the Protection of Fight and Martyrdom Monu-
       ments, n.d.

1193. Gun, Nerin E. The Day of the Americans. New York:
       Fleet, 1966.
            The liberation of Dachau.

1194a. Gutman, Yisrael, ed. The Holocaust in Documents. New
       York: Anti-Defamation League, 1982.

1194b. Gutman, Yisrael and Rothkirchen, Livia. The Catastrophe of
       European Jewry: Antecedents, History, Reflections, Se-
       lected Papers. Jerusalem: Yad Vashem, 1976.

1195. Haesler, Alfred A. The Lifeboat Is Full: Switzerland and
       the Refugees, 1933-1945. New York: Funk & Wagnalls,
       1969.

1196. Halperin, Irving. Messengers from the Dead. Philadelphia:
       Westminster, 1971.

1197. Handler, Andrew, ed. Holocaust in Hungary: An Anthology
       of Jewish Responses. University, Ala.: University of
       Alabama Press, 1981.

1198. Hanusiak, Michael. Lest We Forget. Toronto: Progress,
       1976.
            Ukrainian massacres of Jews, with photographs.

1199. Hardman, Leslie H. The Survivors: The Story of the Belsen
       Remnant. London: Vallentine, Mitchell, 1958.

1200. Hartman, Abraham. Neither to Laugh Nor to Weep. Boston:
       Beacon, 1968.
          Discusses Armenian genocide.

1201. Heger, Heinz. The Men with the Pink Triangle. Boston:
       Alyson, 1980.
          One of the rare books on homosexuals in the concen-
       tration camps.

1202. Heilbut, Anthony. Exiled in Paradise, German Refugee Art-
       ists and Intellectuals in America. New York: Viking,
       1983.

1203. Heimler, Eugene. Concentration Camp. New York: Pyra-
       mid, 1961.

1204. Henry, Clarissa and Hillel, Marc. Of Pure Blood. New
       York: McGraw-Hill, 1976.
          History of the German Lebensborn agencies and Nazi
       adoptions of Aryan looking Jewish and Slavic children.

1205. Herling, Gustav. A World Apart. Westport, Conn.: Green-
       wood Press, 1974 (1951).

1206. Herrmann, Lazar. The Darkest Hour: Adventures and Es-
       capes by Leo Lania. London: Gollancz, 1942.

1207. Herrmann, Simon H. Austauschlager Bergen-Belsen. Tel
       Aviv: Irgun Qlej Merkaz Europe, 1944.

1208. Heymont, Irving. Among the Survivors of the Holocaust,
       1945: The Landsberg DP Camp Letters of Major Irving
       Heymont, United States Army. New York: KTAV, 1982.
          Eyewitness' letters to the author's wife about immediate
       postwar conditions at Landsburg am Lech camp, formerly
       a Dachau branch camp.

1209. Hilberg, Raul. The Destruction of the European Jews. Chi-
       cago: Quadrangle, 1961.
          Monumental history, considered a classic; lacks section
       on Jewish resistance; systematic compendium on the sub-
       ject of its title; well documented; with tables, charts and
       notes; no bibliography.

1210. _____, ed. Documents of Destruction: Germany and Jew-
       ry, 1933-1945. Chicago: Quadrangle, 1971.

1211. _____, et al., eds. The Warsaw Diary of Adam Czernia-
       kow: Prelude to Doom. New York: Stein & Day, 1979.
          A day-to-day account book of the chairman of the War-
       saw Judenrat (Jewish Council), from September 6, 1939 to
       July 23, 1942.

1212. Hirschfeld, G., ed. German Exile in Great Britain. London:
      German Historical Institute, 1983.

1213. Hirshaut, Julien. Jewish Martyrs of Pawiak. New York:
      Schocken, 1982.
           Pawiak was the infamous Polish prison.

1214. Holocaust. Jerusalem: Keter, 1974.

1215. Horowitz, Irving L. Genocide, State Power and Mass Murder.
      New Brunswick, N.J.: Transaction, 1977.

1216. Hyams, Joseph. A Field of Buttercups. Englewood Cliffs,
      N.J.: Prentice-Hall, 1968.
           About J. Korczak, the pediatrician who voluntarily died
      with the Warsaw ghetto children.

1217. Hymers, R.L. Holocaust II. Van Nuys, Cal.: Bible Voice,
      1978.

1218. International Committee of Red Cross. Report of the ICRC
      on Its Activities During the Second World War (September
      1, 1939-June 30, 1947). 3 vols. Geneva: ICRC, 1948.

1219. _____. The Work of the ICRC for Civilian Detainees in
      German Concentration Camps for 1939 to 1945. Geneva:
      ICRC, 1947.

1220. Jackman, Jarrell C. and Borden, Carla M., eds. The Muses
      Flee Hitler: Cultural Transfer and Adaptation, 1930-1945.
      Washington, D.C.: Smithsonian Institution, 1983.
           Good collection of essays, especially the one about in-
      tellectual emigrés in Great Britain by Bernard Wasserstein.

1221. Jewish Anti-Fascist Committee of the U.S.S.R., et al. The
      Black Book: The Nazi Crime Against the Jewish People.
      New York: Duell, Sloan & Pearce, 1946.
           One of earliest illustrated documentations of the Holo-
      caust.

1222. Joffo, Joseph. A Bag of Marbles. Boston: Houghton Mifflin,
      1974.
           Two Jewish boys' experiences in Nazi-occupied France,
      written by one of them.

1223. Kalb-Beller, Zalek. L'immigré Herschel Schaerbeeker reconte.
      Paris and Brussels: Pierre de Meyere, 1978.

1224. Kárný, Miroslav. Tajemství a legendy třetí říše (The Secrets
      and the Legends of the Third Reich). Prague: Mladá
      fronta, 1983.

718. Lorain, Pierre. L'armement clandestin. Paris: L'emancipat-
      rice, 1972.
         See also entry under Addenda.

719. Lorant, Stefan. I Was Hitler's Prisoner: A Diary. New
      York: Putnam's, 1935.
         Early warning by famous journalist and author.

720. Lorit, Sergius C. The Last Days of Maximilian Kolbe. New
      York: New City, 1980.

721. Löwenthal, Richard and Mühlen, Patrick von, eds. Widerstand
      und Verweigerung in Deutschland, 1933-1945. Berlin:
      Dietz, 1982.

722. Macek, Vladko. In the Struggle for Freedom. University
      Park: Pennsylvania State University Press, 1957.

723. Macintosh, Charles. From Cloak to Dagger: An SOE Agent
      in Italy, 1943-1945. London: Kimber, 1982.

724. Macksey, Kenneth. The Partisans of Europe in the Second
      World War. New York: Stein & Day, 1975.
         Claims that partisans' contributions to victory were sel-
      dom essential.

725. Maclaren, Roy. Canadians Behind Enemy Lines, 1939-1945.
      Vancouver: University Press, 1981.

726. Malý, Jaromír and Melichar, Jozef. Dachau, symbol české
      síly, vzdoru a obětí. (Dachau, Symbol of Czech Strength,
      Defiance and Sacrifices). Prague: Vilímek, 1945.

727. Manwell, Roger and Fraenkel, Heinrich. The July Plot. Lon-
      don: Pan, 1966.

728. _____ and _____. The Men Who Tried to Kill Hitler.
      New York: Pocket Books, 1966.

729. Marshall, Bruce. The White Rabbit, from the Story Told by
      Wing Commander F.F.E. Yeo-Thomas. London: Pan, 1954.

730. Mason, Herbert M.J. To Kill the Devil: The Attempt on the
      Life of Adolf Hitler. New York: Norton, 1978.

731. Massing, Paul W. All Quiet in Germany. London: Gollancz,
      1935.

732. Masterman, J.C. The Double-Cross System in the War of
      1939-1945. New Haven: Yale University Press, 1972.

Seven "soundings" into Nazi history, including one about the "Family Camp" at Birkenau.

1225. Katsh, Abraham I., ed. Warsaw Diary of Chaim A. Kaplan. New York: Macmillan, 1973.

1226. Katz, Joseph. One Who Came Back: The Diary of a Jewish Survivor. New York: Herzl, 1973.

1227. Katz, Robert. Black Sabbath: A Journey Through a Crime Against Humanity. New York: Macmillan, 1969.

1228. Ka-Tzetnik (Cetynski, Karol). Atrocity. Secaucus, N.J.: Lyle Stuart, 1963.

1229. Kazasov, Dimo. Burni godini, 1918-1944 (Stormy Years, 1918-1944). Sofia: Naroden Pechat, 1949.

1230. Keneally, Thomas. Schindler's List. New York: Penguin, 1983.
      Portrait of daring and cunning German industrialist who saved Jews from the gas chambers.

1231. Kenrick, Donald and Puxon, Grattan. Destiny of Europe's Gypsies. New York: Basic Books, 1972.

1232. Kessel, Sim. Hanged at Auschwitz. New York: Stein & Day, 1972.

1233. Kiedrzynska, Wanda. Matériel pour la bibliographie des camps de concentration hitleriens. Warsaw: Academie des Sciences, 1964.

1234. Kielar, Wieslaw. Anus Mundi: 1500 Days in Auschwitz-Birkenau. New York: Times, 1980.
      One of the best memoirs by an early Polish inmate, a political prisoner.

1235. Kinnaird, Clark. This Must Not Happen Again! The Black Book of Fascist Horror. New York: Pilot Press, 1945.

1236. Klein, Gerda. The Holocaust and Renewal: Promise of a New Spring. Chappaqua, N.Y.: Rossel Books, 1982.

1237. Knapp, Stefan. The Square Sun. London: Museum Press, 1956.

1238. Kochan, Lionel. Pogrom: 10 November 1938. London: Deutsch, 1957.

1239. Kohn, Murray J. The Voice of My Blood Cries Out. New York: Shengold, 1979.

1240. Kolb, Eberhard. Bergen-Belsen. Hannover: Literature &
       Zeitgeschehen, 1962.

1241. Konzentrationslager Buchenwald. Weimar: Thüringer Volks-
       verlag, 1949.

1242. Korczak, Janusz. Ghetto Diary. New York: Schocken,
       1978.
       Memoirs of an admirable pediatrician of the Warsaw
       ghetto.

1243. _____. The Warsaw Ghetto Memoirs of Janusz Korczak.
       Washington, D.C.: University Press of America, 1979.

1244. Korman, Gerd, ed. Hunter and Hunted: Human History of
       the Holocaust. New York: Dell, 1973.

1245. Kranitz-Sanders, Lillian. Twelve Who Survived: An Oral
       History of the Jews of Lodz, Poland, 1930-1954. New York:
       Irvington, 1982.
       Includes a sixty-minute tape.

1246. Krantz, Morris and Auster, Louis. Hitler's Death March.
       New York: Zebra, 1978.

1247. Kranzler, David. Japanese, Nazis and Jews. New York:
       Yeshiva University Press, 1978.

1248. Kraus, Ota and Kulka, Erich. The Death Factory: Docu-
       ments on Auschwitz. Oxford: Pergamon, 1966.

1249. _____ and _____. Massmord und Profit. Berlin: Dietz,
       1963.

1250. _____ and _____. Noc a mlha (Night and Fog).
       Prague: Naše vojsko, 1958.

1251. Krausnick, Helmut and Broszat, Martin. Anatomy of the SS
       State. London and New York: Granada, 1982.
       See entry 256 for annotation.

1252. Kren, George M. and Rappaport, Leon H. Holocaust and the
       Crisis of Human Behavior. New York: Holmes & Meier,
       1980.

1253. Kühnrich, Heinz. Der KZ-Staat, Rolle und Entwiklung der
       faschistischen Konzentrationslagern, 1933-1945. Berlin:
       Dietz, 1960.

1254. Kulka, Erich. The Holocaust Is Being Denied. Tel-Aviv:
       Committee of Auschwitz Camp Survivors in Israel, 1977.

1255. Kuper, Jack. Child of the Holocaust. New York: Signet, 1980.

1256. Kuper, Leo. Genocide: Its Political Use in the Twentieth Century. New Haven, Conn.: Yale University Press, 1982.

"Genocide"--coined by Raphael Lemkin in 1944--referred to Axis occupation policies and then at the Nuremberg trials as an international crime. Case studies of Armenians, Jews, Gypsies, Soviet citizens, Indonesians, Cambodians, etc.

1257. Lachs, Manfred. The Ghetto of Warsaw. London: Woburn, 1942.

1258. Lafitte, François. The Internment of Aliens. London: Penguin, 1940.

1259. Lagus, Karel and Polák, Josef. Město za mřížemi (City Behind Bars). Prague: Naše vojsko, 1964.

About Terezín.

1260. Langer, Lawrence L. Versions of Survival: The Holocaust and the Human Spirit. Albany, N.Y.: State University of New York Press, 1982.

1261a. Láník, Jožko. Oswiecim, hrobka štyroch miliónov ludí (Auschwitz, Grave of Four Million People). Bratislava, Czechoslovakia: Poverenictvo SNR pre informácie, 1945.

1261b. Lapide, Pinchas E. The Last Three Popes and the Jews. London: Souvenir Press, 1967.

1262. Laqueur, Walter. Farewell to Europe. Boston: Little, Brown, 1981.

This is a novel, yet listed here because it focuses on a little-researched aspect of the Holocaust: 1945 and after for Jews in Germany.

1263. _____. The First News of the Holocaust. New York: Leo Baeck Institute, 1979.

1264. Lederer, Zdenek. Ghetto Theresienstadt. New York: Fertig, 1983 (1953).

Written in 1947 by observant eyewitness. Contains map, statistics of transports to and from Terezín. Most of later accounts are relying on this book.

1265. Lester, Eleonore. Wallenberg: The Man in the Iron Web. Englewood Cliffs, N.J.: Prentice-Hall, 1982.

1266. Lévai, Jenö. Black Book of the Martyrdom of Hungarian Jewry. Zürich: Central European Times, 1948.

1267.   . Fehér könyv; külföldi akciók magyar zsidók men-
        tésére (White Book: Foreign Actions for the Saving of
        Hungarian Jews). Budapest: Officina, 1946.

1268.   . Fekete könyv a magyar zsidóság szenvedéseiröl
        (Black Book About the Sufferings of Hungarian Jewry).
        Budapest: Officina, 1946.

1269.   , ed. Eichmann in Hungary: Documents. Budapest:
        Pannonia, 1961.

1270.   , comp. Hungarian Jewry and the Papacy: Pope
        Pius XII Did Not Remain Silent; Reports, Documents and
        Records from Church and State Archives, Assembled by
        Jenö Lévai. London: Sands, 1968.

1271. Levenstein, Aaron. Escape to Freedom: The Story of the
        International Rescue Committee. Westport, Conn.: Green-
        wood Press, 1983.
              Fifty years of the IRC, including events of World War
        II.

1272. Levi, Primo. Lilit e altri racconti (Lilit and Other Stories).
        Torino: Einaudi, 1981.

1273.   . The Reawakening. A Liberated Prisoner's Long
        March Home Through Europe. Boston: Little, Brown,
        1965.
              Covers the author's anabasis from Auschwitz to Torino,
        his home. Auschwitz was liberated in January, he arrived
        in Italy in August.

1274.   . Se non ora, quando? (If Not Now, When?) Torino:
        Einaudi, 1982.

1275.   . Shema: Collected Poems of Primo Levi. London:
        Menard, 1976.
              Includes a condensed version of "Why Auschwitz? The
        Jews and the Tragedy of the Nazi Camps."

1276.   . Survival in Auschwitz: The Nazi Assault on Hu-
        manity. New York: Collier, 1966 (1959).
              One of the very best memoirs about Auschwitz by an
        Italian inmate.

1277. Levin, Nora. The Holocaust, the Destruction of European
        Jewry, 1933-1945. New York: Schocken, 1973 (1968).
              Scholarly history, with both chronological and country-
        by-country descriptions of the Holocaust; also deals with
        aspects of Jewish resistance and various rescue missions.
        Notes but no bibliography.

1278. Levy, Claude and Tillard, Paul. Betrayal at the Vel d'Hviv.
      New York: Hill & Wang, 1969.

1279. Liebman, Marcel. Als jood geboren (Born a Jew). Antwerp-
      Amsterdam: Standard, 1978.

1280. Liptzin, Solomon. Germany's Stepchildren. Philadelphia:
      Jewish Publication Society of America, 1944.

1281. Littell, Franklin H. The Crucifixion of the Jews: The Fail-
      ure of the Christians to Understand the Jewish Experi-
      ence. New York: Harper & Row, 1976.

1282. _____ and Locke, Hubert G., eds. The German Church
      Struggle and the Holocaust. Detroit: Wayne State Uni-
      versity Press, 1974.

1283. Lower Saxony. Minister of Interior. Das Lager Bergen-
      Belsen: Dokumente und Bilder. Hannover: Fackelträger,
      1981.

1284. Lowrie, Donald A. The Hunted Children. New York: Nor-
      ton, 1963.

1285. Maas, Peter. King of the Gypsies. New York: Viking,
      1975.

1286. Machlejd, Wanda. Experimental Operations on Prisoners of
      Ravensbrück Concentration Camp. Poznan, Poland:
      Wydawnictwo zachodnie, 1960.

1287. Manwell, Roger and Fraenkel, Heinrich. The Incomparable
      Crime. New York: Putnam's, 1967.

1288. Marrus, Michael R. and Paxton, Robert O. Vichy France
      and the Jews. New York: Basic Books, 1981.
          Two distinguished scholars accuse Vichy France of anti-
      Semitic policies.

1289. Maršálek, Hans. Die Geschichte des Konzentrationslagers
      Mauthausen. Vienna: Österreichische Lagergemeinschaft
      Mauthausen, 1980.

1290. _____. Konzentrationslager Gusen. Vienna: Österreich-
      ische Lagergemeinschaft Mauthausen, 1968.

1291. Marton, Kati. Wallenberg. New York: Random House, 1982.

1292. Mechanicus, Philip. Year of Fear: A Jewish Prisoner Waits
      for Auschwitz. New York: Hawthorne, 1968.
          Story from the Netherlands and Westerbrook camp.

1293. Melezin, Abraham. Particulars About the Demographic Proc-
       esses Among the Jewish Population in the Towns of Lodz,
       Cracow and Lublin During the German Occupation Period.
       Lodz, Poland: Centralna Żydowska Komisja Historyczna
       w Polsce, 1946.
       Text is in Polish, with resumé in English.

1294. Melodia, Giovanni. Sotto il segno della svastica (Under the
       Sign of the Swastika). Milan: Mursia, 1979.

1295. Meltzer, Milton. Never to Forget: The Jews of the Holo-
       caust. New York: Dell, 1976.
       Short, practical survey.

1296. Mendelsohn, John, ed. The Holocaust: Selected Documents.
       18 vols. New York: Garland, 1982.
       A monumental work of essential importance; includes
       volumes on war crime trials.

1297. Mermelstein, Mel. By Bread Alone, the Story of A-4685.
       Los Angeles: Crescent, 1979.
       Czechoslovak Holocaust victim's story.

1298. Mid-European Law Project. Forced Labor and Confinement
       Without Trial in Bulgaria. Washington, D.C.: Mid-
       European Studies Center, 1952.
       Parallel studies exist on Hungary, Poland, Rumania and
       Yugoslavia.

1299. Mitscherlich, Alexander and Mielke, Fred. Doctors of Infamy,
       the Story of the Nazi Medical Crimes. New York: Schu-
       man, 1949.

1300. Moczarski, Kazimierz. Conversations with an Executioner,
       the Incredible 225-Day-Long Interview with the Man Who
       Destroyed the Warsaw Ghetto. Englewood Cliffs, N.J.:
       Prentice-Hall, 1981.

1301. Molho, Michael (Rabbi), ed. In Memoriam: Hommage aux vic-
       times juifs des Nazis en Grèce. Salonica: Communauté
       israélite de Thessalonique, 1948.

1302. Monneray, Henri. La persécution des Juifs dans les pays de
       l'Est. Paris: Editions du Centre, 1949.

1303. _____. La persécution des Juifs en France et dans les
       autres pays de l'Ouest. Paris: Editions du Centre, 1947.

1304. Monnerjahn, Engelbert. Häftling Nr. 29,392. Vallendar-
       Schönstatt, W. Ger.: Patria, 1975.

1305. Mortkowitz-Olczakowa, Hanna. Mister Doctor, the Life of
      Janusz Korczak. London: Peter Davies, 1965.

1306. Moskovitz, Sarah. Love Despite Hate, Child Survivors of the
      Holocaust and Their Adult Lives. New York: Schocken,
      1983.

1307. Müller, Filip. Eyewitness Auschwitz: Three Years in the
      Gas Chambers at Auschwitz. New York: Stein & Day,
      1979.
         Unique memoir of a Slovak Jew who survived after work-
      ing at the gas chambers for three years.

1308. Musiol, Theodor. Dachau, 1933-1945. Katowice, Poland:
      Institut Slaski, n.d.

1309. Musmanno, Michael A. The Eichmann Kommandos. Philadel-
      phia: Macrae Smith, 1961.

1310. Naumann, Bernd. Auschwitz. New York: Praeger, 1966.

1311. Neuhäusler, Johannes (Bishop). What Was It Like in the
      Concentration Camp Dachau? Munich: Trustees for the
      Monument of Atonement in the Concentration Camp at
      Dachau, 1960.

1312. Neumann, Yirmeyahu Oscar. Im Schatten des Todes: Ein
      Tatsachenbericht vom Schicksalskampf des slowakischen
      Judentums. Tel Aviv: Olamenu, 1956.

1313. Neusner, Jacob. Stranger at Home: The Holocaust, Zionism
      and American Judaism. Chicago: The University of Chi-
      cago Press, 1981.

1314. Novák, Václav, et al., eds. Terezínské listy (Terezín News).
         Czech anthology with resumés in Russian, English and
      German; published irregularly by the Terezín Monument in
      Ústí nad Labem, Czechoslovakia.

1315. Novitch, Miriam. L'extermination des Tziganes. Paris: AMIF,
      1969.

1316. _____. La vérité Sur Treblinka. Paris: Beresnich, 1967.

1317. Nyiszli, Miklós. Auschwitz, a Doctor's Eyewitness Account.
      New York: Fawcett, 1960.
         Memoirs of a Hungarian physician forced to collaborate
      in the Nazi medical experiments.

1318. Oberski, Jona. Childhood. Garden City, N.Y.: Doubleday,
      1983.
         Autobiographical story of another youngster from Am-

sterdam who, unlike Anne Frank, survived and tells of his
impressions of the Westerbrook and Bergen Belsen concentration camps. Short but powerful story through the eyes
of a child aged four to eight.

1319. Overduin, Jacobus. Faith and Victory in Dachau. Cather-
ines, Ont.: Paideia, [1978].

1320. Paris, Edmond. Genocide in Satellite Croatia, 1941-1945.
Chicago: American Institute for Balkan Affairs, 1960.

1321. Paxton, Robert O. Vichy France: Old Guard and New Order, 1940-1944. New York: Knopf, 1972.

1322. Pearl, Cyril. The Dunera Scandal, the WW 2 Injustice Britain
and Australia Tried to Forget. London: Angus & Robert-
son, 1983.
    The story of German and Austrian anti-Nazi refugees,
including Jews, shipped on the Dunera from Great Britain
to Australia and kept behind barbed wires.

1323. Pignatelli, Luigi. Il secondo regno (The Second Reign).
Milan: Longanesi, 1969.

1324. Pilch, Judah, ed. The Jewish Catastrophe in Europe. New
York: American Association for Jewish Education, 1968.
Includes some material on Jewish partisans.

1325. Pisar, Samuel. Of Blood and Hope. Boston: Little, Brown,
1981.

1326. Plant, Richard. The Pink Triangle: Gays in the Third
Reich. New York: Holt, Rinehart & Winston, 1983.

1327. Poliakov, Leon. Harvest of Hate, the Nazi Program for the
Destruction of the Jews of Europe. New York: Schocken,
1979.
    Good short survey of the Holocaust.

1328. _____ and Sabille, Jacques. Jews Under the Italian Occupation. New York: Fertig, 1983 (1955).
    Short text with ample documentation, including facsimiles,
based on files of the German, Italian and French adminis-
trations; deals with Italian occupation in France, Yugoslavia and Greece.

1329. _____ and Wulf, Josef. Das Dritte Reich und die Juden.
Berlin: Colloquium, 1955.

1330a. Porter, Jack N. Confronting History and Holocaust, Collected
Essays, 1972-1982. Washington, D.C.: University Press
of America, 1983.

1330b. _____, ed. Genocide and Human Rights: A Global Anthol-
       ogy. Washington, D.C.: University Press of America,
       1982.

1331. Prati, Pino da. Il Triangolo rosso del deportado politico no.
      6017 (The Red Triangle of Political Deportee No. 6017).
      Milan: Gastaldi, 1946.

1332. Presser, Jacob. The Destruction of the Dutch Jewry. New
      York: Dutton, 1969.

1333. Procop, C.S. In Memoriam. Bucharest: Titan, 1946.

1334. Proudfoot, Malcolm J. European Refugees, 1939-1952: A
      Study of Forced Population Movement. Evanston, Ill.:
      Northwestern University Press, 1956.

1335. Rabinowitz, Dorothy. About the Holocaust: What We Know
      and How We Know. New York: American Jewish Commit-
      tee, 1979.

1336. _____. New Lives: Survivors of the Holocaust Living
      in America. New York: Avon, 1977.

1337. Ramati, Alexander. Barbed Wire on the Isle of Man, the War-
      time British Internment of Jews. New York: Harcourt
      Brace Jovanovich, 1980.
         Novelized but true story.

1338. _____. While the Pope Kept Silent. London and Boston:
      Allen & Unwin, 1978.
         See also entry 781.

1339. Rassinier, Paul, ed. The Drama of the European Jews. Sil-
      ver Spring, Md.: Steppingstones, 1976.

1340. Rector, Frank. The Nazi Extermination of Homosexuals.
      New York: Stein & Day, 1981.

1341. Reder, Rudolf. Belzec. Cracow: Wojewodzka žydowska komis-
      ja historyczna, 1946.

1342. Reitlinger, Gerald R. Final Solution: The Attempt to Exter-
      minate the Jews of Europe, 1939-1945. New York: A.S.
      Barnes, 1961 (1953).

1343. Reznikoff, Charles. Holocaust. Santa Barbara: Black Spar-
      row, 1977.

1344. Ringelblum, Emmanuel. Notes from the Warsaw Ghetto: The
      Journal of Emmanuel Ringelblum. New York: McGraw-

Hill, 1958.
Informative notes by an historian in the ghetto.

1345. _____. Polish-Jewish Relations During the Second World
War. New York: Fertig, 1976.

1346. Robinson, Jacob. Psychoanalysis in a Vacuum: Bruno Bettelheim and the Holocaust. New York: YIVO Institut,
1970.
Rebuttal to Bettelheim's The Informed Heart.

1347. _____, ed. Holocaust and After: Sources and Literature
in English. New Brunswick, N.J.: Transaction, 1973.
Done with the cooperation of Yad Vashem and the YIVO
Institute; important for entries up to 1971.

1348. _____ and Bauer, Yehuda, eds. Guide to Unpublished
Material of the Holocaust Period. 3 vols. Jerusalem:
Ahva Coop. Press, 1970-1975.

1349. _____ and Friedman, Philip, eds. Guide to Jewish History
Under Nazi Impact. New York: YIVO Institut, 1960.

1350. _____ and Sachs, Henry, eds. The Holocaust: The Nuremberg Evidence: Documents, Digest, Index & Chrono-
logical Tables. New York: YIVO Institut, 1976.

1351. Roiter, Howard. Voices from the Holocaust. New York:
Frederick Fell, 1975.

1352. Rose, Peter I., ed. The Ghetto and Beyond. New York:
Random House, 1969.

1353. Rosenbaum, Irving J. The Holocaust and Halakhah. New
York: KTAV, 1976.

1354. Rosenfeld, Harvey. Raoul Wallenberg, Angel of Rescue.
Buffalo, N.Y.: Prometheus Press, 1982.

1355. Rossel, Seymour. Holocaust. New York: Franklin Watts,
1981.

1356. Rothbart, Markus. I Wanted to Live to Tell a Story. New
York: Vantage, 1980.

1357. Rothchild, Sylvia, ed. Voices from the Holocaust. New
York: New American Library, 1981.

1358. Rothkirchen, Livia. The Destruction of Slovak Jewry: A
Documentary History. Jerusalem: Yad Vashem, 1961.
In Hebrew, summary in English.

1359. _______, ed. Yad Vashem Studies on the European Jewish Catastrophe and Resistance. 14 vols. New York: KTAV, n.d.

Above editor's name is transcribed from Hebrew either as Rothkirchen or as Rotkirchen.

1360. Rubin, Arnold P. Hitler and the Nazis: The Evil That Men Do. New York: Bantam, 1979.

1361. Rückerl, A. N.S. Vernichtungslager. Munich: Deutscher Taschenbuch Verlag, 1977.

1362. Rutheford, Ward. Genocide: The Jews in Europe, 1939-45. New York: Ballantine, 1973.

1363. Ryan, Michael D., ed. Human Responses to the Holocaust, Perpetrators, Victims, Bystanders and Resistance. Lewiston, N.Y.: E. Mellen, 1981.

Papers of the 1979 conference on the church struggle and the Holocaust, sponsored by the National Conference of Christians and Jews.

1364. Sandberg, Moshe. My Longest Year: In the Hungarian Labour Service and in the Nazi Camps. Jerusalem: Yad Vashem, 1968.

1365a. Schleunes, Karl A. The Twisted Road to Auschwitz: Nazi Policy Toward German Jews, 1933-1945. Urbana: University of Illinois Press, 1970.

1365b. Schoenberner, Gerhard. The Yellow Star: The Persecution of the Jews of Europe, 1933-1945. New York: Bantam, 1973.

Illustrated; chapter on Jewish resistance, especially in the Warsaw ghetto.

1366a. Schramm, Hanna. Menschen in Gurs, Memories of a Concentration Camp in France, 1940-1941. Worms, Ger.: H. Heintz, 1977.

1366b. Schwarberg, Günther. Der Juwelier von Majdanek. Hamburg: Stern, 1981.

Fate of Slovak Jewish watchmaker; includes story of Majdanek war crime trial.

1367. Schwarz, Leo W., ed. The Root and the Bough: The Ethic of an Enduring People. New York: Rinehart, 1949.

Collection of early essays from Poland and the western USSR.

1368. Sehn, Jan, ed. Concentration Camp Oswiecim-Brzezinka

(Auschwitz-Birkenau). Warsaw: Wydawnictwo Prawnicze, 1957.

1369. Selzer, Michael. Deliverance Day: The Last Hours at Dachau. Philadelphia: Lippincott, 1978.

1370. Semprun, Jorge. The Long Voyage. New York: Grove, 1964.

1371. Shabbetai, K. As Sheep to the Slaughter? The Myth of Cowardice. New York and Tel Aviv: World Association of Bergen Belsen Survivors' Associations, 1963.
       Rebuttal to Arendt, Bettelheim and Hilberg, with a Foreword by Gideon Hausner.

1372. Shapell, Nathan. Witness to the Truth. New York: David McKay, 1974.

1373. Sharnik, Alexei Z. Memoirs from the East. Budapest: Patria, 1945.

1374. Sherwin, Byron and Ament, Susan. Encountering the Holocaust, an Interdisciplinary Survey. Chicago: Impact Press, 1979.

1375. Shulman, Abraham. The Case of the Hotel Polski. New York: Schocken, 1982.

1376. Shur, Irene and Littell, Franklin H. Reflections on the Holocaust. Philadelphia: American Academy of Political Science, 1980.

1377. Simonov, Constantin. Maidanek--Un camp d'extermination. Paris: Editions sociales, 1945.

1378. Sington, Derrick. Belsen Uncovered. Toronto: Nelson, 1946.

1379. Smith, Marcus J. The Harrowing of Hell: Dachau. Albuquerque: University of New Mexico Press, 1972.

1380. Smolen, Kazimierz, ed. Selected Problems from the History of KL Auschwitz. Auschwitz: Panstwowe Muzeum, 1979.

1381. _____, et al., eds. From the History of KL Auschwitz. New York: Fertig, 1982.
       See entry 830 for annotaiton.

1382. Šormová, Eva. Divadlo v Terezíně, 1941/1945 (Theatre in Terezín, 1941-1945). Terezín, Czechoslovakia: Památník Terezín, 1973.

1383. Sosnowski, Kiryl. The Tragedy of Children Under Nazi Rule.
       New York: Fertig, 1983 (1962).

1384. Spanjaard, Barry A. Don't Fence Me in: An American Teen-
       ager in the Holocaust. Saugus, Cal.: B & B Publ.,
       1981.

1385. Sperber, Manes. Than a Tear in the Sea. New York: Ber-
       gen Belsen Memorial Press, 1967.

1386. Starkopf, Adam. There Is Always Time to Die. New York:
       Schocken, 1981.

1387. Steinitz, Lucy Y. Living After the Holocaust. New York:
       Bloch, 1975.

1388. Stern, Ellen N. Elie Wiesel: Witness for Life. New York:
       KTAV, 1982.
       Biography of the well-known author-survivor.

1389. Strauss, Herbert A., ed. Jewish Immigrants of the Nazi
       Period in the USA. 6 vols. New York: K.G. Saur,
       1978- .
       Sponsored by the Research Foundation for Jewish Im-
       migration.

1390. Strom, Margot S. and Parsons, William S. Facing History
       and Ourselves. Watertown, Mass.: Intentional Educa-
       tion, 1982.
       Secondary school syllabus and readings.

1391. Stroop, Jürgen. The Stroop Report: The Jewish Quarter of
       Warsaw Is No More. New York: Pantheon, 1979.

1392. Suzman, Arthur. Six Million Did Die. Johannesburg: South
       African Jewish Board of Deputees, 1978.

1393. Svatá, Jarmila. Milenci SS smrti (Lovers of the SS Death).
       Prague: Svoboda, 1945.

1394. Szajkowski, Zosa. Analytical Franco-Jewish Gazetteer, 1939-
       1945. New York: Frydmann, 1966.

1395. Taylor, John R. Strangers in Paradise: The Hollywood Emi-
       grés, 1933-1950. New York: Holt, Rinehart & Winston,
       1983.

1396. Tenenbaum, Joseph. Race and Reich. New York: Twayne,
       1956.

1397. Thalman, Rita and Feinermann, Emmanuel. Crystal Night, 9-

10 November, 1938. New York: Coward-McCann & Geoghegan, 1974.

1398.   Thomas, Gordon and Witts, Max M. Voyage of the Damned.
        Greenwich, Conn.: Fawcett, 1975.

1399.   Thorne, Leon. Out of the Ashes. New York: Bloch, 1976.

1400.   Tokayer, Marvin and Schwartz, Mary. The Fugu Plan: The
        Untold Story of the Japanese and the Jews During World
        War II. London: Hamlyn, 1981.

1401.   Trepman, Paul. Among Men and Beasts. New York: A.S.
        Barnes, 1978.

1402.   Trunk, Isaiah. Jewish Responses to Nazi Persecution: Col-
        lective and Individual Behavior in Extremis. New York:
        Stein & Day, 1981.

1403.   _____. Judenrat: The Jewish Councils in Eastern Europe
        Under Nazi Occupation. New York: Stein & Day, 1977.
             An answer to Arendt. Encyclopedic format covers ap-
        proximately 400 Jewish councils. National Book Award
        winner.

1404.   _____. Lodzher Ghetto: An Historical and Sociological
        Study. New York: YIVO Institut, 1962.

1405.   Tsion, Daniel (Rabbi). Pet godini pod fashistki gnet: spo-
        meni (Five Years Under Fascist Terror: Remembrances).
        Sofia: n.p., 1945.

1406.   Turkow, Jonas. Janusz Korczak, el apostol de los niños.
        Buenos Aires: Ejecutivo sudamericano del Congreso Judio
        Mundial, 1967.

1407.   Tushnet, Leonard. The Pavement of Hell: Three Leaders of
        the Judenrat. New York: St. Martin's, 1974.

1408.   _____. To Die with Honor. Secaucus, N.J.: Citadel,
        1965.

1409.   U.S. Army. Dachau. Atlanta, Ga.: Center for Research in
        Social Change at Emory University, 1982 (1945).
             Reprint of a first-hand report by the U.S. Seventh Ar-
        my and others right after the liberation of Dachau, with
        photographs. This is one of five entries in the Witness to
        the Holocaust Series.

1410.   _____. The Seventy-First Came to Gunskirchen Lager.
        Secaucus, N.J.: Citadel, 1983.

Liberators' impressions of Gunskirchen, a branch of the Mauthausen concentration camp in Austria.

1411. Van Riet, Victor. <u>Mauthausen, 188 marches et la mort.</u>
       Brussels: André de Rache, 1977.

1412. Vaneck, Ludo. <u>Het boek der kampen (The Book of Camps).</u>
       Strombeck-Bever, The Netherlands: De Schorpionen,
       1969.

1413. Vinokurov, Joseph, et al., eds. <u>The Babi Yar Book of Re-
       membrance.</u> Philadelphia: Publishing House of Peace,
       1983.
           In Russian, English and Yiddish, illustrated, listing
       approximately 2,000 names of Jews killed at Babi Yar in
       1941; the majority of names are still unknown.

1414. Votoček, Otakar and Kostková, Zdenka. <u>Terezín.</u> Prague:
       Odeon, 1980.
           The history of Terezín, before, during and after the
       Nazi occupation; richly illustrated; written in Czech.

1415. <u>Washington Post</u> Editors. <u>Holocaust: The Obligation to Re-
       member.</u> Washington, D.C.: <u>Washington Post</u>, 1983.
           A sixty-eight page oversize memorial of the April 1983
       Holocaust survivors' gathering speeches and editorials.

1416. Weil, Bruno. <u>Francia a traves de las alambradas.</u> Buenos
       Aires: Claridad, 1941.

1417. Weinstein, A.A. <u>A Barbed Wire Surgeon.</u> New York: Mac-
       millan, 1948.

1418. Weinstock, Eugene. <u>Beyond the Last Path.</u> New York: Bonit
       Gaer, 1947.

1419. Weissberg, Alexander. <u>The Accused.</u> New York: Simon &
       Schuster, 1951.

1420. _____. <u>Desperate Mission: Joel Brand's Story.</u> New York:
       Criterion, 1958. British title: <u>Advocate for the Dead.</u>

1421. Wellers, George. <u>L'étoile jaune à l'heure de Vichy: De Dran-
       cy à Auschwitz.</u> Paris: Fayard, 1973.

1422. Wells, Leon W. <u>The Death Brigade.</u> New York: Schocken,
       1980 (1946).

1423. _____. <u>The Janowska Road.</u> New York: Macmillan, 1963.
       Report of a young boy in Lwov.

1424a. Werbell, Frederick E. (Rabbi) and Clarke, Thurston. Lost
       Hero: The Mystery of Raoul Wallenberg. New York:
       McGraw-Hill, 1982.

1424b. Wiernik, Yankel. A Year in Treblinka. New York: General
       Jewish Workers' Union of Poland, 1945.

1425. Wiesel, Elie, et al. Dimensions of the Holocaust. Evanston,
       Ill.: Northwestern University Press, 1978.

1426. _____, ed. Report to the President: President's Commis-
       sion on the Holocaust. Washington, D.C.: GPO, 1979.

1427a. Winnick, Myron, ed. Hunger Disease. New York: Wiley,
       1979.
            Jews in Warsaw.

1427b. Witkowski, Jozef. Hitlerowski oboz koncentracyjni dle malolet-
       nich v Lodzi (Hitler's Concentration Camp for Those Un-
       der Age in Lodz). Breslau, Pol.: Zaklad narodowy im.
       Ossolinskych, 1975.

1428. Wnuk, Jozef and Radomska-Strzemecka, Helena. Dzieci pol-
       skie oskarzaja, 1939-1945 (Polish Children Accuse 1939-1945).
       Lublin, Pol.: Wydawatelstwo lubelskie, 1975.

1429. World Committee for the Relief of the Victims of German Fas-
       cism. The Reichstag Fire Trial: The Second Brown Book
       of the Hitler Terror. New York: Fertig, 1969 (1934).

1430. World Jewish Congress. Black Book of the Nazi Crimes
       Against the Jewish People. Atlanta: Nexus, 1982 (1946).

1431. Wormser-Migot, Olga. L'ère des camps. Paris: Union gen-
       eral d'éditions, 1973.

1432. _____. Le système concentrationnaire Nazi, 1933-1945.
       Paris: Presses universitaires de France, 1968.

1433. _____ and Michel, Henri, eds. Tragédie de la déportation,
       1940-1945: Témoignages de survivants des camps de con-
       centration allemands. Paris: Hachette, 1954.

1434. Wytwycky, Bohdan. The Other Holocaust: Many Circles of
       Hell. Washington, D.C.: The Novak Report, 1980.

1435. Yad Vashem. Yad Vashem Bulletins 1-10. Jerusalem: Yad
       Vashem, n.d.
            Bound edition of first ten volumes, covering 1957-1961.

1436. YIVO Institute. Imposed Jewish Governing Bodies Under Nazi

Nazi Rule. YIVO Colloquium, December 2-5, 1967. New York: YIVO Institute, 1972.

1437. _____. YIVO Annual of Jewish Social Science. New York: YIVO Institute, 1946.

1438. Zajacová, Viera. Slováci v Mauthausenu (Slovaks in Mauthausen). Bratislava, Czechoslovakia: Epocha, 1970.

1439. Zák, Jiří, ed. Buchenwald varuje: Dokumenty, vzpomínky, svědectví (Buchenwald Warns: Documents, Remembrances, Testimonies). Prague: Státní nakladatelství politické literatury, 1962.

1440. Zolli, Eugenio. Before the Dawn. New York: Sheed & Ward, 1954.

1441. Zylberberg, Michael. A Warsaw Diary, 1939-1945. Bridgeport, Conn.: Hartmore House, 1969.

7. H O L O C A U S T -- W O M E N

1442. Abramowicz, Zofia. Tak bylo (That's How It Was). Lublin:
Wydawnictwo lubelskie, 1962.

1443. Balicka-Kollowska, Helena. Mur mial dwie strony (The Wall
Had Two Sides). Warsaw: Ministerstwo obrony naro-
dowej, 1958.

1444. Bar Oni, Byrna. The Vapor. Chicago: Visual Impact, 1976.
Young Polish girl's sad adventures among the partisans.

1445. Berg, Mary (Wattenberg). Warsaw Ghetto, a Diary. New
York: Fischer, 1945.

1446. Berkowitz, Sarah B. Where Are My Brothers? New York:
Helios, 1965.
Includes report on Bergen Belsen.

1447. Birenbaum, Halina. Hope Is the Last to Die. Boston: G.K.
Hall, 1971.

1448. Campion, Joan. Gisi Fleischmann and the Jewish Fight for
Survival. Bethlehem, Penn.: Dvorion Books, 1983.
Struggle of a Slowak woman to save Jews; includes de-
tails of the "European Plan" and dealings with Dieter von
Wisliczeny of the Gestapo.

1449. Delbo, Charlotte. None of Us Will Return: Auschwitz and
After. Boston: Beacon, 1978.
Slim but powerful memoir from the French resistance
and various camps; compared to Picasso's "Guernica."

1450. Dränger, Gusta (Dawidsohn-Drängerowa). Pamietnik Justyny
(Justina's Diary). Cracow: Centralna żydowska komisja
historyczna, 1946.

1451. Dribben, Judith S. A Girl Called Judith Strick. New York:
Cowles, 1970.
Story of a Jewish resister and concentration camp Häft-
ling.

1452. Dufurnier, Denise. Ravensbrück, the Women's Camp of
      Death. London: George Allen & Unwin, 1948.

1453. Fénelon, Fania. Playing for Time. New York: Berkley,
      1979.
      Memoir of the French singer who was member of the
      women's orchestra in Auschwitz.

1454. Ferderber-Salz, Bertha. And the Sun Kept Shining. New
      York: Schocken, 1980.
      A courageous woman's calvary through Auschwitz, Ber-
      gen Belsen and a concise picture of the post-Holocaust
      reception of returned Jews.

1455. Gabor, Georgia M. My Destiny: Survivor of the Holocaust.
      Arcadia, Cal.: American Publishing, 1981.

1456. Geisel, Erika, ed. Vielleicht war das alles erst der Anfang:
      Hanna Levy-Hass, Tagebuch aus dem KZ Bergen-Belsen,
      1944-1945. Berlin: Rotbuch, 1979.
      Yugoslav Jewish partisan in Bergen Belsen; also in-
      cludes long recent interview with her.

1457. Gluck, Gemma La Guardia. My Story. New York: David
      McKay, 1961.
      New York mayor's sister tells of her experiences as a
      concentration camp prisoner.

1458. Grant, Myrna. The Journey. Wheaton, Ill.: Tyndale, 1978.
      Strange tale of Jewish woman becoming Baptist mission-
      ary during the Holocaust; geopolitical background informa-
      tion is frequently wrong.

1459. H., Janka [sic]. W ghetcie i obozie, Pamietnik dwunastoletniej
      dziewczyny (In the Ghetto and the Concentration Camp,
      the Memoir of a Twelve Year Old Girl). Cracow: Woje-
      wodzka komisja historyczna, 1946.

1460. Haas, Gerda S. These I Do Remember: Fragments from the
      Holocaust. Salt Lake City, Utah: Wheelwright, 1982.

1461. Hart, Kitty. I Am Alive. London: Transword, 1946.

1462. _____. Return to Auschwitz. New York: Atheneum,
      1982.

1463. Hersh, Gizelle and Mann, Peggy. "Gizelle, Save the Chil-
      dren!" New York: Everest House, 1980.
      Four sisters from Rumania in Auschwitz.

1464. Heyman, Eva. The Diary of Eva Heyman. Jerusalem: Yad

Vashem, 1974.
Young girl's touch story depicting, with great insight, anguish before deportation.

1465. Huttenbach, Henry R. Life of Herta Mansbacher: Portrait of a Jewish Teacher, Heroine and Martyr. New York: Hermon, 1980.

1466. Jackson, Livia E. Elli, Coming of Age in the Holocaust. New York: Times Books, 1980.

1467. Ka-Tzetnik (Cetynski, Karol). House of Dolls. London and New York: Granada, 1982.
Somewhat novelized story of prostitution in the camps.

1468. Kopecky, Lilli. In the Shadow of the Flames: Six Lectures on the Holocaust. Atlanta: Center for Research in Social Change at Emory University, 1982.
Discusses Auschwitz-Birkenau, anti-Semitism and neo-Nazism.

1469. Košutová, Olga. U Svatobořic, zápisky a povídky z internačního tábora (At Svatobořice, Memoirs and Tales from an Internment Camp). Brünn, Czechoslovakia: Družstvo moravského kola spisovatelů, 1946.

1470. Kovaly, Heda and Kohak, Erazim. The Victors and the Vanquished. New York: Horizon, 1973.
Memoirs of woman under Nazi and Communist persecutions.

1471. Laska, Vera, ed. Women in the Resistance and in the Holocaust: Voices of Eyewitnesses. Westport, Conn.: Greenwood Press, 1983.
See entry 919 for annotation.

1972. Leitner, Isabella. Fragments of Isabella. New York: Crowell, 1978.
Lyrically written story of four, then three, sisters from Hungary to Auschwitz and then in hiding.

1473. Lengyel, Olga. Five Chimneys. Chicago: Ziff-Davis, 1947.
One of the first and best books by an Auschwitz survivor; reissued numerous times; under the title I Survived Hitler's Ovens by Avon and with the original title by Fertig in New York and by Granada in London in 1983.

1474. Levy-Hass, Hanna. Inside Belsen. Totowa, N.J.: Littlefield, Adams, 1983.
See entry 1456 for annotation.

1475. Lewinska, Pelagia. Twenty Months at Auschwitz. Secaucus,
       N.J.: Lyle Stuart, 1968.

1476. Liégeois, Constance. Calvarie de femmes. Ciney, Belgium:
       1945.

1477. Lingens-Reiner, Ella. Prisoner of Fear. London: Gollancz,
       1948.

1478. Lubetkin, Zivia. In the Days of Destruction and Revolt.
       Tel Aviv: Hakibbutz Hamevchad, 1981.
          By one of the heroines of the Warsaw ghetto uprising.

1479. Michelson, Frida. I Survived Rumbuli. New York: Schock-
       en, 1981.
          The persecution of Latvian Jews, and the author's hid-
       ing.

1480. Minney, Rubeigh J. I Shall Fear No Evil: The Story of Dr.
       Alina Brewda. London: Kimber, 1966.
          Biography of gynecologist Dr. Alina Brewda-Bielostocki
       who perished at Auschwitz; also deals with medical experi-
       ments in the camps.

1481. Moskin, Marietta. I Am Rosemarie. New York: John Day,
       1972.

1482. Neuman, Judith Sternberg. In the Hell of Auschwitz: The
       Wartime Memoirs of Judith Sternberg Neuman. Jericho,
       N.Y.: Exposition Press, 1963.

1483. Neumann, Oskar. Gisi Fleischmann: The Story of a Heroic
       Woman. Tel Aviv: World WIZO Department of Organization
       and Education, 1970.

1484. Pawlowicz, Sala. I Will Survive. New York: Norton, 1962.

1485. Perl, Gisella. I Was a Doctor in Auschwitz. New York:
       Arno, 1979 (1948).
          A strong statement on medical perversities by an eye-
       witness physician.

1486. Reiner, Ella L. Prisoners of Fear. London: Gollancz, 1948.

1487. Rolnikasová, Maria. Nemohu mlčet (I Can Not Remain Silent).
       Prague: Naše vojsko, 1968.
          Diary of a 14 year old Lithuanian girl from the Wilno
       ghetto.

1488. Salus, Grete. Niemand, nichts--ein Jude: Theresienstadt,
       Auschwitz, Oederan. Darmstadt, W. Ger.: Verlag Darm-
       städter Blätter, 1981.

1489. Sassoon, Agnes. Agnes: How My Spirit Survived. Edge-
       ware, Middlesex, Eng.: Lawrence Cohen, 1983.
       Heartrending story of a Slovak girl and her anabasis
       from Bratislava to Bergen Belsen and eventually to Israel.

1490a. Schafranov, Sofia. I campi della morte in Germania (Camps
       of Death in Germany). Milan: Sonzogno, 1945.

1490b. Schlamm, Vera. Pursued. San Francisco: Hineni Ministries,
       1972.

1491. Siegal, Aranka. Upon the Head of a Goat: A Childhood in
       Hungary. New York: Farrar, Straus & Giroux, 1981.
       Poignant memoir of teenager until deportation.

1492. Szmaglewska, Seweryna. Smoke over Birkenau. New York:
       Holt, 1947.

1493. Weiss, Reska. Journey Through Hell: A Woman's Account of
       Her Experiences at the Hands of the Nazis. London:
       Vallentine, Mitchell, 1961.

1494. Zyskind, Sara. Stolen Years. New York: New American Li-
       brary, 1981.
       Life of a child of from eleven to seventeen in the ghet-
       to, Auschwitz and slave labor camp of Mittelstein.

1495. Zywulska, Krystyna. I Came Back. New York: Roy, 1951.
       Auschwitz memoir of Polish woman; the recent German
       edition (Wo vorher Birken waren, Munich: Kindler, 1979)
       contains also her poems from the concentration camp.

8. W O M E N   I N   H I D I N G

1496. Brand, Sandra. I Dared to Live. New York: Shengold,
      1978.
      A woman's hair-raising experiences trying to survive
      with false identity papers in Nazi-occupied Poland.

1497. David, Janina. A Square of Sky. A Touch of Earth: A
      Wartime Childhood in Poland. New York: Penguin, 1981
      (1964, 1966).

1498. Demetz, Hana. The House on Prague Street. New York:
      St. Martin's, 1980.
      This somewhat novelized true story covers a half-Jewish
      girl's survival in Nazi-ruled Bohemia.

1499. Feld, Marilla. I Chose to Live. New York: Manor, 1979.
      The bitter adventures of a courageous Polish dancer
      determined to stay alive.

1500. Frank, Anne. The Diary of a Young Girl. Garden City,
      N.Y.: Doubleday, 1952.
      The well-known story of the Dutch girl; actually less
      powerful than many others.

1501. Fromm, Bella. Blood and Banquets: A Berlin Social Diary.
      New York: Harper & Bros., 1942.
      An early warning by a German woman who managed to
      get out in time.

1502. Gurdus, Luba K. The Death Train. New York: Schocken,
      1978.
      Polish mother's calvary in hiding and at Majdanek; il-
      lustrated by the author.

1503. Kaminska, Ruth T. I Don't Want to Be Brave Anymore.
      Washington, D.C.: New Republic, 1978.
      The life of a famous actress' daughter under the Nazis
      and the Soviets.

1504. Klein, Gerda W. All but My Life. New York: Hill & Wang,
      1957.

A sensitively written story of a girl in hiding and at a labor camp.

1505. Koehn, Ilse. Mischling Second Degree, My Childhood in Nazi Germany. New York: Bantam, 1978.

1506. Kulkielko, Renya. Escape from the Pit. New York: Sharon, 1947.
       The constant struggle of a young girl to stay alive.

1507. Minco, Marga. Bitter Herbs, a Little Chronicle. New York: Oxford University Press, 1960.
       A literary gem by a Dutch girl.

1508. Reiss, Johanna. The Upstairs Room. New York: Bantam, 1979.
       Two Dutch children hidden by a farmer.

1509. Rubinstein, Erna. The Survivor in Us All: A Memoir of the Holocaust. Hamden, Conn.: Archon Books, 1983.
       Story of four Polish sisters who survived the Holocaust.

1510. Somerhausen, Anne. Written in Darkness: A Belgian Woman's Record of the Occupation, 1940–1945. New York: Knopf, 1946.

1511. Zuker-Bujanowska, Liliana. Liliana's Journal, Warsaw, 1939–1945. New York: Dial, 1980.
       A teenager's trials and tribulations in the Warsaw ghetto, including a marriage to a Polish resister who was killed, and hiding with false identity papers.

9. PRE-1945 KNOWLEDGE OF THE HOLOCAUST

1512. Apenszlak, Jacob, ed. The Black Book of Polish Jewry: An Account of the Martyrdom of Polish Jewry Under the Nazi Occupation. New York: Fertig, 1982 (1943).
See entry 1051 for annotation.

1513. Bauer, Yehuda. American Jewry and the Holocaust. Detroit: Wayne State University Press, 1981.

1514. Blaettler, Franz (pseud.). Warsaw 1942. Zürich: F.G. Micha, 1945.
Author witnessed the killing of Jews by the thousands in 1941–1942, including women and children. Book was not allowed to be published during the war.

1515. Bucher, Rudolf. Zwischen Verrat und Menschlichkeit. Frauenfeld, Switz.: Huber, 1967.
Author was a Swiss physician who witnessed the killing of Jews in Warsaw and Smolensk on one of the four Swiss medical missions to the Eastern front, this one in the winter of 1941–42; he lectured about the killings in 1942 in Switzerland.

1516. Ciechanowski, Jan. Defeat in Victory. Garden City, N.Y.: Doubleday, 1947.
As Polish ambassador to Washington, the author witnessed the conversation between President Franklin D. Roosevelt and the Polish resistance courier Jan Karski, who reported on the extermination of the Jews from firsthand knowledge; the meeting took place in early 1942.

1517. Dinnerstein, Leonard. America and the Survivors of the Holocaust. New York: Columbia University Press, 1982.

1518. Dobkowski, Michael N. The Politics of Indifference: A Documentary History of Holocaust Victims in America. Washington, D.C.: University Press of America, 1982.

1519. Ehrenberg, Hans P. Autobiography of a German Pastor. London: Strident Christian Movement Press, 1943.

1520. Falconi, Carlo. The Silence of Pius XII. Boston: Little,
       Brown, 1970.

1521. Feingold, Henry L. The Politics of Rescue: The Roosevelt
       Administration and the Holocaust, 1938-1945. New Bruns-
       wick, N.J.: Rutgers University Press, 1975.

1522. Friedländer, Saul. Pius XII and the Third Reich, a Docu-
       mentation. New York: Knopf, 1966.

1523. Friedman, Saul. No Haven for the Oppressed: United States
       Policy Toward Jewish Refugees, 1938-1945. Detroit:
       Wayne State University Press, 1973.
          Covers the general Western apathy to the plight of the
       Jews.

1524. Gilbert, Martin. Auschwitz and the Allies. New York: Holt,
       Rinehart & Winston, 1981.
          One of the latest scholarly works dealing with this dis-
       turbing subject.

1525. Israel, Fred L., ed. The War Diary of Breckenridge Long:
       Selections from the Years 1939-1944. Lincoln: University
       of Nebraska Press, 1966.
          Breckenridge Long was assistant secretary of state in
       charge of special war problems at the time the news re-
       garding the Nazi extermination of the Jews was confirmed
       in the Fall of 1942.

1526. Karski, Jan. Story of a Secret State. Boston: Houghton
       Mifflin, 1944.
          See entry 672 for annotation.

1527. Laqueur, Walter. The Terrible Secret: Suppression of the
       Truth About Hitler's "Final Solution." Boston: Little,
       Brown, 1980.
          Concise, informative, stunning; unfortunately lacks bib-
       liography.

1528. Ludwig, Carl. Die Flüchtlingspolitik der Schweiz in den Jah-
       ren 1932 bis 1955. Bern: Lang, 1966.

1529. Morley, John F. Vatican Diplomacy and the Jews During the
       Holocaust, 1939-1943. New York: KTAV, 1980.
          Written by a priest.

1530. Morse, Arthur D. While Six Million Died, a Chronicle of
       American Apathy. New York: Random House, 1967; New
       York: Overlook Press, 1983.

1531. Murphy, Paul I. La Popessa. New York: Warner, 1983.

Biography of Sister Pascalina, the confidante of Pius XII. In one chapter on the Jews, author claims that the Holy See saved the lives of 400,000 Jews; undocumented.

1532. Rhodes, Anthony. The Vatican in the Age of the Dictators, 1922-1945. London: Hodder & Stoughton, 1973.

1533. Ross, Robert W. So It Was True: The American Protestant Press and the Nazi Persecution of the Jews. Minneapolis: University of Minnesota Press, 1980.

1534. Sharf, Andrew. The British Press and the Jews Under Nazi Rule. London: Oxford University Press, 1964.

1535. Shub, Boris, ed. Hitler's Ten Year War on the Jews. New York: Institute of Jewish Affairs, 1943.

1536. U.S. Office of Strategic Services. Research and Analysis Branch. Concentration Camps in Germany. Washington, D.C.: GPO, 1944.

1537. U.S. War Refugee Board. German Extermination Camps: Auschwitz and Birkenau. Washington, D.C.: GPO, 1944.

1538. Vrba, Rudolf and Bestic, Alan. I Cannot Forgive. New York: Grove, 1964.
Vrba and another man escaped from Auschwitz and notified the outside world about the exterminations.

1539. Wasserstein, Bernard, M.J. Great Britain and the Jews of Europe, 1939-1945. New York: Oxford University Press, 1979.

1540. Wise, Stephen S. As I See It. New York: Jewish Opinion Publication Corp., 1944.

1541. _____. Challenging Years, the Autobiography of Stephen Wise. New York: Putnam's, 1949.
Rabbi Wise was head of the American Jewish Congress and of the World Jewish Congress.

1542. Wyman, David S. Paper Walls: America and the Refugee Crisis, 1938-1941. Amherst: University of Massachusetts Press, 1968.

10. W A R   C R I M E S

1543. Andrews, Allen. Exemplary Justice. London: Harrap, 1976.

1544. Andrus, Burton C. I Was the Nuremberg Jailer. New York:
       Coward-McCann, 1969.

1545. Appleman, John A. Military Tribunals and International
       Crimes. Westport, Conn.: Greenwood Press, 1971 (1954).

1546. Arendt, Hannah. Eichmann in Jerusalem: A Report on the
       Banality of Evil. New York: Viking, 1965.
            Controversial opus regarding the blame for the Holo-
       caust; offers philosophical concepts connected with anti-
       Semitism and the "Final Solution."

1547. Barrington, J. Harcourt, ed. The "Zyklon B" Trial: Trial
       of Bruno Tosch and Two Others. London: William
       Hodge.
            Vol. VIII of the War Crimes Trials Series, David M.
       Fyfe, General Editor.

1548. Bauer, Fritz. Die Kriegsverbrecher vor Gericht. Zürich:
       Europe, 1945.

1549. Bayle, François. Croix gammée contre caducée. Les expéri-
       ances humaines en Allemagne pendant la deuxième guerre
       mondiale. Neustadt [?], n.p., 1950.
            This is a strange entry technically. The Library of
       Congress has #43 of allegedly only 100 copies printed;
       a few other copies are available in United States
       libraries. There is no publisher or date noted in the
       book, yet it is a 1,521-page illustrated tome; it is a sys-
       tematic and thorough treatment of the various medical ex-
       periments conducted by the Nazis in and out of concen-
       tration camps, indispensable for any research on the topic.
       Bayle is a physician who was on the French Scientific
       Commission for War Crimes for the twenty-three Nazi doc-
       tors' trial in Nuremberg, from November 1946 through Au-
       gust 1947.

1550. Belgium. Ministry of Justice. Les Crimes de guerre commis

sous l'occupation de la Belgique, 1940-1945. La persécution antisemitique en Belgique. Liège: Thones, 1947.

1551. Benton, Wilbour E. and Grimm, George, eds. Nuremberg:
German Views of the War Trial. Dallas: Southern Metho-
dist University Press, 1955.
Includes bibliography.

1552. Bethell, Nicholas. The Last Secret. London: Deutsch,
1974.

1553. Bezymenskii, Lev A. Tracing Martin Bormann. Moscow:
Progress, 1966.

1554. Black Book: The Nazi Crime Against the Jewish People.
New York: Duell, Sloan & Pearce, 1946.

1555. Blum, Howard. Wanted! The Search for Nazis in America.
New York: Quadrangle, 1977.
The first book calling attention to Nazis, some of them
war criminals, immigrating to and achieving citizenship in
the U.S. by not disclosing their Nazi backgrounds.

1556. Borkin, Joseph. The Crime and Punishment of I.G. Farben.
New York: Free Press, 1978.

1557. Bosch, William J. Judgement on Nuremberg. Chapel Hill:
University of North Carolina Press, 1970.

1558. Bower, Tom. Barbie: Butcher of Lyon. New York: Pantheon, 1984.
The second book on Barbie after his capture in Febru-
ary 1983.

1559. _____. Blind Eye to Murder: Britain, America and the
Purging of Nazi Germany--A Pledge Betrayed. London:
Granada, 1983.

1560. _____. The Pledge Betrayed: America and Britain and
the Denazification of Postwar Germany. Garden City,
N.Y.: Doubleday, 1982.
Same as above British edition; title comparison is in-
teresting. Skillful study analyzing why denazification
failed.

1561. Brand, George, ed. The Velpke Baby Home Trial: Trial of
Heinrich Gerike and Seven Others. London: William
Hodge, 1950.
Vol. VII of the War Crimes Trials Series, David M.
Fyfe, General Editor.

1562.   Braunbuch: Kriegs- und Nazi-Verbrecher in der Bundesre-
        publik. Berlin: Archivverwaltung der DDR, 1965.

1563.   Bross, Werner. Gespräche mit Göring während des Nüren-
        berger Prozesses. Flensburg, W. Ger.: Wolff, 1950.

1564.   Calvocoressi, Peter. Nuremberg. New York: Macmillan,
        1948.

1565.   Cameron, John, ed. The "Peleus" Trial: Trial of Heinz Eck,
        August Eck, August Hoffman, Walter Weisspfenning,
        Hans Richard Lenz and Wolfgang Schwender. London:
        William Hodge, 1948.
            Vol. I of the War Crimes Trials Series, David M. Fyfe,
        General Editor.

1566.   Central Commission for Investigation of German Crimes in
        Poland. German Crimes in Poland. 2 vols. New York:
        Fertig, 1982.
            Originally published in England, 1946-47. Contains
        wealth of material on Jewish and other victims of the Nazi
        occupation, especially on Auschwitz-Birkenau, Treblinka,
        Chelmno (Kulmhof), Belzec, Stutthof, Ravensbrück, the
        Warsaw uprising, Soviet POW's and more.

1567.   Congrès Juif Mondial. Le massacre des Juifs de Jassy.
        Bucharest: Le Congrès, 1946.

1568a. Conot, Robert E. Justice at Nuremberg: The First Compre-
        hensive Dramatic Account of the Trial of the Nazi Leaders.
        New York: Harper & Row, 1983.
            Details the trial itself and the picture behind the scenes
        as well; notable bibliography.

1568b. Cooper, R.W. The Nuremberg Trial. Harmondsworth, Eng.:
        Penguin, 1947.

1569.   Creel, George. War Criminals and Punishment. New York:
        R.M. McBride, 1944.

1570.   Cuddon, Eric, ed. The Dulag [sic] Luft Trial: Trial of
        Erich Killinger and Four Others. London: William Hodge,
        1952.
            Volume X of the War Crimes Trials Series, David M.
        Fyfe, General Editor. Now listed as vol. IX. Discusses
        British POW's and their captors' trial in 1945.

1571.   Datner, Szymon. Crimes Against POWs. Warsaw: Zachodnia
        agencja prasowa, 1964.

1572.   Davidson, Eugene. Trial of the Germans: An Account of the

Twenty-Two Defendants Before the International Tribunal
at Nuremberg, 1945-1946. New York: Macmillan, 1972.

1573. Delius, F.C. Unsere Siemens-Welt. Berlin: Rotbuch, 1972.

1574. Eichmann Trial. The Attorney General of Israel vs. Adolf,
Son of Adolf Karl Eichmann. Jerusalem: Ministry of Jus-
tice, 1962.
Minutes of the trial in English translation.

1575. Elam, Henry, ed. The Stalag Luft III Trial: Trial of Max
Wielen and Seventeen Others. London: William Hodge.
Vol. XIII of the War Crimes Trials Series, David M.
Fyfe, General Editor.

1576. Erdstein, Erich and Bean, Barbara. Inside the Fourth Reich.
New York: St. Martin's, 1977.

1577. Fabre-Luce, Alfred. Le mystère du Maréchal: Le Procès
Pétain. Geneva: Bourquin, 1946.
Trial of French Marshal Pétain by sympathetic commen-
tator.

1578. Farago, Ladislas. Aftermath: Martin Bormann and the
Fourth Reich. New York: Simon & Schuster, 1974.

1579. Ferencz, Benjamin B. Less Than Slaves: Jewish Forced
Labor and the Quest for Compensation. Cambridge,
Mass.: Harvard University Press, 1979.

1580. Fishman, Jack. The Seven Men of Spandau. New York:
Rinehart, 1954.

1581. Fitzgibbon, C. Denazification. London: Michael Joseph,
1969.

1582. France. Service d'Information des Crimes de Guerre. La
persécution raciale. Paris: Le Service, 1947.

1583. Frank, Hans. Im Angesicht des Galgens. Munich: F.A.
Beck, 1953.
Memoirs written before his execution by Generalgou-
verneur of Poland in 1946.

1584. Friedman, Tuviah. The Hunter. Garden City, N.Y.: Doubleday, 1961.
Autobiography of the person who tracked Eichmann for
fifteen years.

1585. Fyfe, David M., General Editor. War Crimes Trials. 15 vols.
London: William Hodge, 1948 [1952].

Series covers histories of defendants' crimes, partial transcripts of trials, documents and illustrations. The series, in numerical order of the volumes, is covered under entries 1565, 1639, 1651, 1610, 1670, 1656, 1561, 1547, 1652, 1510, 1609, 1674, 1575, 1631 and 1608. Note, however, that entries without a publication date still did not appear and are unlikely to do so.

1586. Gallagher, Richard. Nuremberg: The Third Reich on Trial. New York: Avon, 1961.

1587. Gilbert, G.M. Nuremberg Diary. New York: Farrar, Straus & Young, 1947.

1588. Glock, Charles, et al. The Apathetic Majority. New York: Harper & Row, 1966.

1589. Glueck, Sheldon. The Nuremberg Trial and Aggressive War. New York: Knopf, 1946.

1590. _____. War Criminals, Their Prosecution and Punishment. New York: Kraus, 1966 (1944).

1591. Goebbels, Joseph. The Secret Conferences of Dr. Goebbels. New York: Dutton, 1970.

1592. Harel, Isser. The House on Garibaldi Street. New York: Bantam, 1976.
The story of Eichmann's capture in Buenos Aires by participant.

1593. Harris, Whitney A. Tyranny on Trial: The Evidence at Nuremberg. Dallas: Southern Methodist University Press, 1954.

1594. Hausner, Gideon. Justice in Jerusalem. New York: Harper & Row, 1966.
By Israeli prosecutor of Eichmann.

1595. Hess, Ilse. England--Nürenberg--Spandau, Ein Schicksal in Briefen. Leoni am Starberger See, Ger.: Druffel, 1952.
By Frau Rudolf Hess.

1596. Heydrich, Lina. Leben mit einem Kriegsverbrecher. Pfaffenhofen, Germany: Ludwig, 1976.
By Frau Reinhard Heydrich.

1597. Infield, Glenn B. Skorzeny, Hitler's Commando. New York: St. Martin's, 1981.

1598. Institute of Jewish Affairs. Statute of Limitations and the

Prosecution of Nazi Crimes in the Federal German Republic.
London: Institute of Jewish Affairs, in association with the
World Jewish Congress, 1969.

1599. International Military Tribunal. Office of the United States
Chief Counsel for Prosecution of Axis Criminality. Nazi
Conspiracy and Aggression. 11 vols. Washington, D.C.:
GPO, 1946. Supplements A and B, 1947-1948, 2 vols.
Documents prepared by the American and British pro-
secutions for the major war criminals' trial; contains over
2,000 items, selected from 100,000.

1600. _____. Trials of the Major Criminals Before the International Military Tribunal. 42 vols. Nuremberg: International Military Tribunal, 1947-1949.
The official publication of the trial records in English,
from pretrial deliberations to sentencing; with documents.

1601. Jackson, Robert H. The Nuremberg Case. New York:
Knopf, 1947.

1602. Jaspers, Marc. La culpabilité allemande. Paris: Minuit,
1948.

1603. Jaworski, Leon. After Fifteen Years. Houston: Gulf, 1961.

1604. Kahn, Leo. Nuremberg Trials. New York: Ballantine, 1972.

1605. Kelley, Douglas M. 22 Cells in Nuremberg. New York:
Greenberg, 1947.

1606. Kempner, Robert Max W. Edith Stein und Anne Frank, Zwei
von hunderttausend: Die Enthüllungen über die NS-
verbrecher in Holland vor dem Schwurgericht in München.
Die Ermordung der "nichtarischen" Mönche und Nonnen.
Freiburg, Basel, Wien: Herder, 1968.

1607. Kent, George O., ed. A Catalog of Files and Microfilms of
the German Foreign Ministry Archives, 1920-1943. 3 vols.
Stanford, Cal.: Hoover Institution, 1962-1966.

1608. Kintner, Earl W., ed. The Doctors' Trial: Trial of Karl
Brandt and Twenty-Two Others. London: William Hodge.
Vol. XV of the War Crimes Trials Series, David M.
Fyfe, General Editor.

1609. _____, ed. The Justice Trial: Trial of Josef Alstotter
and Fifteen Others. London: William Hodge.
Vol. XI of the War Crimes Trials Series, David M. Fyfe,
General Editor.

1610. _____, ed. The Hadamar Trial: Trial of Alfons Klein, Adolf Wahlmann, Heinrich Ruoft [and Four Others]. London: William Hodge, 1949.
   Vol. IV of the War Crimes Trials Series, David M. Fyfe, General Editor.

1611. Klarsfeld, Beate. Die Geschichte des P.G. 2633930 Kiesinger. Darmstadt, Ger.: Joseph Melzer, 1969.

1612. _____. Wherever They May Be! New York: Vanguard, 1975.
   The pursuit of war criminals, especially of Barbie, by the author, a German Christian.

1613a. Knieriem, August von. The Nuremberg Trials. Chicago: Regnery, 1959.

1613b. Knoop, Hans. The Menten Affair. New York: Macmillan, 1978.
   Pieter Nicolas Menten and the Holocaust trial.

1614. Kruse, Falco. NS-Processe und Restauration. Frankfurt am Main: Kritische Justiz, 1978.

1615. Kühnrich, Heinz. Judenmörder Eichmann, Kein Fall der Vergangenheit. Berlin: Dietz, 1961.

1616. _____, ed. SS im Einsatz, Eine Dokumentation über die Verbrechen der SS. Berlin: Deutscher Militärverlag, 1967.

1617. Lamb, Max and Sanford, Harry. The Last Nazi. New York: Tower, 1980.

1618. Lang, Jochen von, ed. Eichmann Interrogated: Transcripts from the Archives of the Israeli Police. New York: Farrar, Straus & Giroux, 1983.

1619. Langbein, Hermann. Der Auschwitz-Prozess: Eine Dokumentation. 2 vols. Vienna: Europa, 1965.
   The 1963-1965 Auschwitz trial; parallel edition by Europäische Verlagsanstalt in Frankfurt am Main.

1620. Lem, Salvatore S.L. Crimini di guerra e delitti contro l'umanità (War Crimes and Offenses Against Humanity). Rome: La Civiltà, 1948.

1621. Levy, Alan. Wanted: Nazi Criminals at Large. New York: Berkley, 1962.

1622. Lewis, John R. Uncertain Judgement: A Bibliography of War Crime Trials. Santa Barbara: ABC-Clio, 1979.

1623. Lichtenstein, Heiner. Majdanek, Reportage eines Prozesses,
      mit einem Nachwort von Simon Wiesenthal. Frankfurt am
      Main: Europäische Verlagsanstalt, 1979.

1624. Majdanek. Rozprawa przed specjalnym sadem karnym w
      Lubline. (Hearing before the Special Criminal Court in
      Lublin). Cracow: Czytelnik, 1945.
          The November 1944 Majdanek trial in Lublin.

1625a. Manchester, William. The Arms of Krupp. New York: Ban-
       tam, 1970.

1625b. Maser, Werner. Nuremberg, a Nation on Trial. London:
       Allen Lane, 1979.

1626. Mason, Henry L. The Purge of Dutch Quislings: Emergency
      Justice in the Netherlands. The Hague: Nejhoff, 1952.

1627. Maugham, Viscount. UNO and War Crimes. London: John
      Murray, 1951.

1628. Mendelssohn, Peter. Nuremberg Documents: Some Aspects
      of German War Policy, 1939-45. London: George Allen &
      Unwin, 1946.

1629. Merle, Marcel. Le procès de Nuremberg. Paris: A. Pedone,
      1949.

1630a. Miale, Florence R. and Selzer, Michael. The Nuremberg
       Mind: The Psychology of the Nazi Leaders. New York:
       Quadrangle, 1975.

1630b. Murphy, Brendan. The Butcher of Lyon: The Story of the
       Infamous Nazi, Klaus Barbie. New York: Harper & Row,
       1983.
          The first book on Barbie after his capture in 1983.

1631. Muszkat, Marian, ed. The Trial of Arthur Greiser. London:
      William Hodge.
          Vol. XIV of the War Crimes Trials Series, David M.
      Fyfe, General Editor.

1632. Naumann, Bernd. Auschwitz--A Report on the Proceedings
      Against Robert Karl Ludwig Mulka and Others Before the
      Court of Frankfurt. New York: Praeger, 1966.
          About the 1963-1965 Auschwitz trial; introduction by
      Hannah Arendt.

1633. Neave, Airey. Nuremberg: A Personal Record of the Trial
      of the Major Nazi Criminals. London: Hodder & Stough-
      ton, 1978.

1634. Neumann, Inge S. A Bibliography of the European War
      Crimes Trials. New York: Carnegie Endowment for In-
      ternational Peace, 1951.
          Compiled by Neumann for the Committee on War Crimes
      Research of the Carnegie Endowment for International
      Peace, and including materials in the Wiener Library in
      London; law oriented, over half of the entries annotated;
      total of 113 typed pages, but with a cut-off date of 1950.
      Reissued in 1978 by Greenwood Press.

1635. Noble, Iris. Nazi Hunter Simon Wiesenthal. New York: J.
      Messner, 1979.
          Biography for younger readers of Wiesenthal who dis-
      likes the epithet "Nazi hunter" as he is a seeker of justice.

1636. Nuremberg Military Tribunals. Trials of War Criminals Before
      the Nuremberg Military Tribunals Under Control Council
      Law No. 10, October, 1946 to April, 1949. 15 vols.
      Washington, D.C.: GPO, 1949-1953.
          Condensed records from original 300,000 pages plus
      documents of twelve cases: Medical, Milch, Justice, Pohl,
      Flick, I.G. Farben, Hostage, Rusha, Einsatzgruppen,
      Krupp, Ministries and High Command. Full transcripts at
      the Library of Congress and National Archives.

1637. Olsen, Jack. Silence on Monte Sole. New York: Putnam's,
      1968.

1638. Pearlman, Moshe. The Capture and Trial of Adolf Eichmann.
      New York: Simon & Schuster, 1963.

1639. Phillips, Raymond, ed. The Belsen Trial: Trial of Josef
      Kramer and Forty-Four Others. London: William Hodge,
      1949.
          Vol. II of the War Crimes Trials Series, David M. Fyfe,
      General Editor. Note in entry 1663 the 1983 reprint of
      H.M.S.O. edition on same topic.

1640. Polevoi, Boris I. The Final Reckoning: Nuremberg Diaries.
      Chicago: Imported Publications, 1978.

1641. Polish Government in Exile. German Crimes Against Poland,
      Official Report ... to the International Military Tribunal.
      London: The Government, 1945.

1642. Prisoners of War, Conventions Between the United States of
      America and Other Powers. Washington, D.C.: GPO,
      1932.

1643. Raynolds, Quentin. Minister of Death: The Eichmann Story.
      New York: Viking, 1960.

1644. Robinson, Jacob. And the Crooked Shall Be Made Straight:
      The Eichmann Trial, the Jewish Catastrophe and Hannah
      Arendt's Narrative. New York: Macmillan, 1965.
            Contradicts Hannah Arendt's theory about the guilt of
      the Jews.

1645. _____ and Sachs, Henry, eds. The Holocaust: The Nur-
      emberg Evidence: Documents, Digest, Index, and Chrono-
      logical Tables. New York: YIVO Institute, 1976.

1646. Roth, Günther and Wolff, Kurt H. The American Denazifica-
      tion of Germany. Columbus: Ohio State University Press,
      1954.

1647. Rückerl, Adalbert. The Investigation of Nazi Crimes, 1945-
      1978: A Documentation. Hamden, Conn.: Archon Books,
      1980.
            War crime investigations by German and Allied courts in
      Eastern Germany and Austria; statistics and legal bases of
      war crime trials; by former POW and public prosecutor.

1648a. Russell of Liverpool, Lord. The Scourge of the Swastika.
      New York: Ballantine, 1956; London: Corgi, 1981.

1648b. Ryan, Allan A. Jr. Klaus Barbie and the United States Gov-
      ernment: The Report, with Documentary Appendix, to the
      Attorney General of the United States. Frederick, Md.:
      University Publications of America, 1983.

1649. Salomon, Ernst von. The Answers to the 131 Questions of
      the Allied Military Government "Fragebogen." London:
      Putnam's, 1954.

1650. Sereny, Gitta. Into That Darkness: From Mercy Killing to
      Mass Murder. New York: McGraw-Hill, 1974.
            Biography of Franz Stangl, commandant of the Treblinka
      extermination camp.

1651. Sleeman, Colin, ed. The Gozawa Trial: Trial of Captain
      Gozawa Sadaichi and Nine Others. London: William Hodge,
      1949.
            Vol. III of the War Crimes Trials Series, David M.
      Fyfe, General Editor.

1652. _____ and Silkin, S.C., eds. The "Double Tenth" Trial:
      Trial of Lt. Col. Sumido Haruzo and Twenty Others.
      London: William Hodge, 1950.
            Projected as Vol. IX of the War Crimes Trials Series,
      David M. Fyfe, General Editor. Now listed as vol. VIII.

1653. Smith, Bradley F. Reaching Judgement in Nuremberg. New
      York: Meridian, 1977.

1654. _____. The Road to Nuremberg. New York: Basic
       Books, 1981.
           Procedures how Allies agreed on war crime trials.

1655. Speer, Albert. Spandau. New York: Macmillan, 1976.

1656. Stevens, E.H., ed. Trial of Generaloberst Nikolaus von
       Falkenhorst. London: William Hodge, 1949.
           Vol. VI of the War Crimes Trials Series, David M.
       Fyfe, General Editor.

1657. Stevenson, William. The Bormann Brotherhood. New York:
       Harcourt Brace Jovanovich, 1973.

1658. Taylor, Telford. Trial Report to the Secretary of the Army
       on the Nuremberg War Crimes Trials Under Council Law
       No. 10. Washington, D.C.: GPO, 1949.

1659. Thomas, Hugh. The Murder of Rudolf Hess. London: Hod-
       der & Stoughton, 1979.

1660. Trivanovitch, Vaso. The Case of Drazha Mikhailovich, High-
       lights of the Evidence Against the Chetnik Leader. New
       York: United Committee of South-Slavic Americans, 1946.

1661. United Nations. International Law Commission. The Charter
       and Judgement of the Nuremberg Tribunal. New York:
       United Nations, 1949.

1662. _____. War Crimes Commission. History of the United
       Nations War Crimes Commission and the Development of the
       Laws of War. London: HMSO, 1948.

1663. _____. Law Reports of Trials of War Criminals: Selected
       and Prepared by the United Nations War Crimes Commis-
       sion. 15 vols. London: HMSO, 1945-1948.
           Includes reports on eighty nine cases, among others
       some concentration camp ones, with summary of debates
       and judgements, with legal commentaries; indexed. The
       [Bergen] Belsen Trial was reprinted separately by H.
       Fertig, 1983.

1664. United States Congress. House of Representatives. Report
       of the Select Committee on the Katyn Forest Massacre.
       Washington, D.C.: GPO, 1952.

1665. _____. Committee on Foreign Affairs. Punishment of War
       Criminals. Hearings ... on H.J. Res. 93, a Joint Resolu-
       tion Requesting the President to Appoint a Commission to
       cooperate with the United nations [sic] War Crimes Com-
       mission ... in the Preparation of Definite Plans for the

Punishment of war criminals of the Axis Countries, March
22 and 26, 1945. Washington, D.C.: GPO, 1945.

1666a. United States. Department of the Army. Guide to Captured
German Records in the Custody of the Department of the
Army Agencies in the United States. Washington, D.C.:
Department of the Army, 1951. Mimeographed.
Not exclusively war crime records.

1666b. United States Military Tribunal. Trials of War Criminals Before the Nuremberg Military Tribunals Under Control
Council Law No. 10. 15 vols. Washington, D.C.: GPO,
1951-1952.
Additional documents and transcripts are in the International Law Library of Columbia University in New York.

1667a. United States. National Archives. Guides to German Records
Microfilmed at Alexandria, Virginia. 42 vols. Washington,
D.C.: GPO, 1958-1964.
Prepared with the cooperation of the American Historical
Association.

1667b. _____, Weinberg, Gerhard L., et al., eds. Guide to Captured German Documents. Washington, D.C.: GPO, 1952.
Mimeographed.

1668. _____, Weinberg, Gerhard L., ed. Supplement to the Guide
to Captured German Documents. Washington, D.C.: GPO,
1959. Mimeographed.

1669. United States. Office of the Judge Advocate. Complete List
of War Crime Trials. Washington, D.C.: GPO, 1950.
Outdated.

1670. Webb, A.M., ed. The Natzweiler Trial: Trial of Wolfgang
Zeuss and Nine Others. London: William Hodge, 1949.
Vol. V of the War Crimes Trials Series, David M. Fyfe,
General Editor.

1671. Weinberg, Gerhard L., et al., eds. Guide to Captured German Documents. See entry 1669.

1672. _____. Supplement to the Guide to Captured German Documents. See entry 1668.

1673. Weingartner, James J. Crossroads of Death: The Story of
the Malmédy Massacre and Trial. Berkeley: University
of California Press, 1979.

1674. Wheeler-Bennett, [John] W., ed. Trial of Field Marshal Albert Kesselring. London: William Hodge.
Vol. XII of the War Crimes Trials Series, David M. Fyfe, General Editor.

1675. Whiting, Charles. The Hunt for Martin Bormann. New York: Ballantine, 1973.

1676. _____. Otto Skorzeny. New York: Ballantine, 1972.

1677. Wiesenthal Foundation, Amsterdam and Federation of Jewish Victims of Nazi Crimes, eds. Essays About Nazi Crimes. New York: M.S. Rosenberg, 1977.

1678. Wiesenthal, Simon. The Murderers Among Us. New York: Bantam, 1973.
A second volume is in preparation. Both deal with cases of tracking down war criminals and gathering evidence against them.

1679. Willis, James F. Prologue to Nuremberg. The Politics and Diplomacy of Punishing War Criminals of the First World War. Westport, Conn.: Greenwood Press, 1982.

1680. Zeiger, Henry A. The Case Against Adolf Eichmann. New York: New American Library, 1960.

1681. Ziemke, E.F. The U.S. Army in the Occupation of Germany, 1944-1946. Washington, D.C.: GPO, 1975.

1682. Zink, H. The United States in Germany, 1944-1955. Westport, Conn.: Greenwood Press, 1974.

11. ART AND PHOTOGRAPHS

1683. Abells, Chana. The Children We Remember, Photographs
      from the Archives of Yad Vashem, Jerusalem, Israel.
      Rockville, Md.: Kar-Ben, 1983.
      Considering the richness of material at Yad Vashem,
      this is a slim tome.

1684. Ausubel, Nathan. Pictorial History of the Jewish People,
      from Bible Times to Our Own Day Throughout the World.
      New York: Crown, 1954.

1685. Blatter, Janet and Milton, Sybil, eds. Art of the Holocaust.
      New York: Rutledge, 1981.

1686. Boguslawska-Swiebocka, Renata and Ceglowska, Teresa, eds.
      KL Auschwitz. Warsaw: Krajowa agencja wydawnicza,
      1980.

1687a. Constanza, Mary S. The Living Witness: Art in the Con-
      centration Camps and Ghettos. New York: Macmillan,
      1982.

1687b. Couvaras, Costa G. Photo Album of the Greek Resistance.
      San Francisco: Wire Press, 1978.

1688. Delarbre, Leon. Dora, Auschwitz, Buchenwald, Bergen-
      Belsen, croquis clandestins. Paris: M. de Romilly, 1945.

1689. Dobroszycki, Lucjan and Kirschenblatt-Gimblett, Barbara.
      Image Before My Eyes: A Photographic History of Jewish
      Life in Poland, 1864-1939. New York: Schocken, 1979.

1690. Domanski, Jerzy, ed. Oswiecim, Malarstvo, rzezba, grafika
      (Auschwitz, Painting, Carving, Graphic Arts). Cracow:
      Wydawnictwo artystyczno-graficzne, 1959.

1691. Eschwege, Helmut. Die Synagoge in der deutschen Ge-
      schichte. Dresden: Verlag der Kunst, 1980.

1692. Frackiewicz, J. Oswiecim w fotografii artystycznej. Ausch-
      witz: Panstwowe Muzeum, 1965.

1693a. Frank, Volker. Antifaschistische Mahnmale in der DDR:
        Ihre Kunstlerische und Architektonische Gestaltung.
        Leipzig: E.S. Seeman, 1970.

1693b. Frommhold, E. Kunst in Widerstand: Malerei, Graphic, Plas-
        tik, 1922-1945. Dresden: Verlag der Kunst, 1968.

1694a. Gans, Mozes H., ed. Memorbook, Pictorial History of Dutch
        Jewry from the Renaissance to 1940. Detroit: Wayne
        State University Press, 1977.

1694b. Gilbert, Martin. The Holocaust, Maps and Photographs. New
        York: Hill & Wang, 1978.
        Small booklet packed with information, including statis-
        tics.

1695. Gottlieb, Malke and Mlotek, Chana, eds. Twenty-Five Ghetto
        Songs with Music and Translation. New York: Workmen's
        Circle, 1968.

1696. Green, Gerald, ed. The Artists of Terezín. New York:
        Schocken, 1978.

1697. Grossman, Mendel. With Camera in the Ghetto. New York:
        Schocken, 1977.

1698. Heartfield, John. Photomontages of the Nazi Period. New
        York: Universe, 1977.

1699. Hellman, Peter, ed. Auschwitz Album, a Book Based Upon
        an Album Discovered by a Concentration Camp Survivor,
        Lily Meier. New York: Random House, 1981.

1700. Heřman, Jan. Jewish Cemeteries in Bohemia and Moravia.
        Prague: Council of Jewish Committees in the ČSR, n.d.

1701. Hořec, Jaromír. ...i děti šly na smrt (...Even Children
        Went Off to Die). Prague: Naše vojsko, 1960.
        Photographs, with text in Czech, Russian, English,
        French and German.

1702. Insdorf, Annette. Indelible Shadows: Film and the Holo-
        caust. New York: Vintage, 1983.
        A study of seventy-five fictional and documentary films
        about the Holocaust by Yale professor; produced in Europe
        and the United States; with filmography and sources for
        rentals.

1703. Jour, Jean. Les camps nazis en images, 1944-1945. Brus-
        sels: Libro-Sciences, 1978.

1704. Kantor, Alfred. The Book of Alfred Kantor. New York:
       McGraw-Hill, 1971.
       Simple but expressive drawings and watercolors from
       Auschwitz and transports; highly informative, with artist's
       additional explanations.

1705. Koscielnicka, Mieczyslawa. Twornosc artystyczna: Malarstvo
       (Artistic Creation: Painting). Auschwitz: Panstwowe
       Muzeum, 1961.

1706. Kulišová, Táňa, et al. Terezín. Naše vojsko, 1967.
       About children in Terezín, with drawings and poems.

1707. Kuna, Milan. Hudba v koncentračních táborech (Music in
       Concentration Camps). Terezín, Czechoslovakia: Památník
       Terezín, 1982.

1708. _____. Kunst in Theresienstadt, 1941-1945. Terezín,
       Czechoslovakia: Památník Terezín, 1972.

1709. Lazar, Auguste (Foreword). Ravensbrück. Berlin: Kon-
       gress, 1959.
       Photographs with German, Russian, French and English
       text.

1710. Lorant, Stefan. Sieg Heil: An Illustrated History of Ger-
       many from Bismarck to Hitler. New York: Norton, 1974.

1711. Matanle, Ivor. Adolf Hitler: A Photographic Documentary.
       New York: Crescent, 1983.

1712. Newmann, Robert. The Pictorial History of the Third Reich.
       New York: Bantam, 1961.

1713a. Novák, Václav, ed. Terezín. Prague: Naše vojsko, 1983.
       Photographs, with text in Czech, Russian, German,
       English and French.

1713b. Novitch, Miriam, et al. Spiritual Resistance: Art from Con-
       centration Camps, 1940-1945. A Selection of Drawings and
       Paintings from the Collection of Kibbutz Lohamei Haghetaot,
       Israel. Philadelphia: Jewish Publication Society of Amer-
       ica, 1981.

1714. Pryce-Jones, David. Paris in the Third Reich: A History of
       the German Occupation, 1940-1944. New York: Holt,
       Rinehart & Winston, 1981.

1715a. Salomon, Charlotte. Charlotte: A Diary in Pictures. New
       York: Harcourt, Brace, 1963.

1715b. Sandel, J. Perished Jewish Artists. Warsaw: Yiddish Buch,
       1957.
       In Yiddish.

1716a. Savitski, M.A. Figures of the Heart. Chicago: Imported
       Publications [from the U.S.S.R.], 1983.
       Portfolio of thirteen color prints by Buchenwald sur-
       vivor, with text in English, Russian, French, English and
       German.

1716b. Schmidt, Diether, ed. In letzter Stunde, 1933-1945. Dres-
       den: Verlag der Kunst, 1964.

1717a. Shulman, Abraham. The Old Country: The Lost World of
       East European Jews. New York: Scribner's, 1974.

1717b. Steiner, Bedrich, ed. Tragédia slovenských Židov: doku-
       menty a fotografie (The Tragedy of Slovak Jews: Docu-
       ments and Photographs). Bratislava, Czechoslovakia:
       Ústredný sväz židovských náboženských obcí, 1949.

1718. Szajkowski, Zosa. An Illustrated Sourcebook on the Holo-
       caust. 3 vols. New York: KTAV, 1977-79.

1719. Toll, Nelly. Without Surrender: Art of the Holocaust.
       Philadelphia: Running Press, 1978.

1720. Umění v Terezíně, 1941-1945 (Art in Terezín, 1941-1945).
       Frýdland, Czechoslovakia: Ruch, 1972.
       Catalog of an exhibit.

1721. Ungar, Otto. Terezínské obrazy a kresby (Terezín Pictures
       and Drawings). Terezín: Památník Terezín, 1970.

1722. Union of American Hebrew Congregations. Spiritual Resist-
       ance: Art from the Concentration Camps, 1940-1945.
       Philadelphia: Jewish Publication Society of America, 1981.

1723a. United States Office of War Information. KZ: A Pictorial Re-
       port from Five Concentration Camps. Atlanta: Emory
       University, 1983 (1945).
       Originally distributed by the U.S. Office of War Infor-
       mation to the German population; now reissued with Ger-
       man, English and Spanish text.

1723b. Vinecour, Earl and Fishmann, Chuck. Polish Jews: The
       Final Chapter. New York: New York University Press,
       1977.
       Photographs of what was left of Jewish schools and
       synagogues in Poland after World War II.

1724. Vishniak, Roman. Polish Jews: A Pictorial Record. New
      York: Schocken, 1968.

1725. _____. A Vanished World. New York: Farrar, Straus &
      Giroux, 1984.
      About 200 photographs from the 16,000 negatives hidden
      in Europe; about German and Eastern European Jewish life.

1726. Volavková, Hana, ed. ...I Never Saw Another Butterfly ...
      Children's Drawings and Poems from Terezín Concentration
      Camp, 1942-1944. New York: Schocken, 1978.

1727. _____, ed. Terezín 1942-1944: Dětské kresby na zastávce
      k smrti (Terezín 1942-1944: Children's Drawings at the
      Stop to Death). Prague: State Jewish Museum, 1959.

1728. Yad Vashem. Holocaust. Jerusalem: Yad Vashem, n.d.

1729. _____. Testimony: Art of the Holocaust. Jerusalem:
      Yad Vashem, 1982.

1730. YIVO Institute. The Warsaw Ghetto in Pictures, Illustrated
      Catalog. New York: YIVO Institute, 1970.

1731. Zbiorowy, Tom. Twornosc Artystyczna: Rzezba (Artistic
      Creation: Carving). Auschwitz: Panstwowe Muzeum,
      1962.

12. PHILOSOPHY AND INTERPRETATION

1732. Barton, Allen H. Communities in Disaster: A Sociological
      Analysis of Collective Stress Situations. Garden City,
      N.Y.: Doubleday, 1969.

1733. Berkowitz, Eliezer. Faith After the Holocaust. New York:
      KTAV, 1973.
          By a well-known rabbi.

1734. Bettelheim, Bruno. The Informed Heart: Autonomy in a
      Mass Age. New York: Avon, 1971 (1960).
          Controversial book concerning the guilt for the Holo-
      caust.

1735. _____ and Janowitz, Morris. Dynamics of Prejudice. New
      York: Harper, 1950.

1736. Brenner, Reeve R. The Faith and Doubt of Holocaust Sur-
      vivors. New York: Free Press, 1980.

1737. Cantril, Hadley. Human Nature and Political Systems. New
      Brunswick, N.J.: Rutgers University Press, 1961.

1738. Cargas, Harry J. A Christian Response to the Holocaust.
      Denver: Stonehenge, 1981.

1739. _____, ed. When God and Man Failed: Non-Jewish Views
      of the Holocaust. New York: Macmillan, 1981.

1740. Cohen, Arthur A. A Tremendum: A Theological Interpreta-
      tion of the Holocaust. New York: Crossroad, 1981.

1741. _____, ed. Arguments and Doctrines, a Reader of Jewish
      Thinking in the Aftermath of the Holocaust. New York:
      Harper & Row, 1970.

1742. Cohen, Elie A. Human Behavior in the Concentration Camp.
      New York: Norton, 1953.
          By a Dutch psychologist and survivor of three years
      in Auschwitz.

1743. Dawidowicz, Lucy S. The Holocaust and the Historians.
        Cambridge, Mass.: Harvard University Press, 1981.

1744. Eckardt, Roy and Alice L. Long Night's Journey into Day:
        Life and Faith After the Holocaust. Detroit: Wayne State
        University Press, 1982.

1745. Eger, Edith E. Coping and Growth: A Theoretical and Em-
        pirical Study for Groups Under Moderate to Severe Stress.
        Holocaust Studies Series. New York: Irvington, 1982.

1746. Fackenheim, Emil L. God's Presence in History: Jewish Af-
        firmation and Philosophic Reflections. New York: Harper
        & Row, 1972.

1747. Faurisson, Robert. The Holocaust Debate, Revisionist His-
        torians Versus Six Million Jews. New York: Revisionary
        Press, 1980.

1748. Fleischner, Eva, ed. Auschwitz: Beginning of a New Era?
        Reflections on the Holocaust. New York: KTAV, 1977.

1749. Frankl, Victor E. From Death Camp to Existentialism: A
        Psychiatrist's Path to a New Therapy. Boston: Beacon,
        1959.
             Author's solution: logotherapy and love. Following
        edition bears title Man's Search for Meaning, an Introduc-
        tion to Logotherapy. New York: Washington Square
        Press, 1969 (1963).

1750. Friedländer, Saul. Kurt Gerstein: The Ambiguity of God.
        New York: Knopf, 1969.

1751. Fromm, Erich. The Anatomy of Human Destructiveness. New
        York: Holt, Rinehart & Winston, 1973.

1752. Griffin, Susan. Pornography and Silence. New York: Harp-
        er & Row, 1981.
             One chapter deals with the Holocaust.

1753. Grosser, George M., et al. The Threat of Impending Disas-
        ter: Contributions to the Psychology of Stress. Cam-
        bridge, Mass.: MIT Press, 1964.

1754. Horney, Karen. The Neurotic Personality of Our Time. New
        York: Norton, 1937.

1755. Horowitz, Irving L. Taking Lives: Genocide and State Pow-
        er. New Brunswick, N.J.: Rutgers University Press,
        1981.

1756. Jaspers, Karl. The Question of German Guilt. New York:
       Dial, 1947.

1757. Jocz, Jakob. Jewish People and Jesus Christ After Ausch-
       witz. Grand Rapids, Mich.: Baker, 1981.

1758. Krystal, Henry, ed. Massive Psychic Trauma. New York:
       International University Press, 1969.

1759. McGarry, Michael B. Christology After Auschwitz. Paramus,
       N.J.: Paulist Press, 1977.

1760. Matussek, Paul. Internment in Concentration Camps and Its
       Consequences. Berlin and New York: Springer, 1975.

1761. Meinecke, Friedrich. The German Catastrophe: Reflections
       and Recollections. Cambridge, Mass.: Harvard University
       Press, 1950.

1762. Mitscherlich, Alexander and Margareta. The Inability to
       Mourn. New York: Grove, 1975.

1763. Neher, André. The Exile of the Word: From the Silence of
       the Bible to the Silence of Auschwitz. Philadelphia: Jew-
       ish Publication Society of America, 1980.

1764. Neusner, Jacob, ed. Understanding Jewish Theology. New
       York: KTAV, 1973.

1765. Niemoeller, Martin. Here Stand I. Chicago: Willett, 1937.

1766. Norborg, Sverre. From Plato to Hitler: Interpretations of
       History. Minneapolis: Burgess, 1940.

1767. Ossendorf, Karel. Beobachtungen an kriegsgeschädigten
       Kindern, under besonderer Berücksichtigung des Kindes
       aus dem KZ. Basel: Auszug, 1949.

1768. Pawleczynska, Anna. Values and Violence in Auschwitz: A
       Sociological Analysis. Berkeley: University of California
       Press, 1979.

1769. Peck, Abraham J., ed. Jews and Christians After the Holo-
       caust. Philadelphia: Fortress, 1982.

1770. Quaytman, Wilfred, ed. Holocaust Survivors: Psychological
       and Social Sequelae. New York: Human Science, 1980.

1771. Rabinsky, Leatrice and Mann, Gertrude. Journey of Con-
       science: Young People Respond to the Holocaust. Cleve-
       land: Collins, 1979.

1772. Roth, John K. A Consuming Fire. Atlanta: John Knox, 1979.

1773. Rubenstein, Richard L. After Auschwitz: Radical Theology and Contemporary Judaism. Indianapolis: Bobbs-Merrill, 1966.

1774. _____. The Cunning of History: The Holocaust and the American Future. New York: Harper & Row, 1975. Brief but concise analysis of the Holocaust and its role in history.

1775. Samuel, Maurice. The Great Hatred. New York: Knopf, 1948.

1776. Snell, John L., ed. The Nazi Revolution: Germany's Guilt or Germany's Fate? Lexington, Mass.: D.C. Heath, 1959.

1777. Swaab, Maurice. Final Solution: The Modern Jewish Problem and Solution. New York: William-Frederick, 1973.

1778. Vaughan, Elisabeth H. Community Under Stress: An Internment Camp Culture. Princeton, N.J.: Princeton University Press, 1949.

1779. West, Rebecca. The Meaning of Treason. New York: Viking, 1949.

1780. Wiesel, Elie. One Generation After. New York: Avon, 1972. Addressed to new generations.

1781. _____. A Jew Today. New York: Random House, 1978.

1782. Wiesenthal, Simon. The Sunflower. New York: Schocken, 1976.

1783. Young-Bruehl, Elisabeth. Hannah Arendt: For Love of the World. New Haven: Yale University Press, 1982.

13. L I T E R A T U R E

1784. Aichinger, Ilse. Herod's Children. New York: Atheneum, 1963.

1785. Alexander, Edward. The Resonance of Dust: Essays on Holocaust Literature and Jewish Fate. Columbus: Ohio State University Press, 1979.

1786. Appelfeld, Aharon. Tzili, the Story of a Life. New York: Dutton, 1983.
      Story of a young girl in hiding.

1787. Asher, Sandy. Daughters of the Law. Beaufort, S.C.: Beaufort, 1960.
      For young readers.

1788. Bainbridge, Beryl. Young Adolf. New York: Braziller, 1978.
      A novel of Hitler's younger years, based partly on his sister-in-law's memoirs.

1789. Berger, Zdena. Tell Me Another Morning. New York: Harper, 1959.

1790. Bilik, Dorothy S. Immigrant Survivors: Post Holocaust Consciousness in Recent Jewish American Fiction. Middletown, Conn.: Wesleyan University Press, 1981.

1791. Blumenthal, Ilse (Weiss). Mahnmal: Gedichte aus dem KZ. Hamburg: Wegner, 1957.

1792. Borowski, Tadeusz. This Way to the Gas, Ladies and Gentlemen. New York: Penguin, 1976.
      Based on author's experiences at Auschwitz; powerful.

1793. Bosmajian, Hamida. Metaphors of Evil: Contemporary German Literature and the Shadow of Nazism. Iowa City: University of Iowa Press, 1979.

1794. Campion, Joan. Mission to Fulfill. Miami Springs, Fla.: Writer's Service, 1982.

A chronicle play in two acts about Gisi Fleischmann, Jewish resistance worker in Slovakia.

1795. Čapek, Karel. The White Plague [Play]. London: Oxford University Press, 1951 (1937); by the author of R.U.R.

1796. Chaneles, Sol. Three Children of the Holocaust. New York: Avon, 1974.
      Winner of the 1982 W.H. Smith Literary Award.

1797. Eisner, Jack. The Survivor. New York: Morrow, 1980.

1798. Ember, Mária. Hajtükanyar (The U-Turn). 2 vols. Budapest: Szépirodalmi könyvkiadó, 1977.
      The anguish of deportation for a young boy and his life in a labor camp.

1799a. Epstein, Leslie. King of the Jews. New York: Coward-McCann & Geoghegan, 1979.
       Novel with deep insight into the role of the Judenrat and its members.

1799b. Ezrahi, Sidra D. By Words Alone: The Holocaust in Literature. Chicago: The University of Chicago Press, 1980.

1800a. Fine, Ellen S. Legacy of Night: The Literary Universe of Elie Wiesel. Albany: State University of New York Press, 1982.

1800b. Frank, Anne. Anne Frank's Tales from the Secret Annex. New York: Washington Square Press, 1982.

1801. Friedlander, Albert H., ed. Out of the Whirlwind: A Reader of Holocaust Literature. Garden City, N.Y.: Doubleday, 1968.
      Over thirty essays by well-known and less-known authors.

1802. Fuks, Ladislav. Mr. Theodore Mundstock. New York: Orion, Grossman, 1968.

1803. Glatstein, Jacob, et al., eds. Anthology of Holocaust Literature. New York: Atheneum, 1973.

1804. Green, Gerald. Holocaust: A Novel of Survival and Triumph. New York: Bantam, 1978.
      The novel on which the TV miniseries was based, thus sparking a revival of public interest in the Holocaust.

1805. Grossman, Ladislav. The Shop on Main Street. Garden City, N.Y.: Doubleday, 1970.

1806. Habe, Hans. The Mission. New York: Signet, 1967.

1807. Hersey, John. The Wall. New York: Knopf, 1950.

1808. Heyen, William. The Swastika Poems. New York: Vanguard, 1977.

1809. Hochhuth, Rolf. The Deputy. New York: Grove, 1964.

1810. Hugo, Richard. The Hitler Diaries. New York: Morrow, 1983.

1811. Jacot, Michael. The Last Butterfly. Indianapolis: Bobbs-Merrill, 1974.

1812. Kanfer, Stefan. The Eighth Sin. New York: Random House, 1978.

1813. Karmel, Ilona. An Estate of Memory. Boston: Houghton Mifflin, 1969.

1814. Kiš, Danilo. Garden, Ashes. New York: Harcourt Brace Jovanovich, 1965.

1815. Kosinski, Jerzy. The Painted Bird. New York: Bantam, 1972.

1816. Kugelmass, Jack and Boyarin, Jonathan, eds. From a Ruined Garden, the Memorial Books of Polish Jewry. New York: Schocken, 1983.
        Selections from Yiddish memorial volumes by researchers of the YIVO Institute.

1817. Kuznetsov, Anatoly. Babi Yar. New York: Dell, 1966.

1818. Langer, Lawrence L. The Age of Atrocity: Death in Modern Literature. Boston: Beacon, 1978.

1819. _____. The Holocaust and Literary Imaginaiton. New Haven: Yale University Press, 1975.

1820. Laqueur, Walter. The Missing Years. Boston: Little, Brown, 1979.
        Novel of Jewish life in pre-Hitler Germany. The sequel, Farewell to Europe, is entry 1262.

1821. Levin, Ira. The Boys from Brazil. New York: Dell, 1977.

1822a. Levin, Meyer. Eva: A Novel of the Holocaust. New York: Behrman, 1979.

1822b. Litvinoff, Emanuel. <u>Falls the Shadow</u>. New York: Stein &
       Day, 1983.

1823. Lustig, Arnošt. <u>A Prayer for Katerina Horowitzova</u>. New
       York: Avon, 1975.

1824. _____. <u>Darkness Casts No Shadow</u>. New York: Avon,
       1978.

1825. _____. <u>Diamonds of the Night</u>. Washington, D.C.: In-
       scape, 1978.

1826. _____. <u>Night and Hope</u>. New York: Avon, 1978.

1827. Malaparte, Curzio. <u>Kaput</u>. New York: Dutton, 1946.

1828. _____. <u>Nicht Wahr?</u> New York: Penguin, 1978.

1829. Mann, Erika. <u>The Lights Go Down</u>. New York: Farrar &
       Rinehart, 1940.

1830. Marland, Michael and Willcox, Roben, eds. <u>While They
       Fought: An Anthology of Prose and Verse Exploring the
       Lives of Those Who Did Not Fight, but Who Had to Endure
       the Second World War</u>. London: Longman, 1980.

1831. Morgenstern, Soma. <u>The Third Pillar</u>. New York: Farrar,
       Straus & Cudahy, 1954.

1832. Murray, Michele. <u>The Crystal Nights</u>. New York: Dell,
       1973.

1833. Napora, Paul. <u>Auschwitz</u>. San Antonio, Tex.: Naylor, 1967.
       Poetry.

1834. _____. <u>Death at Belsen</u>. San Antonio, Tex.: Naylor,
       1967.
       Poetry.

1835. Peroutka, Ferdinand. <u>Oblak a valčík (Clouds and a Waltz)</u>.
       Toronto: Sixty-Eight Publishers, 1976.

1836. Rosenfield, Alvin H. <u>A Double Dying: Reflections on Holo-
       caust Literature</u>. Bloomington: Indiana University Press,
       1980.

1837. _____ and Greenberg, Irving, eds. <u>Confronting the Holo-
       caust, the Impact of Elie Wiesel</u>. Bloomington: Indiana
       University Press, 1978.

1838a. Rothenberg, Joshua, ed. <u>And They Will Call Me</u>.... Waltham,

Mass.: Department of Near Eastern and Judaic Studies, Brandeis University, 1982.

1838b. Sachs, Nelly. O the Chimneys. New York: Farrar, Straus & Giroux, 1967.
  Compassionate poetry by one who escaped Holocaust.

1839. Schwarz-Bart, André. The Last of the Just. New York: Atheneum, 1960.

1840. Shaw, Robert. The Man in the Glass Booth: A Drama in Two Acts. New York: Samuel French, 1968.

1841. Skloot, Robert, ed. Theatre of the Holocaust. Madison: University of Wisconsin Press, 1982.
  Includes four plays: Shimon Winkelberg's Resort 76, Harold and Edith Lieberman's Throne of Straw, George Tabori's The Cannibals, and Charlotte Delbo's Who Will Carry the Word?

1842. Steinbeck, John. The Moon Is Down. New York: Viking, 1981.
  Norwegian resistance.

1843. Styron, William. Sophie's Choice. New York: Random House, 1979.

1844. Tomkiewicz, Mina. Of Bombs and Mice. Cranbury, N.J.: A.S. Barnes, 1970.

1845. Uris, Leon. Mila 18. Garden City, N.Y.: Doubleday, 1961.
  Novel of the Warsaw Ghetto uprising.

1846. Wieskopf, Franz C. The Firing Squad. New York: Knopf, 1944.

1847. Wiesel, Elie. Night. New York: Pyramid, 1961.

1848. _____. The Trial of God. New York: Random House, 1979.

1849. _____. Zahmen or the Madness of God, a Play. New York: Random House, 1975.

1850. Wiesenthal, Simon. Max and Helen. New York: Morrow, 1982.
  Based on a true case from the author's Documentation Center.

1851. Wouk, Herman. War and Remembrance. New York: Pocket Books, 1980.

1852a. Wurio, Eva L. To Fight in Silence. New York: Holt, Rinehart & Winston, 1973.

1852b. Yaffe, James. The Voyage of the Franz Joseph. New York: Putnam's, 1970.

1853. Ziemian, Joseph. The Cigarette Sellers of Three Crosses Square. New York: Avon, 1977.

1854. Zimmels, Hirsh J. The Echo of the Holocaust in Rabbinic Literature. New York: KTAV, 1977.

A D D E N D A

Jews and Anti-Semitism

1855. Mendelsohn, Ezra. The Jews of East Central Europe Between
the World Wars. Bloomington: University of Indiana
Press, 1983.

Nazism

1856a. Allen, Peter. The Windsor Secret: New Revelations of the
Nazi Connection. New York: Stein and Day, 1984. British title The Crown and the Swastika: Hitler, Hess and
the Duke of Windsor. London: Robert Hale, 1983.

1856b. Blackburn, Gilmer W. Education in the Third Reich: Race
and History in Nazi Textbooks. Albany: State University
of New York Press, 1984.

1857. Childers, Thomas. The Nazi Voter: The Social Foundations
of Fascism in Germany, 1919-1933. Chapel Hill: University of North Carolina, 1983.

1858. Friedlander, Saul. Reflections on Nazism, an Essay on Kitsch
and Death. New York: Harper & Row, 1984.

1859. Gordon, Sarah. Hitler, Germans, and the "Jewish Question."
Princeton, N.J.: Princeton University Press, 1984.

1860. Henry, Frances. Victims and Neighbors: A Small Town in
Nazi Germany Remembered. South Hadley, Mass.: Bergin
& Garvey, 1984.

1861. Kater, Michael H. The Nazi Party: A Social Profile of Members and Leaders, 1919-1945. Cambridge, Mass.: Harvard
University Press, 1983.

1862. Paine, Lauran. German Military Intelligence in World War II.
       New York: Stein and Day, 1984. British title The Ab-
       wehr. London: Robert Hale, 1984.

1863. Shirer, William L. The Nightmare Years, 1930-1940. Boston:
       Little, Brown, 1984.
           The second volume of memoirs by knowledgeable foreign
       correspondent.

                              Resistance

1864. Burney, Christopher. Solitary Confinement and Dangerous
       Democracy. London: Macmillan, 1983 (1952).
           Two works bound in one volume; deals with Buchen-
       wald, 1942-1944.

1865a. Cruickshank, Charles. SOE in the Far East. New York:
       Oxford University Press, 1983.
           Based on agents' accounts and files; author claims that
       the course of World War II in the Far East could have been
       changed had SOE (Special Operations Executive) been given
       wider powers by British authorities.

1865b. Foot, Michael R.D. SOE 1940-1946. London: B.B.C. Pub-
       lishing Co., 1984.
           European activities of the Special Operations Executive
       by expert scholar.

1866. Hodges, Andrew. Alan Turing: The Enigma, a Biography.
       New York: Simon & Schuster, 1983.
           Biography of Bletchley Park mathematician, highly in-
       strumental in breaking the Enigma code and intellectual
       progenitor of digital computers; written by mathematician.

1867. Kozaczuk, Wladislaw. Enigma: How the German Machine
       Cipher Was Broken and How It Was Read by the Allies in
       World War II. Frederick, Md.: University Publications
       of America, 1984.

1868. Lorain, Pierre. Clandestine Operations: The Arms and
       Techniques of the Resistance, 1941-1944. New York:
       Macmillan, 1983.
           For French original, see entry 718. Translated by
       David Kahn. English title Secret Warfare. London:
       Orbis, 1984.

1869. Pape, Richard. Boldness Be My Friend. London: Granada,
       1984 (1953).

One of best escape histories of World War II from Nazi
prison camps, involving the support of resisters in the
Netherlands, Germany, Poland and Czechoslovakia.

1870. West, Nigel. MI 6, British Secret Intelligence Service Oper-
       ations, 1909-1945. London: Weidenfeld and Nicolson,
       1983.
       History of the British overseas Secret Intelligence
       Service, with emphasis on World War II.

Resistance--Women

1871. Vinke, Herman. The Short Life of Sophie Scholl. New York:
       Harper and Row, 1984.
       Deals with short-lived German student resistance and
       its leader.

Jewish Resistance

1872. Druks, Herbert. Jewish Resistance During the Holocaust.
       New York: Irvington, 1983.

1873. Krakowski, Shmuel. The War of the Doomed: Jewish Armed
       Resistance in Poland, 1942-1944. New York: Holmes &
       Meier, 1984.

Holocaust

1874. Agel, Jerome and Boe, Eugene. Deliverance in Shanghai.
       New York: Dembner Books, 1983.

1875. Bamberger, Ib Nathan. The Viking Jews: A History of the
       Jews of Denmark. New York: Shengold, 1983.

1876. Braham, Randolph L., ed. Contemporary Views on the Holo-
       caust. Hingham, Mass.: Kluwer Nijhoff Publishing, 1983.

1877. Breitowicz, Jakob. Through Hell to Life. New York: Shen-
       gold, 1983.

1878. Browning, Christopher R. Essays on the Emergence of the
       Final Solution. New York: Holmes & Meier, 1984.

1879. Brownlow, Donald Grey and DuPont, John Eleuthere. Hell
       Was My Home: The True Story of Arnold Shay, Survivor
       of the Holocaust. West Hanover, Mass.: Christopher
       Publishing House, 1983.

1880. Dobroszycki, Lucjan, ed. The Chronicle of the Lodz Ghetto,
       1941-1944. New Haven and London: Yale University
       Press, 1984.
            Monumental and unique work; written secretly by a
       group of ghetto residents and now edited by an eyewitness
       who is a YIVO Institute historian.

1881. Friedling, Sheila, ed. The Pit and the Trap. New York:
       Holocaust Library, 1983.

1882. Gruber Ruth. Haven, The Unknown Story of 1,000 World
       War II Refugees. New York: Coward, McCann and
       Geoghegan, 1983.

1883. Hancock, Ian (Yanko le Redžosko). Land of Pain: Five
       Centuries of Gypsy Slavery. Buda, Texas (Box 856):
       International Gypsy Committee, 1982.
            One of the few entries on Gypsy history; includes bib-
       liography.

1884. Hilberg, Raul. The Destruction of the European Jews. 3
       vols. New York: Holmes & Meier, 1984.
            This is revised and definitive edition of entry 1209;
       unabridged, with maps, tables, appendices, bibliography
       and index, 1,000 pp. The same publisher is also prepar-
       ing a general reader's edition of about 400 pages, and a
       student edition of about 350 pages.

1885. Klarsfeld, Serge. Vichy--Auschwitz: Le rôle de Vichy dans
       la solution finale de la question juive en France, 1942.
       Paris: Fayard, 1983.

1886. Leuhter, Sara, ed. Guide to Wisconsin Survivors of the
       Holocaust: A Documentary Project of the Wisconsin Jewish
       Archives. Madison: State Historical Society of Wisconsin,
       1983.

1887. May, Antoinette. Witness to War: A Biography of Margaret
       Higgins. New York: Beaufort Books, 1983.
            Higgins arrived in Dachau before the liberating armies
       in 1945.

1888. Oshry, (Rabbi) Ephraim. Responsa for the Holocaust. New
       York: Judaica Press, 1983.

1889. Pinsker, Sanford and Fischel, Jack, eds. Holocaust Studies

Annual: America and the Holocaust. Greenwood, Fla.: Penkevill, 1984.

1890. Sachar, Abram L. The Redemption of the Unwanted, from the Liberation of the Death Camps to the Founding of Israel. New York: St. Martin's, 1983.

Holocaust--Women

1891. Hillesum, Etty. An Interrupted Life: The Diaries of Etty Hillesum, 1941-1943. New York: Pantheon, 1983.
A woman's search for her identity and her Jewishness before deportation to Auschwitz.

Pre-1945 Knowledge of the Holocaust

1892. Abella, Irving and Troper, Harold. None Is Too Many: Canada and the Jews of Europe, 1933-1948. New York: Random House, 1983.
Deals with Canada's refusal to accept Jewish immigrants before and during World War II.

1893. Penkower, Monty Noam. The Jews Were Expendable: Free World Diplomacy and the Holocaust. Champaign-Urbana: University of Illinois Press, 1983.

War Crimes

1894. Loftus, John. The Belarus Secret. New York: Penguin, 1983.
Revelations about the post-World War II smugglings of hundreds of Nazis out of Europe; contains a 32-page postscript about the case of Klaus Barbie, the "Butcher of Lyons."

1895. MacPherson, Malcolm C. The Blood of His Servants: The True Story of One Man's Search for His Family's Friend and Executioner. New York: Times Books, 1984.
Bibi Krumholz' successful lifetime manhunt for his family's killer--the famous Pieter Menten case.

1896. Sayer, Ian and Botting, Douglas. Nazi Gold: The Story of

the World's Greatest Robbery and Its Aftermath. London:
Granada, 1984.
>   The history of the evacuation and burial of $2.5 billion
>   worth of Reichsbank treasures and foreign currency re-
>   serves to a Bavarian Alpine fortress of Hitler. According
>   to the author, parts fell into the hands of Nazi individuals
>   and of a few American soldiers, but this was covered up
>   by the United States.

1897. Tusa, Ann and Tusa, John. The Nuremberg Trial. London:
Macmillan, 1983.
>   Latest of many books on the subject; based on massive
>   research in Washington archives and British Public Records
>   Office at Kew; compact but well worth the effort of read-
>   ing.

Art and Photographs

1898. American Office of War Information. KZ--Bildbericht aus
fünf Konzentrationslagern. Atlanta: Emory University,
Witness to the Holocaust Project, 1983 (1945).
>   This pictorial document was distributed to German popu-
>   lation in 1945; it shows photographs from Buchenwald,
>   Gardelegen, Ohrdruf, Bergen-Belsen and Nordhausen.
>   Text in German, English and Spanish.

1899. Gursan-Salzmann, Ayse. The Last Jews of Radauti. New
York: Dial, 1983.
>   Significant photographs of a vanished Romanian commu-
>   nity.

1900. Karas, Joza. Music of Terezín. New York: Pendragon, 1984.

1901. Zeman, Zbyněk. Heckling Hitler: Caricatures of the Third
Reich. London: Orbis, 1984.

Philosophy and Interpretation

1902. Katz, Steven T. Post-Holocaust Dialogues: Critical Studies
in Modern Jewish Thought. New York: New York University Press, 1983.

1903. Letgers, Lyman H., ed. Western Society After the Holocaust.
Boulder, Colo.: Westview, 1983.

1904.   Rausch, David A. A Legacy of Hatred: Why Christians
        Must Not Forget the Holocaust. Chicago: Moody, 1984.

Literature

1905.   Bowlby, Alex. Roman Candle. London: Weidenfeld and
        Nicolson, 1983.

1906.   Jünger, Ernst. On the Marble Cliffs. New York: Penguin,
        1984 (1939).

1907.   Ritchie, J.M. German Literature Under National Socialism.
        Totowa, N.J.: Barnes and Noble, 1983.

A U T H O R   I N D E X

References correspond to entry number, not to page number.

Abel, Theodore 92, 93
Abella, Irving 1892
Abells, Chana 1683
Abramov, M. 435
Abramowicz, Zofia 1442
Achille-Delmas, François 94
Ackerman, Nathan W. 1
Adamovich, Ales 436
Adamson, Hans C. 437
Adler, Cyrus 1043
Adler, H.G. 2, 1044, 1045, 1046
Agel, Jerome 1874
Ager, Trygve M. 650
Aichinger, Ilse 1784
Ainsztein, Reuben 954, 955
Alcorn, Robert H. 438
Alexander, Edward 1785
Allen, Peter 1856a
Allen, William S. 95
Alquen, Gunther d' 96
Alsop, Stewart 439
Altschuler, David A. 1047
Ament, Susan 1374
American Association for a
    Democratic Germany 440
American Jewish Committee
    3, 4
American Jewish History As-
    sociation 1048
American Office of War Infor-
    mation 1898
Amery, Jean 1049
Amery, Julian 441
Amicale de Neuengamme 442
Amicale de Ravensbrück 884
Andenes, Johs. 443
Andreas-Friedrich, Ruth 444

Andrews, Allen 1543
Andreyev, V. 445
Andrus, Burton C. 1544
Anger, Per 1050
Apenszlak, Jacob 956, 1051, 1512
Apitz, Bruno 1052
Appelfeld, Aharon 1786
Appleman, John A. 1545
Aptecker, George 1053
Arad, Yitzak 957, 958, 1054
Arendt, Hannah 97, 1546
Arieti, Silvano 1055
Armstrong, John A. 446
Aron, Isaac 1056
Aron, Robert 447
Aronsfeld, Caesar C. 5
Aronson, Gregor 99
Aronson, Shlomo 98
Asher, Sandy 1787
Astrup, Helen 885
Auster, Louis 1246
Ausubel, Nathan 1684
Auty, Phyllis 448, 449
Avni, Haim 7
Ayconberry, Pierre 99
Azanjac, Dušan 450

Bade, Wilfrid 100
Badia, G. 101
Bailly, Jacques C. 451
Bainbridge, Beryl 1788
Baker, Leonard 1057
Banchen, Bernt 452
Balfour, Michael 453
Ballemilla Portuondo, Aurelio
    454
Balicka-Kollowska, Helena 1443

Ball-Kaduri, Kurt J.   8
Bamberger, Ib Nathan   1875
Banas, Josef   9
Bancroft, Mary   886
Barkai, Meyer   959
Barker, Elisabeth   455
Barkley, Alben   1058
Barnard, Jean J.   1076
Bar-Oni, Byrna   1444
Bar-On, Zwi   960
Barrington, J. Harcourt   1547
Barron, L. Smythe   102
Barry, R.H.   456
Barta, František   457
Barton, Allen H.   1732
Bartoš, Antonín   695
Bartoszowski, Wladyslaw   458,
    459, 460, 461, 1059
Baschwitz, Kurt   103
Basok, Moshe   1042
Bauer, Fritz   1548
Bauer, Yehuda   961, 962, 1060,
    1061, 1062, 1063, 1064, 1348,
    1513
Baum, Bruno   462
Baum, Rainer C.   1065
Bauminger, Arieh L.   463
Baxter, Richard   104
Bayle, François   1549
Bazna, Elyesa   464
Bean, Barbara   1576
Beck, Friedrich A.   105
Becker, Howard   106
Beevor, J.G.   466
Begma, Vasilii   465
Belgium. Ministry of Justice
    1550
Bell, Leland V.   107
Bellak, Georgina   887
Bellanger, Claude   467
Beloff, Max   1066
Belth, Nathan C.   10, 11
Benčík, Antonín   468
Bennecke, Heinrich   108
Benneckenstein, Paul M.   109
Bennett, Jeremy   469
Benton, Wilbour E.   1551
Benuzzi, Felice   470
Benze, Rudolf   110
Berben, Paul   471, 472, 1067
Berdych, Václav   473

Berg, Mary   1445
Berger, Alexander   474
Berger, Zdena   1789
Bergh, Siegfried van den   1068
Berkovits, Eliezer   1070, 1733
Berkowitz, Sarah B.   1446
Bergmann, Martin S.   1069
Bernadac, Christian   888, 1071,
    1072, 1073, 1074
Bernadotte, Folke   1075
Bernard, Henri   475, 476, 477,
    478
Bernard, Jean J.   1076
Bertelsen, Aage   479
Bertrand, Simone   889
Besgen, Achim   111
Best, S. Payne   480
Bestic, Alan   1538
Bethell, Nicholas   1552
Bethge, Eberhard   481
Bettelheim, Bruno   1077, 1734,
    1735
Bewley, Charles   112
Beyer, Wilhelm R.   482
Beyerchen, Alan D.   113
Bezwinska, Jadwiga   963, 1078
Bezymenskii, Lev A.   1553
Bial, Morrison D.   964
Bidault, Georges   483
Bielenberg, Christabel   114
Bierman, John   1079
Bilik, Dorothy S.   1790
Billig, Joseph   1080
Binion, Rudolph   115
Birenbaum, Halina   1447
Biss, Andreas   1081
Black, Floyd H.   1082
Blackburn, Gilmer W.   1856b
Blaettler, Franz   1514
Bláha, František   1084
Blair, B.   12
Blair, C.N.M.   484
Blatter, Janet   1685
Blet, Pierre   1085
Bleuel, Hans P.   116
Bley, Wulf   117
Bloch, Charles   118
Bloch, Pierre   485
Bloch, Sam E.   1086
Blum, Howard   1555
Blumenson, Martin   486

Blumenthal, Ilse 1791
Blumenthal, Nachman 965, 1087, 1088
Boe, Eugene 1874
Boehm, Eric H. 966
Boguslawska-Swiebocka, Renata 1686
Bogusz, Josef 487, 1089
Bokun, Branko 488
Bolkonsky, Sidney 119
Bonhoeffer, Dietrich 489, 490
Bor, Josef 1090, 1091
Borden, Carla M. 1220
Borinski, Friedrich 120
Borkin, Joseph 121, 1556
Bor-Komorowski, Tadeusz 491
Bormann, Martin 122
Bornstein, Ernst I. 1092
Borowski, Tadeusz 1792
Borwicz, Michal M. 1093, 1094
Borzkowski, Tuvia 967
Bosanquet, Mary 492
Bosch, William J. 1557
Bosmajian, Hamida 1793
Botting, Douglas 1896
Bourdrel, Philippe 13
Bower, Tom 1558, 1559, 1560
Bowlby, Alex 1905
Bowman, Derek 1095
Boyajian, Dickram H. 1096
Boyarin, Jonathan 1816
Bracher, Karl D. 123
Braden, Thomas 439
Bradley, John 493
Braham, Randolph L. 1097, 1098, 1099, 1100, 1876
Brand, George 1561
Brand, Joel 1101
Brand, Sandra 1496
Brandenburg, Hans C. 124
Braubach, Max 494
Breitowicz, Jakob 1877
Brennan, William 1102, 1103
Brenner, Reeve R. 1736
Breur, Dunya 890
Brickhill, Paul 495, 496
Brinskii, Anton P. 497
Broad, Pery 1104
Bross, Werner 1563
Broszat, Martin 125, 126, 227, 256, 1251

Brown, Anthony C. 498, 499
Browning, Christopher R. 1105, 1878
Brownlow, Donald Grey 1879
Bubeníčková, Růžena 1106
Buber-Neumann, Margarete 891
Bucher, Rudolf 1515
Buchheim, Hans 128, 129, 130
Buchheit, Gert 131
Buchmann, Erika 892
Buckley, Christopher 500
Buckmaster, Maurice 501
Bullock, Alan 132
Burg, J.G. 1107
Bürger, Kurt 502
Burgess, Alan 503
Buriánek, František 504
Burney, Christopher 1864
Busson, Suzanne 893
Butler, Josephine 894
Butler, Rohan D. 133
Butler, Rupert 134, 135, 505
Byrnes, Robert F. 14

Cahen, Fritz M. 506
Cahiers d'Auschwitz 1108
Calvocoressi, Peter 507a, 1564
Cameron, John 1565
Campion, Joan 1448, 1794
Cantril, Hadley 1737
Čapek, Karel 1795
Cargas, Harry J. 1738, 1739
Carr, William 136a
Carré, Mathilde Lily 895
Cecil, Robert 136b
Ceglowska, Teresa 1686
Central Commission for Investigation of German Crimes in Poland 1566
Central Intelligence Agency 507b
Chaim, Bezalel 1109, 1110
Chambard, Claude 508
Chaneles, Sol 1796
Chapman, F. Spenser 509
Charny, Israel W. 1111
Chartok, Roselle 1112
Charvat, Joseph 1113
Chary, Frederick B. 1114
Chatel, Nicole 896
Childers, Thomas 1857

Chauvet, Paul   510
Cholawski, Shalom   968, 969
Choumoff, Pierre S.   1115
Cianfarra, Camille M.   137
Ciechanowski, Jan M.   511, 1516
Clare, George   1116
Clarke, Comer   1117
Clayton, Aileen   897
Cline, Marjorie W.   512a
Clissold, Stephen   512b
Clogg, R.   449
Cobb, Richard   513
Cohen, Arthur A.   1740, 1741
Cohen, Elie A.   1118, 1742
Cohen, Martin A.   15
Cohn, Norman   16, 1119
Collier, Basil   514, 515
Collis, Robert   1120
Colvin, Ian   516
Compton, James V.   138
Cong, Joel   17
Congrès Juif Mondial   1567
Conot, Robert E.   1568a
Conrad, Norton   496
Constanza, Mary S.   1687a
Conway, John S.   139
Cookridge, Edward H.   517, 518, 519
Cooper, Lady Diana   898
Cooper, R.W.   1568b
Cotta, Michèle   520
Cottier, Georges M.M.   521
Couvaras, Costa G.   1687b
Cowburn, Benjamin H.   522
Crankshaw, Edward   140
Crawford, Fred R.   1121
Creel, George   1569
Cruickshank, Charles   523a, 523b, 1865a
Cuddon, Eric   1570
Curtiss, John S.   18
Cvetkova, Nadežda   899
Czech, Danuta   524, 1078, 1122

Dabrowska, Danuta   1123
Dallin, Alexander   141
Dalton, Hugh   525
Dank, Milton   526
Dansette, Adrien   527

Darling, Donald   528
D'Astier, Emmanuel   529
Datner, Szymon   1571
David, Janina   1497
Davidson, Basil   530, 531
Davidson, Eugene   1572
Davies, A.P.   532
Dawidowicz, Lucy S.   1124, 1125, 1743
Deacon, Richard   533, 534
Deakin, Frederick W.   535, 536
Deborin, G.   537
Dedijer, Vladimir   538
Delarbre, Leon   1688
Delarue, Jacques   142
De Lawnay, J.   539
Delbo, Charlotte   1449
Delius, F.C.   1573
Delzell, Charles F.   1126
Demant, Ebbo   1127
Demetz, Hana   1498
Derry, Sam I.   540
Deschner, Gunther   143
Des Pres, Terence   1128
Deuel, Wallace R.   144
Deutsch, Harold C.   145, 541a
Deutschkron, Inge   1129
Devoto, Andrea   147
Dewar, Diana   541b
D'Harcourt, Pierre   542
Diamant, David   970
Diamond, Sandor A.   148
Dicks, Henry V.   149
Diels, Rudolf   150
Dietrich, Otto   151
Dimont, Max I   19
Dimsdale, Joel E.   1130
Dinnerstein, Leonard   20, 1517
Dissman, Willi   152
Distel, Barbara   543
Dixon, Aubrey   544
Djilas, Milovan   545
Dobkowski, Michael N.   153, 1518
Dobroszycki, Lucjan   1123, 1689, 1880
"Docteur X"   1131
Dodd, Martha   155
Dodd, William E.   156
Doležal, Jiří   547, 548
Domanski, Jerzy   1690

Donat, Alexander 1132, 1133
Donovan, John 1134
Dorian, Emil 1135
Dornberg, John 158a, 158b
Dourlein, Pieter 549
Dränger, Guste 1450
Dreyfus, Paul 550
Dribben, Judith S. 1451
Druks, Herbert 1872
Dubois, Josiah E., Jr. 1136
Duboscq, Geneviève 900
Dufurnier, Denise 1452
Du Jinchay, R. 551
Dulles, Allen W. 552, 553
Dunin-Wazowicz, Krzysztof 554
Dunker, Ulrich 21
DuPont, John Eleuthere 1879
Duszak, Stanislav 1137

Eban, Abba 22
Ebeling, Hans 159
Eckart, Dietrich 160
Eckardt, Alice L. 1744
Eckardt, Roy 1744
Eckman, Lester 971
Edgar, Donald 555
Edwards, Robert 556
Eger, Edith E. 1745
Eggers, Reinhold 557
Ehrenberg, Hans P. 1519
Ehrenburg, Ilya 1138
Ehrlich, Blake 558
Ehrmann, František 1139
Eisenberg, Azriel 1140, 1141
Eisner, Jack 1797
Eitinger, L. 1142
Ekart, Antoni 1143a
Elam, Henry 1575
Eliach, Yaffa 1143b
Elkin, Judith L. 23
Elkins, Michael 972
Elling, Hanna 901
Elliot-Bateman, Michael 559
Ember, Mária 1798
Enzor, R.C.K. 161
Epstein, Helen 1144
Epstein, Leslie 1799a
Erdstein, Erich 1576
Eschwege, Helmut 973, 1145, 1691

Espinola, Francisco 560
Esterer, Ingeborg 1146
Eudes, Dominique 561
Evans, A.J. 563
Everett, Susanne 162
Ezrahi, Sidra D. 1799b

Fabre-Luce, Alfred 1577
Fackenheim, Emil L. 24, 1746
Falconi, Carlo 1520
Farago, Ladislas 564, 1578
Faurisson, Robert 1747
Federation of Czechoslovakian Jews 1147
Federation of Jewish Committees in Yugoslavia 1148
Feig, Konnilynn G. 1149
Fein, Erich 1150
Fein, Helen 1151
Feinermann, Emmanuel 1397
Feingold, Henry L. 1521
Feld, Marilla 1499
Felice, Renzo de 1152
Fénelon, Fania 1453
Fenyo, Mario D. 163
Ferderber-Salz, Bertha 1454
Ferencz, Benjamin B. 1579
Fernandez Artucio, Hugo 164
Fest, Joachim C. 165, 166
Fiala, Bohumír 565
Field, Geoffrey C. 25
Fielding, Xan 566
Fine, Ellen S. 1800a
Finker, Moshe 1153
Fischel, Jack 1889
Fischer, Conan 167
Fisher, Jules S. 1154
Fishman, Jack 567, 1580
Fishman, Joshua T. 26
Fishmann, Chuck 1723b
Fitzgibbon, Constantine 568, 1581
Fitzgibbon, Louis 1155
Flannery, Edward H. 27
Fleischner, Eva 1748
Fleming, Peter 168
Flender, Harold 569
Flicke, W.F. 570
Foot, Michael R.D. 571, 572, 573, 574, 1865b
Ford, Corey 575, 576

Forman, James 577
Forssmann, Werner 169
Fourcade, Marie-Madeleine 902
Frackiewicz, J. 1692
Fraenkel, Heinrich 578, 579,
    727, 728, 1287
Fraenkel, Josef 1156
France. Service d'Information
    des Crimes de Guerre 1582
Francos, Ania 903
Franěk, Rudolf 1157
Frank, Anne 1500, 1800b
Frank, Hans 1583
Frank, Volker 1693a
Frankl, Victor E. 1158, 1749
Frenay, Henri 580
Friedlander, Albert H. 1159,
    1801
Friedlander, Henry 1160, 1161
Friedländer, Saul 170, 1162,
    1522, 1750, 1858
Friedlander, W. 171
Friedling, Sheila 1881
Friedman, Ina R. 1163
Friedman, Philip 974, 1164,
    1165, 1166, 1167, 1349
Friedman, Saul S. 1168, 1523
Friedman, Tuviah 1584
Frisby, Julian 453
Frischauer, Will 172, 581
Fromm, Bella 1501
Fromm, Erich 1751
Frommhold, E. 1693b
Frumkin, Jacob 28
Frye, Alton 173
Fuchik, Julius 582
Fuchs, Gottlieb 583
Fuchs, Lawrence 29
Fuks, Ladislav 1802
Fuller, Jean O. 584, 585, 904,
    905, 906
Fyfe, David M. 1585
Fyodorov, A. 586

Gabor, Georgia M. 1455
Galante, Pierre 587
Gallagher, J.P. 588
Gallagher, Richard 1586
Gallagher, Thomas 589
Gallin, Mary A. 590
Gallo, Max 174

Gangulee, Nagendranath 175
Gans, Mozes H. 1694a
Garcia, Max 1169
Gardiner, Muriel 907
Gardner, K. 591
Garfinkels, Betty 1170
Garlinski, Jozef 592, 593, 594,
    595
Garrett, Richard 596, 597
Gasman, Daniel 176
Geehr, Richard S. 30
Geisel, Erika 1456
Geraghty, Tony 598
Gersdorff, Ursula von 177
Gershon, Karen 1171
Gerz, Jochen 1172
Geve, Thomas 1173
Gibinski, H. 1174
Gilbert, G.M. 1587
Gilbert, Martin 1175, 1176,
    1524, 1694b
Gilboa, Yehoshua A. 31, 1177
Gilchrist, Andrew 599
Gillman, Peter and Leni 1178
Gisevius, Hans B. 178, 600
Giskes, H.J. 601
Gjelsvik, Tore 602
Glassman, Bernard 32
Glassman, Samuel 33
Glatstein, Jacob 1803
Glieder, Mikhail 603
Glock, Charles 1588
Gluck, Gemma La Guardia 1457
Glueck, Sheldon 1589, 1590
Goddard, Donald 604
Goebbels, Joseph 179, 1591
Goldberg, Izaac 62, 1179
Goldberg, Michel 1180
Goldstein, Bernard 1181
Goldstein, Charles 975
Goldstein, David 976
Goldston, Robert C. 180, 1182
Gollwitzer, Helmut 1183
Gordon, Bertram M. 605
Gordon, Harold J. 181
Gordon, Sarah 1859
Gossens, Hector 606
Gostner, Erwin 1184 /
Gottlieb, Malke 1695
Gottlieb, Moshe R. 977
Graber, G.S. 182, 183, 607, 608

Graml, Hermann   609
Grant, Myrna   1458
Graupe, Heinz M.   34
Gray, Martin   1185
Gray, Ronald   184
Green, Gerald   1696, 1804
Greenberg, Irving   1837
Griffin, Susan   1752
Grimm, George   1551
Grinberg, Natan   1186
Grobman, Alex   1187
Gross, Leonard   1188
Grosser, George M.   1753
Grosshans, Henry   185
Grossman, Chaike   978
Grossman, Ladislav   1805
Grossman, Mendel   1697
Grossman, Vasily   1138, 1189
Groves, Leslie   610
Gruber, Ruth   1882
Gruber, Samuel   979
Grudzinska-Gross, Irena   611
Grunberger, Richard   186, 187
Grünewald, Paul   612
Grunfeld, Frederic V.   188
Gryn, Edward   1190
Grzesinski, Albert C.   189
Grzesiuk, Stanislaw   1191
Gueguen-Dreyfus, Georgette
   613
Gumkowski, J.   1192
Gun, Nerin E.   190, 1193
Gurdus, Luba K.   1502
Gurian, Waldemar   191
Gursan-Salzmann, Ayse   1899
Guterman, Norbert   54
Gutman, Yisrael (Israel)   980,
   981, 982, 1194a, 1194b
Gutteridge, Richard   983

H., Janka   1459
Haag, Lina   908
Haas, Gerda S.   1460
Habe, Hans   1806
Hackett, John W.   614
Haesler, Alfred A.   1195
Haestrup, Jørgen   615, 616,
   617
Haffner, Sebastian   192
Hahlweg, W.   618
Hájková, Dagmar   909

Hajšman, Jan   619
Hale, Oron J.   193
Hallie, Philip   620
Halperin, Irving   1196
Hamilton, James D.   194
Hamilton, Richard F.   195
Hamilton-Hill, Donald   621
Hamlin, David   196
Hamšík, Dušan   622
Hamson, Denys   623
Hanák, Vladimír   624
Hancock, Ian   1883
Handler, Andrew   1197
Hanfstaengl, Ernst   197, 198
Hanser, Richard   199, 625
Hanusiak, Michael   1198
Hardman, Leslie H.   1199
Harel, Isser   1592
Harris, Whitney A.   1593
Hart, Kitty   1461, 1462
Hartman, Abraham   1200
Hartshorne, Edward Y.   200
Hastings, Max   626
Haukelid, Knut   627
Hauner, Milan   201
Hausner, Gideon   1594
Hay, Malcolm   35
Hayes, Carlton, J.H.   628
Hayes, Paul M.   202
Heartfield, John   1698
Heger, Heinz   1201
Heiber, Helmut   203, 204, 205
Heiden, Konrad   206, 207
Heilbrunn, Otto   544, 629
Heilbut, Anthony   1202
Heilig, Bruno   630
Heimler, Eugene   1203
Heller, Celia S.   36
Hellman, Peter   631, 1699
Henry, Clarissa   1204
Henry, Frances   1860
Herling, Gustav   1205
Herman, Jan   1700
Herrmann, Lazar   1206
Herrmann, Simon H.   1207
Hersey, John   1807
Hersh, Gizelle   1463
Herwarth von Bittenfeld, Hans
   H.   208
Herzstein, Robert E.   209, 210,
   211

Hess, Ilse 1595
Heston, Leonard L. 212
Heydrich, Lina 1596
Heyen, William 1808
Heyman, Eva 1464
Heymont, Irving 1208
Hilberg, Raul 1209, 1210,
    1211, 1884
Hillel, Marc 1204
Hillesum, Etty 1891
Hillgruber, Andreas 213
Hilton, Stanley E. 214
Hinsley, F.H. 632
Hirsch, Phil 215
Hirschfeld, G. 1212
Hirschman, Ira A. 984, 985
Hirshaut, Julien 1213
Hitler, Adolf 216, 217, 218,
    219, 220
Hochhuth, Rolf 1809
Hochmuth, Ursel 633
Hodges, Andrew 1866
Hoettl, Wilhelm 634, 986
Hofer, Walter 221
Hoffmann, Heinrich 222, 223,
    314
Hoffmann, Peter 635, 636
Höhne, Heinz 224, 637
Holmes, Colin 37
Holub, Ota 638, 639
Homze, Edward L. 225
Horbach, Michael 640
Hořec, Jaromír 1701
Horn, Wolfgang 226
Horney, Karen 1754
Hornsay, Denis D.F.C. 910
Horowitz, Irving L. 1215,
    1755
Horton, Dick 641
Hory, Ladislaus 227
Hossbach, Friedrick 228
Hostache, René 642
Houskova, Hana 911
Howarth, David 643, 644
Howarth, Patrick 645, 646
Howe, George 647
Howell, Edgar M. 648
Howes, Stephen 649
Hoye, Bjarne 650
Hugo, Richard 1810
Hunt, Antonia 912

Hurewitz, Jacob C. 38
Husák, Gustav 651
Hutak, J.B. 652
Huttenbach, Henry R. 1465
Hutton, Joseph B. 229
Hyams, Joseph 1216
Hyde, H. Montgomery 653, 913
Hymers, R.L. 1217

Ignatov, P. 654
Igra, Samuel 230
Ihlau, Olaf 655
Infield, Glenn B. 231, 1597
Insdorf, Annette 1702
Institute of Jewish Affairs 1598
International Committee of Red
    Cross 1218, 1219
International Military Tribunal
    1599, 1600
Internazionale Fäderation der
    Widerstandkämpfer 656
Iranek-Osmecki, George 657
Iranek-Osmecki, Kazimierz 658
Irving, David 232, 233
Isaac, Jules 39
Israel, Fred L. 1525
Ivanov, Miroslav 659
Ivanov, V.V. 854

Jackman, Jarrell C. 1220
Jackson, Daphne 914
Jackson, Livia E. 1466
Jackson, Robert 581
Jackson, Robert H. 1601
Jacot, B.L. 885
Jacot, Michael 1811
Jahoda, Maria 1
Jakuse, Ruth 543
Janovská, Jarmila 915
Janowitz, Morris 1735
Jansen, Jon 234
Jaspers, Karl 1756
Jaspers, Marc 1602
Jaworski, Leon 1603
Jenks, William A. 235
Jewish Anti-Fascist Committee of
    the U.S.S.R. 1221
Jocz, Jakob 1757
Joffo, Joseph 1222
Joffroy, Pierre 660
John, Otto 661

Johnpoll, Bernard K. 41
Johns, Philip 662
Jones, Reginald V. 663, 664
Jones, W.M. 665
Jong, Louis de 236a, 666,
    667, 668
Jour, Jean 1703
Jucovy, Milton E. 1069
Julitte, Pierre 669
Jünger, Ernst 1906

Kahanovich, Moshe 987
Kahn, Albert 343
Kahn, David 236b
Kahn, Leo 1604
Kalb-Beller, Zalek 1223
Kamenetsky, Ihor 237, 238,
    670
Kaminska, Ruth T. 1503
Kanfer, Stefan 1812
Kantor, Alfred 1704
Karas, Joza 1900
Karmel, Ilona 1813
Kárný, Miroslav 1224
Karov, D. 671
Karski, Jan 672, 1526
Kastner, Rudolph 673
Kater, Michael H. 1861
Katsh, Abraham I. 1225
Katz, Alfred 988
Katz, Jacob 42, 43, 44
Katz, Joseph 1226
Katz, Robert 674, 1227
Katz, Steven T. 1902
Ka-Tzetnik 1228, 1467
Kazasov, Dimo 1229
Keegan, John 239
Kehr, Helen 240
Kelley, Douglas M. 1605
Kempner, Benedicta M. 916
Kempner, Robert M.W. 1606
Kempowski, Walter 241
Keneally, Thomas 1230
Kenrick, Donald 1231
Kent, George O. 242, 1607
Kernish, Joseph 965
Kersten, Felix 243
Kersten, Jakob 675
Kessel, Joseph 244
Kessel, Sim 1232
Kessler, Harry Graf 245

Kiedrzynska, Wanda 917a, 1233
Kielar, Wieslaw 1234
Kielmansegg, Johann A. 246
Killinger, Manfred von 247
Kinnaird, Clark 1235
Kintner, Earl W. 1608, 1609,
    1610
Kirkpatrick, Clifford 248
Kirschenblatt-Gimblett, Barbara
    1689
Kiš, Danilo 1814
Kisch, Guido 45
Klarsfeld, Beate 1611, 1612
Klarsfeld, Serge 1885
Klausner, Carla L. 80
Klein, Alexander 676
Klein, Françoise 677
Klein, Gerda W. 1236, 1504
Klem, Per 437
Klönne, Arno 678a
Klose, Werner 249
Kluger, Ruth 989
Knapp, Stefan 1237
Knieriem, August von 1613a
Knight, Frida 678b
Knight-Patterson, W.M. 250
Knoop, Hans 1613b
Knout, David 990
Koch-Kent, Henri 679
Kochan, Lionel 46, 47, 1288
Kocwa, Eugenia 917b
Koehl, Robert L. 251
Koehn, Ilse 1505
Koenigsberg, Richard A. 252
Koeves, Tibor 253
Kogon, Eugen 680
Kohak, Erazim 1470
Kohn, Hans 254
Kohn, Moshe 991
Kohn, Murray J. 1239
Kohn, Nahum 992
Kolb, Eberhard 1240
Komité der antifaschistischen
    Widerstandskämpfer in der
    DDR 681, 682
Komjathy, Anthony 255
Konopka, Vladimír 683
Kopecky, Lilli 1468
Korbonski, Stefan 685
Korczak, Janusz 1242, 1243
    (see also 1216, 1305, 1406)

Korman, Gerd 1244
Kortchak, Roika 993
Koscielnicka, Mieczyslawa 1705
Kosinski, Jerzy 1815
Kostková, Zdenka 1414
Košutová, Olga 1469
Kousoulas, D. George 686
Kovaly, Heda 1470
Kovpak, Sidor A. 687
Kowalski, Isaac 994
Kozaczuk, Wladislaw 1867
Krakowski, Shmuel 1873
Kramarz, Joachim 688
Kranitz-Sanders, Lillian 1245
Krantz, Morris 1246
Kranzler, David 1247
Kraus, Ota 1248, 1249, 1250
Krausnick, Helmut 256, 1251
Krebs, Albert 257
Krejčí, Sylva and Oskar 689
Kren, George M. 1252
Křen, Jan 548
Krispyn, Egbert 690
Krüger, Horst 258
Kruse, Falco 1614
Kruuse, Jens 691
Krylová, Libuše 692
Krystal, Henry 1758
Kubizek, August 259
Kublin, Hyman 48
Kuehnl, Reinhard 260
Kugelmass, Jack 1816
Kühnrich, Heinz 693, 1253,
    1615, 1616
Kulišová, Táňa 1706
Kulka, Erich 1248, 1249, 1250,
    1254
Kulkielko, Renya 1506
Kulski, Julian E. 694
Kuna, Milan 1707, 1708
Kunc Radimír 695
Kuper, Jack 1255
Kuper, Leo 1256
Kurzman, Dan 995
Kuznetsov, Anatoly 1817
Kyzya, Luke 465

Lacaze, André 696
Lachs, Manfred 1257
Lackó, Miklós 261
Lafitte, François 1258

Lagus, Karel 1259
Lamb, Max 1617
Lambert, Gilles 996
Lampe, David 697
Land, Barbara M. 262
Landes, Daniel 1187
Lang, Daniel 263
Lang, Jochen von 264, 1618
Langbein, Hermann 1619
Langelaan, George 698
Langer, Lawrence L. 1260,
    1818, 1819
Langer, Walter C. 265
Langhoff, Wolfgang 699
Langley, James M. 574, 700
Langmaid, Janet 240
Lánik, Jožko 1261a
Lapide, Pinchas 1261b
Laqueur, Walter Z. 266, 701,
    702, 1262, 1263, 1527, 1820
Larsen, Stein U. 267
Laska, Vera 918, 919, 1471
Latour, Anny 997
Lavi, Theodore 998
Lazar, Auguste 1709
Lazar, Chaim 971, 999
Lazar-Litai, Chaim 1000
Leasor, James 703, 704
Leber, Annelore 705
Leboucher, Fernande 706
Lebzelter, Gisela 50
Le Chêne, Evelyn 707, 708
Lederer, Zdenek 1264
Lee, A.S.G. 709
Leiser, Clara 336
Leitner, Isabella 1472
Lem, Salvatore S.L. 1620
Lemkin, Raphael 268
Lemmer, Ernst 710
Lend, Evelyn 711
Lengyel, Olga 1473
Leschnitzer, Adolf 51
Leslau, Wolf 52
Leslie, Anita 920
Leslie, Peter 712
Lester, Eleonore 1265
Letgers, Lyman H. 1903
Leuhter, Sara 1886
Leuner, Heinz D. 713
Lévai, Jenö 1266, 1267, 1268,
    1269, 1270

Levenstein, Aaron 1271
Leverkuehn, Paul 714
Levi, Primo 1272, 1273, 1274, 1275, 1276
Levin, Don 960
Levin, Ira 1821
Levin, J. 461
Levin, Meyer 1822a
Levin, Nora 1277
Levy, Alan 1621
Levy, Claude 1278
Levy, Richard S. 269
Levy-Hass, Hanna 1474
Lewin, Ronald 715
Lewin, Zofia 1059
Lewinska, Pelagia 1475
Lewis, John R. 1622
Lewy, Guenter 270
Lichtenstein, Heiner 1623
Liddell Hart, Basil H. 271
Liebman, Marcel 1279
Liègeois, Constance 1476
Lilge, Frederic 272
Lingens-Reiner, Ella 1477
Linn, Edward 1010
Lipgens, Walter 716
Liptzin, Solomon 1280
Littell, Franklin H. 1281, 1282, 1376
Litten, Irmgard 921
Littlefield, Franklin H. 1376
Littlejohn, David 717
Litvinoff, Emanuel 1822b
Locke, Hubert G. 1282
Loftus, John 1894
Lorain, Pierre 718, 1868
Lorant, Stefan 719, 1710
Lorit, Sergius C. 720
Low, Alfred D. 53
Lowenthal, Leo 54
Lowenthal, Marvin 55
Löwenthal, Richard 721
Lower Saxony. Ministry of Interior 1283
Lowrie, Donald A. 1284
Lubetkin, Zivia 1478
Ludecke, Kurt G. 273
Ludwig, Carl 1528
Lustig, Arnošt 1823, 1824, 1825, 1826

Maas, Peter 1285
MacBain, Alistair 576
Macek, Vladko 722
Machlejd, Wanda 922, 1286
Macintosh, Charles 723
MacPherson, Malcolm C. 1895
Macksey, K.J. 274, 724
Maclaren, Roy 725
McMillan, James 675
Malaparte, Curzio 1827, 1828
Malitz, Horst 275
Malý, Jaromír 726
Manchester, William 1625a
Mann, Erika 276, 1829
Mann, Gertrude 1771
Mann, Peggy 989, 1463
Manning, Paul 277
Manwell, Roger 278, 279, 727, 728, 1287
Margalith, Aaron M. 1043
Mark, Bernard 1001, 1002
Marland, Michael 1830
Marr, Wilhelm 56
Marrus, Michael R. 1288
Maršálek, Hans 1289, 1290
Marshall, Bruce 729
Marton, Kati 1291
Maser, Werner 280, 281, 1625b
Mason, Henry L. 1626
Mason, Herbert M.J. 730
Massing, Paul W. 57, 731
Masson, Madeleine 923
Masterman, J.C. 732
Masters, Anthony 1003
Mastný, Vojtěch 733
Matanle, Ivor 1711
Matussek, Paul 1760
Matusiak, Tadeusz 734
Maugham, Viscount 1627
Maurel, Micheline 924
May, Antoinette 1887
May, Harry S. 58
Mayer, Milton 282
Mayerhofer, Emma 925
McGarry, Michael B. 1759
McGovern, James 283
McGovern, William M. 284
McKale, Donald M. 285, 286
Mechanicus, Philip 1292
Meed, Vladka 1004
Meinecke, Friedrich 1761

Melchior, Marcus 735
Melezin, Abraham 1293
Melichar, Jozef 726
Melodia, Giovanni 1294
Meltzer, Milton 1295
Mendelsohn, Ezra 1855
Mendelsohn, John 1296
Mendelssohn, Peter 1628
Mendes-Flohr, Paul R. 59
Merkl, Peter H. 287, 288
Merle, Marcel 1629
Mermelstein, Mel 1297
Meyer, Gertrude 952
Meyer, Peter 60
Meyers, Earl D. 171
Miale, Florence 1630a
Michaelis, Meir 61
Michel, Henri 736, 737, 738, 739, 740, 741, 1433
Michel, Jean 742
Michelson, Frida 1479
Mid-European Law Project (Bulgaria) 1298
Mielke, Fred 1299
Milch, Werner 120
Miller, Russell 743
Milton, Sybil 1161, 1685
Minco, Marga 1507
Minney, Rubeigh J. 1480
Mirchuk, Petro 1005
Mitchell, Otis C. 289, 290
Mitrani, Thérèse 926
Mitscherlich, Alexander and Margareta 1299, 1762
Mlotek, Chana 1695
Moczarski, Kazimierz 1300
Molden, Fritz 744
Molho, Michael 1301
Mollo, Andrew 291
Monneray, Henri 1302, 1303
Monnerjahn, Engelbert 1304
Moravec, František 745
Moreau, Emilienne 927
Morgenstern, Soma 1831
Morley, John F. 1529
Morse, Arthur D. 1530
Mortkowitz-Olczakowa, Hanna 1305
Moskin, Marietta 1481
Moskovitz, Sarah 1306
Moss, W. Stanley 746

Mosse, George L. 86, 292, 293, 294, 295, 296
Moulin, Jean 747
Moulin, Laure 748
Moulis, Miloslav 749
Mountfield, David 750
Moyzisch, L.C. 751
Mühlen, Patrick von 721
Müller, Filip 1307
Munske, Hilde 297
Murawska, Zofia 1190
Mure, David 752
Murphy, Brendan 1630b
Murphy, Paul I. 1531
Murray, Michele 1832
Muser, Erna 928
Musiol, Theodor 1308
Musmanno, Michael A. 1309
Muszkat, M. 1006, 1631
Myerson, Abraham 62
Nagy-Talavera, Nicholas M. 298
Napora, Paul 1833, 1834
Nansen, Odd 753
Naumann, Bernd 1310, 1632
Neave, Airey 754, 755, 930, 1633
Neher, André 1763
Neugroschel, Joachim 63
Neuhäusler, Johann 299, 1311
Neuman, Judith S. 1482
Neumann, Franz 300
Neumann, Inge S. 1634
Neumann, Oskar 1483
Neumann, Peter 301
Neumann, Yirmayahu O. 1312
Neusner, Jacob 1313, 1764
Newmann, Robert 1712
Nicholas, Elisabeth 931
Niemoeller, Martin 1765
Niewyk, Donald L. 64, 65
Nir, Akiva 1007
Nirenstein, Albert 1008
Noakes, Jeremy 302
Noble, Iris 1635
Nogby, Hans 464
Noguères, Henri 756
Nohejl, Miloslav 757
Noireau, Robert 758
Nokleby, Berit 794
Nolte, Ernst 303

Norborg, Sverre 1766
Norton, Conrad 496
Novac, Anna 932
Novák, Václav 1314, 1713a
Novick, Peter 759
Novitch, Miriam 1009, 1315,
   1316, 1713b
Nowak, Jan 760
Nuremberg Military Tribunals
   1636
Nyiszli, Miklós 1317

Oberski, Jona 1318
O'Donnell, James P. 304
Olden, Rudolf 305
Olsen, Jack 1637
Orlow, Dietrich 306, 307, 308
Orska, Irena 933
Oshry, (Rabbi) Ephraim 1888
Ossendorf, Karel 1767
Ourisson, Dounia 934
Outze, Børge 761
Overduin, Jacobus 1319

Paine, Lauran 1862
Papanek, Ernst 1010
Pape, Richard 1869
Papen, Franz von 309
Paris, Edmond 1320
Parsons, William S. 1390
Passmore, Richard 762
Passy, Colonel (André de Wav-
   rin) 763
Patai, Raphael 66, 67
Pawleczynska, Anna 1768
Pawlowicz, Sala 1484
Paxton, Robert O. 1288, 1321
Payne, Robert 310
Pearl, Cyril 1322
Pearson, Michael 764
Pech, Karlheinz 765
Pechel, Rudolf 766
Peck, Abraham J. 1769
Penkower, Monty Noam 1893
Pergner, Edward 767
Perl, Gisella 1485
Perl, William R. 1011
Pearlman, Moshe 1638
Peis, Gunther 425
Perlmutter, Nathan 68
Perlmutter, Ruth Ann 68

Peroutka, Ferdinand 1835
Perrault, Giles 768
Persen, Mirko 769
Persico, Joseph 770
Pestouric, Roger 771
Peterson, Edward N. 311
Petrow, Richard 772
Phillips, Raymond 1639
Picard, Henri 773
Picard, Max 312
Picker, Henry 313, 314
Picket-Wicks, Eric 774
Pignatelli, Luigi 1323
Pilch, Judah 1324
Pilzer, Jay M. 69
Pinsker, Sanford 1889
Pinson, Koppel S. 315
Piotrowski, Stanislaw 316
Pisar, Samuel 1325
Plant, Richard 1326
Platner, Geert 317
Polák, Josef 1259
Polakiewicz, Moshe 956
Polevoi, Boris I. 1640
Poliakov, Leon 1327, 1328, 1329
Polish Government in Exile 1641
Pollins, Harold 70
Ponomarenko, P.K. 775
Pool, James 318
Pool, Susanne 318
Poole, Kenyon E. 319
Popov, Duško 776
Pore, Renate 320
Porter, Jack N. 71, 1012, 1330a,
   1330b
Prager, Moshe 1013
Prati, Pino da 1331
Pravan, V. 777
Pražák, Jiří 622
Presser, Jacob 1332
Pridham, Geoffrey 302
Procop, C.S. 1333
Pritte, Terence 778
Pross, Harry 321
Proudfoot, Malcolm J. 1334
Pryce-Jones, David 1714
Pulzer, Peter G.J. 72
Pünter, Otto 779
Puxon, Grattan 1231

Quarrie, Bruce 322

Quaytman, Wilfred 1770

Rabinowitz, Dorothy 1335, 1336
Rabinsky, Leatrice 1771
Radó, Sándor 780
Radomska-Strzemecka, Helena
    1428
Raeder, Erich 323
Ramati, Alexander 781, 1337,
    1338
Rappaport, Leon H. 1252
Rashke, Richard 1014
Rassimier, Paul 1339
Rausch, David A. 1904
Rauschning, Hermann 782,
    783, 784
Ravine, Jacques 1015
Raynolds, Quentin 1643
Rector, Frank 1340
Reder, Rudolf 1341
Reed, Douglas 324
Rees, J.R. 325
Régis, Roger 785
Reichmann, Eva G. 326
Reid, Miles 786
Reid, P.R. 787, 788
Reiner, Ella L. 1486
Reinharz, Jehuda 59, 73
Reiss, Johanna 1508
Reitlinger, Gerald R. 327,
    328, 1342
Remak, Joachim 329
Renault-Roulier, Gilbert 789,
    790, 791, 792
Reznikoff, Charles 1343
Rezzori, Gregor von 74
Rhodes, Anthony 1532
Rhodes, James M. 330
Ribbentrop, Joachim 331
Rich, Norman 332
Riess, Curt 333
Ringelblum, Emmanuel 1344,
    1345
Rings, Werner 793
Riste, Olav 794
Ristic, Dragica N. 795
Ritchie, J.M. 1907
Ritter, Gerhard 796
Roberts, Stephen H. 334
Roberts, Walter R. 797a
Robinson, Jacob 1346, 1347,

1348, 1349, 1350, 1644, 1645
Robinson, Nehemiah 75
Roblin, Michael 76
Roehm, Ernst 335
Roelfzema, Erik Hazenhoff 797b
Rogers, Lindsay 798
Roiter, Howard 992, 1351
Rolnikasová, Maria 1487
Roon, Ger van 799
Roosevelt, Kermit 800
Rootham, Jasper 801
Roper, Edith 336
Rose, Anna 1016
Rose, Leesha 1017
Rose, Peter I. 1352
Rosen, Donia 935
Rosenbaum, Irving J. 1353
Rosenberg, Alfred 337, 338
Rosenfeld, Harvey 1354
Rosenfield, Alvin H. 1836, 1837
Ross, Robert W. 1533
Rossel, Seymour 91, 1355
Rotenstreich, Nathan 1064
Roth, Günther 1646
Roth, John K. 1772
Rothbart, Markus 1356
Rothchild, Sylvia 1357
Rothenberg, Joshua 1838a
Rothfels, Hans 802, 803
Rothkirchen, Livia 1194, 1358,
    1359
Rothschild, Guy de 1018
Roussell, Aage 804
Rousset, David 805
Roxan, David 339
Rubenstein, Richard L. 1773,
    1774
Rubin, Arnold P. 1360
Rubinstein, Erna 1509
Rückerl, Adalbert 1361, 1647
Rudnicky, K.S. 806
Rupp, Leila J. 262
Russell of Liverpool, Lord 1648a
Rutheford, Ward 1362
Rutkowski, A. 1192
Ryan, Allan A. Jr. 1648b
Ryan, Michael D. 1363

Sabille, Jacques 1328
Sachar, Abram L. 1890
Sacher, Howard M. 77

Sachs, Henry 1350, 1645
Sachs, Nelly 1838b
Sagitz, Walter 340
Saint Claire, Simone 936
Salomon, Charlotte 1715a
Salomon, Ernst von 1649
Salus, Grete 937, 1488
Salvesen, Sylvia 938
Samuel, Maurice 1775
Samuels, Gertrude 1019
Sandberg, Moshe 1364
Sandel, J. 1715b
Sanders, Marion K. 341
Sandilands, John 946b
Sanford, Harry 1617
Sanguedolce, Joseph 807
Sapfirov, Nikolai N. 808
Saralvo, Corrado 809
Sartre, Jean-Paul 78
Sassoon, Agnes 1489
Sautter, Reinhold 342
Savitski, M.A. 1716a
Sayer, Ian 1896
Sayers, Michael 343
Schacht, Hjalmar 344
Schafranov, Sofia 1490a
Schappes, Morris U. 79
Schaul, Dora 811
Schätzle, Julius 810
Schellenberg, Walter 812
Schirach, Baldur von 345
Schlabrendorff, Fabian von
    813, 814
Schlamm, Vera 1290b
Schleunes, Karl A. 1365a
Schmidt, Diether 1716b
Schmidt, Paul 346
Schmitthenner, Walter A. 815
Schnabel, Reimund 347
Schneider, Gertrude 1020
Schoenbaum, David 348
Schoenberner, Gerhard 1365b
Schoenbrun, David 816
Scholl, Inge 817
Schramm, Hanna 1366a
Schramm, Wilhelm von 818
Schreieder, Joseph 819
Schultz, Joseph 80
Schulz, Sigrid 349
Schuschnigg, Kurt von 350
Schuster, Kurt G.P. 820

Schutz, Wilhelm W. 821
Schwarberg, Günther 1366b
Schwartz, Mary 1400
Schwartz, Paul 351
Schwarz, Leo W. 1367
Schwarz, Solomon 81
Schwarz-Bart, André 1839
Schweitzer, Arthur 352
Scott, William E. 822
Seaton, Albert 354
Seabury, Paul 353
Sehn, Jan 1368
Seibert, Theodore 356
Selzer, Michael 1369, 1630a
Semprun, Jorge 1370
Senesh, Hannah 1022
Sereny, Gitta 1650
Sergueiew, Lily 939
Seth, Ronald 357, 823
Seton-Watson, Hugh 824
Shabbetai, K. 1371
Shapell, Nathan 1372
Shapkó, Yekaterina N. 825
Sharf, Andrew 1534
Sharnik, Alexei Z. 1373
Shaw, Robert 1840
Sherman, A.J. 1023
Sherwin, Byron 1374
Shirer, William L. 358, 359,
    360, 1863
Shub, Boris 1535
Shulman, Abraham 1375, 1717a
Shur, Irene 1376
Siegal, Aranka 1491
Siemer, Pat 361
Silianoff, Eugene 587
Silkin, S.C. 1652
Šima, Ladislav 826
Simonov, Constantin 1377
Sington, Derrick 1378
Skidmore, Ian 827
Skloot, Robert 1841
Skorzeny, Otto 362
Slabý, Z.K. 767
Sleeman, Colin 1651, 1652
Smith, Bradley F. 363, 364,
    828, 1653, 1654
Smith, Marcus J. 1379
Smith, R. Harris 829
Smith, Ronald G. 883
Smolen, Kazimierz 830, 831,
    1380, 1381

Turkow, Jones 1406
Turner, Don 851
Turner, Henry A. Jr.   402
Tusa, Ann 1897
Tusa, John 1897
Tushnet, Leonard 1407, 1408
Tyrell, Albrecht 403

Ungar, Otto 1721
Unger, Michael 404
Union of American Hebrew Con-
    gregations 1722
United Nations 1661, 1662,
    1663
U.S. Army 1409, 1410
U.S. Congress 1664, 1665
U.S. Department of the Army
    852, 1666a
U.S. Military Tribunal 1666b
U.S. National Archives 1667a,
    1667b, 1668
U.S. Office of the Judge Ad-
    vocate 1669
U.S. Office of Strategic Serv-
    ices 1536
U.S. Office of War Information
    1723a
U.S. War Refugee Board 1537
Uris, Leon 1845

Vago, Bela 86
Van der Post, Laurens 853
Van Riet, Victor 1411
Vaneck, Ludo 1412
Vaughan, Elisabeth H. 1778
Vechtomova, E.A. 854
Veillon, Dominique 855
Verity, Hugh B. 856
Vershigora, Pavlo 857
Veselý-Štainer, Karel 858
Viereck, Peter 405
Vinecour, Earl 1723b
Vinke, Herman 1871
Vinocour, Jack 1034
Vinokurov, Joseph 1413
Vishniak, Roman 1724, 1725
Volanská, Hela 944
Volavková, Hana 1726, 1727
Volz, Hans 406a
Von der Lühe, Irmgard 945
Von Hassel, Ulrich 859a

Von Staden, Wendelgard 406b
Votoček, Otakar 1414
Voute, Peter 859b
Vrba, Rudolf 1538

Waagener, Sam 860
Wachsman, Z.H. 87
Wagner, Jonathan F. 407
Wagner, Ludwig 408
Waite, Robert G.L. 409, 410
Walker, Lawrence D. 411
Wallimann, Isidor 153
Walter, Eugene V. 861
Walther, Herbert 412
Wanstall, Ken 339
Ward, Donna I. 946a
Warlimont, Walter 413
Warmbrunn, Werner 862
Warner, Lavinia 946b
Warner, Philip 863
Washington Post Editors 1415
Wasserstein, Bernard M.J.
    1220, 1539
Webb, A.M. 1670
Weber, Hermann 414
Wegner, Max 152
Weil, Bruno 1416
Weinberg, David H. 88
Weinberg, Gerhard L. 1671,
    1672
Weingartner, James J. 1673
Weinreich, Max 415a
Weinstein, A.A. 1417
Weinstein, Fred 415b
Weinstock, Eugene 1418
Weiskopf, Franz C. 1846
Weiss, Reska 1493
Weissberg, Alexander 1101,
    1419, 1420
Weiszäcker, Ernst von 416
Wellers, George 1421
Wells, Leon W. 1422, 1423
Werbell, Frederick E. 1424a
West Germany. Ministry of De-
    fense 865
West, Nigel 864a, 864b, 1870
West, Rebecca 1779
Weyl, Stefan 234
Whaley, Barton 417
Wheatley, Ronald 418
Wheeler-Bennett, John W. 419,

420, 421, 422, 1674
White, Ralph 649
Whiting, Charles 866, 867, 868,
    1675, 1676
Whittlesey, Derwent 423
Wiener, Jan G. 869
Wiernik, Yankel 1424b
Wiesel, Elie 1425, 1426, 1780,
    1781, 1847, 1848, 1849
Wiesenthal, Simon 1678, 1782,
    1850
Wiesenthal Foundation, Amster-
    dam 1677
Wighton, Charles 424, 425
Wilborts, Suzanne 947
Wilkinson, James D. 870
Willcox, Roben 1830
Williams, Eric 871, 872
Willis, James F. 1679
Wing, Jennifer Patai 67
Winkler, Dorte 426
Winnick, Myron 1427a
Winterbotham, F.A. 873
Wirth, Louis 89
Wischnitzer, Mark 90
Wise, Stephen S. 1540, 1541
Wistrich, Robert 427
Witkowski, Jozef 1427b
Witts, Max M. 1398
Wnuk, Jozef 1428
Wolf, Lore 948
Wolff, Kurt H. 1646
Woodhouse, Christopher M.
    874
Woods, Rex 875
World Committee (1934) for the
    Relief of the Victims of Ger-
    man Fascism 1429
World Jewish Congress 1430
Wormser-Nigot, Olga 1431,
    1432, 1433
Wouk, Herman 1851
Wulf, Josef 1329
Wunderlich, Frieda 428
Wurio, Eva L. 1852a

Wyman, David S. 1542
Wynne, Barry 949
Wytwicky, Bohdan 1434

Yad Vashem 1035, 1036, 1037,
    1038, 1039, 1040, 1435,
    1728, 1729
Yaffe, James 1852b
Yahil, Leni 876
YIVO Institute 1436, 1437, 1730
Yoors, Jan 877
Young, Gordon 950
Young-Bruehl, Elisabeth 1783

Zahn, Gordon C. 429, 878
Zajacová, Viera 1438
Žák, Jiří 1439
Zassenhaus, Hiltgunt 951
Zavrl, Vida 928
Zawodny, Janusz 879, 880
Zbiorowy, Tom 1731
Zeiger, Henry A. 1680
Zeller, Eberhard 881
Zeman, Zbyněk A.B. 430, 1901
Zentner, Kurt 882
Ziemer, Gregor 431
Ziemian, Joseph 1853
Ziemke, E.F. 1681
Zimmels, Hirsh J. 1854
Zimmermann, Wolf-Dieter 883
Zink, H. 1682
Zinner, Paul E. 432
Zisenwine, David 91
Zollek, A. 433
Zolli, Eugenio 1440
Zorn, Gerda 952
Zörner, G. 953
Zortman, Bruce 434
Zuker-Bujanowska, Liliana 1511
Zuckerman, Isaac 1041
Zuckerman, Itzhak 1042
Zuroff, Efrain 982
Zylberberg, Michael 1441
Zyskind, Sara 1494
Zywulska, Krystyna 1495

ABOUT THE AUTHOR

Vera Laska has first-hand knowledge of the resistance and of concentration camps; she is a survivor of the Auschwitz, Gross Rosen and Nordhausen-Dora concentration camps.

She received her Ph.D. in history from the University of Chicago. She is chairman of the division of social sciences and professor of history at Regis College in Weston, Massachusetts, where she teaches, among others, a course on the resistance and the Holocaust. She writes a history column for several local newspapers and is in demand as a lecturer.

She is the author of numerous articles and books. Her sixth book, just prior to this bibliography, is Women in the Resistance and in the Holocaust.